NEW PUNK CINEMA

Edited by
Nicholas Rombes

EDINBURGH UNIVERSITY PRESS

© Copyright in this edition Edinburgh University Press, 2005
© Copyright in the individual contributions is retained by the authors

Edinburgh University Press Ltd
22 George Square, Edinburgh

Typeset in Sabon by
Hewer Text Ltd, Edinburgh, and
printed and bound in Great Britain by
MPG Books Ltd, Bodmin, Cornwall

A CIP record for this book is available from the British Library

ISBN 0 7486 2034 6 (hardback)
ISBN 0 7486 2035 4 (paperback)

The right of the contributors
to be identified as authors of this work
has been asserted in accordance with
the Copyright, Designs and Patents Act 1988.

CONTENTS

	Notes on the Contributors	vii
	Acknowledgements	xi
	Introduction *Nicholas Rombes*	1
PART I	BACKGROUNDS AND CONTEXTS	
1	Punk Cinema *Stacy Thompson*	21
2	Italian Neo-realist Influences *Jay McRoy*	39
3	The French New Wave: New Again *Timothy Dugdale*	56
4	Sincerity and Irony *Nicholas Rombes*	72
PART II	SCREENING NEW PUNK CINEMA	
5	DVD and the New Cinema of Complexity *Graeme Harper*	89

CONTENTS

	6	Digital Technologies and the Poetics of Performance *Bruno Lessard*	102
	7	Navigating Chaos *Silvio Gaggi*	113
	8	Non-linear Narrative *Bruce Isaacs*	126
	9	Making it Real *Steven Rubio*	139
PART III		CASE STUDIES	
	10	Dogma Brothers: Lars von Trier and Thomas Vinterberg *Shohini Chaudhuri*	153
	11	Mike Figgis: *Time Code* and the Screen *Constantine Verevis*	168
	12	What Was the Neo-Underground and What Wasn't: A First Reconsideration of Harmony Korine *Benjamin Halligan*	180
	13	Repo Man: Reclaiming the Spirit of Punk with Alex Cox *Xavier Mendik*	193
		Bibliography	204
		Index	213

NOTES ON THE CONTRIBUTORS

Shohini Chaudhuri is Lecturer in Contemporary Writing and Film at the University of Essex. Her articles have appeared in *Screen*, *Camera Obscura*, and *Strategies*. Her forthcoming books include *Contemporary World Cinema: Europe, the Middle East, East Asia and South Asia* (Edinburgh University Press) and *Feminist Film Theorists: Laura Mulvey, Kaja Silverman, Teresa de Laurentis, and Barbara Creed* (Routledge Critical Thinkers Series).

Timothy Dugdale teaches in the English Department at the University of Detroit Mercy, where he also serves as Associate Editor of the journal *Post Identity*.

Silvio Gaggi is professor of Humanities and Chair of the Department of Humanities and American Studies at the University of South Florida, where he teaches courses dealing with various aspects of Modern and Post-modern culture. He has published articles on various arts of the twentieth century (painting, film, literature, and theatre) in numerous journals. His books *Modern/Postmodern, A Study in Twentieth-Century Arts and Ideas* (1989) and *From Text to Hypertext: Decentering the Subject in Fiction, Film, the Visual Arts, and Electronic Media* (1997) were both published by the University of Pennsylvania Press.

Benjamin Halligan is a lecturer in the Department of Theatre, Film and Television Studies, York St John, University of Leeds. His critical biography of

Michael Reeves was published by Manchester University Press in 2003 and his study of the European New Waves is forthcoming.

Graeme Harper is Professor and Foundation Chair of the School of Creative Arts, Film and Media at the University of Portsmouth. Founder and co-editor of the journal *Studies in European Cinema* and co-founder of the international European Cinema Research Forum (ECRF), he has served on the research assessment panels of the European Commission and the UK's Arts and Humanities Research Board. His latest books include work on cinema and medicine, cinema and landscape, and surrealist cinema. He is also a fiction writer.

Bruce Isaacs is a final-year Ph.D. student at the University of Sydney, Australia. He is currently working in the area of post-modern American culture and hopes to pursue an interest in creative writing.

Bruno Lessard is a Ph.D. candidate in literature and cinema in the Department of Comparative Literature at the University of Montreal. He has published articles in art and interdisciplinary journals such as *Parachute* and *Intermédialités* and has forthcoming chapters in several essay collections on digital media.

Jay McRoy is an Assistant Professor of English and Coordinator of the Film Studies Certificate Program at the University of Wisconsin, Parkside. His writings on film have appeared in numerous journals and collections, including *Kino Eye, The Journal of Fantastic in the Arts, Paradoxa, Traditions in World Cinema* (Edinburgh University Press, 2004), *Horror Film: Creating and Marketing Film* (University of Mississippi Press, 2004), and *Horror Zone: The Cultural Experience of Contemporary Horror Cinema* (Verso, forthcoming). He is also the editor of *Japanese Horror Cinema* (Edinburgh University Press, 2005).

Xavier Mendik is Director of the Cult Film Archive at University College Northhampton. His publications as author, editor and co-editor include *Dario Argento's Tenebrae* (Flicks Books, 2000), *Unruly Pleasures: The Cult Film and its Critics* (Fab Press, 2000), *Shocking Cinema of the Seventies* (Noir Publishing, 2002), *Underground USA: Filmmaking Beyond the Hollywood Canon* (Wallflower Press, 2002), and *Alternative Europe: Eurotrash and Exploitation Cinema since 1945* (Wallflower Press, 2004). A collection of Mendik's writings on European and American horror cinema is forthcoming from Wallflower Press under the title *Fear Theory*. Beyond his academic research, he is an established documentary writer and producer. He recently completed *Fear Today, Horror Tomorrow*, which examined Eli Roth's film *Cabin Fever*, and is currently completing a documentary on Brian Yuzna for Mosaic Entertainment.

Nicholas Rombes is Associate Professor of English at the University of Detroit Mercy, where he co-founded the Electronic Critique programme and where he co-edits the journal *Post Identity*. His writing on cinema has appeared in journals including *CTheory* and *Post Script*. His book on the Ramones' first album is forthcoming from Continuum Publishers as part of their 33 1/3 series.

Steven Rubio is a former steelworker who left the factory and picked up a doctorate in English from the University of California, Berkeley. A film major in his long-ago youth, he saw the last Sex Pistols, concert to include Sid Vicious, and has waited ever since for someone to ask him to write about punk and movies in the same essay.

Stacy Thompson is an Assistant Professor in the English Department at the University of Wisconsin, Eau Claire, where he teaches courses in critical theory and cinema studies. His articles on punk cinema have appeared in journals including *Cinema Journal* and *College Literature*. Thompson's book, *Punk Productions: Unfinished Business* (SUNY Press, 2004), examines punk history, aesthetics and economics through materialist critique.

Constantine Verevis lectures in film and television in the School of Literary, Visual, and Performance Studies at Monash University, Melbourne. His articles have appeared in publications such as *Framework*, *Australian Studies*, *Film Criticism*, *Hitchcock Annual*, and *Media International Australia*. He is presently working on a book entitled *Film Remakes* for Edinburgh University Press.

ACKNOWLEDGEMENTS

Many thanks to the writers who contributed to this volume, and to the series editors Steven Jay Schneider, Linda Badley and R. Barton Palmer. Special thanks are due to Steven Schneider, who supported this project with enthusiasm from the beginning, and to Linda Badley for her helpful comments and suggestions. I am also grateful to Sarah Edwards at Edinburgh University Press for her support and goodwill, and to Neil Curtis and Eddie Clark for their careful attention to the manuscript.

Gratitude and thanks are also due to my colleagues and students at the University of Detroit Mercy. I am indebted to the members of the English Department's reading group – Michael Barry, John Freeman, Chris Gilliard, Marcel O'Gorman, Heather Hill-Vasquez and Rosemary Weatherston – for lively discussion about many of the issues in this book. I would also like to extend my appreciation to my students at UDM, who continually amaze with their insights and deep sense of critique.

My love goes to my parents, who, it turns out, knew what they were doing when they took me to see *Blazing Saddles* when I was eight. The pleasure of seeing movies and seeing through movies is something I owe to them.

To Lisa, my compatriot, my deepest love and gratitude. Without you, this project would not have been possible. You have always been my one-and-only punk rock girl. And to Niko and Maddy, my love.

Chapter 13 originally appeared, in different form, as 'Fear and Loathing in Beverly Hills' in *Senses of Cinema*, issue 24, Jan. – Feb. 2003 at www.sensesofcinema.com. And chapter 12 is a revised version of 'What is the Neo-Underground and What Isn't: A First Consideration of Harmony Korine', which appeared in *Underground U.S.A.* (2002), S. J. Schneider and X. Mendik (eds), London: Wallflower Press, 150–60.

INTRODUCTION

Nicholas Rombes

> I belong to the blank generation and
> I can take it or leave it each time
> (Richard Hell and the Voidoids, 'Blank Generation')

> We are the middle children of history, with no purpose or place. We have no great war, or great depression. The great war is a spiritual war. The great depression is our lives.
> (Tyler Durden, *Fight Club*)

An advertisement for the Samsung VM-A680 video-phone, featuring a beautiful woman standing beneath a movie marquee that reads 'We All Have a Movie Within. What's Yours?' offers a promise of the phone as movie-camera, and the user as star:

> You already have drama in your life. All you need now is a phone that lets you capture it. Enter Samsung's VM-A680 video phone. It allows you to record up to 15 seconds of digital video and audio as you walk down along the red carpet of your life. You can save it, play it, email it, and send it to your friends.

The advertisement ends with the phrases 'Your life. Now showing', giving new meaning to Andy Warhol's prediction that, in the future, everyone will be famous for fifteen minutes. And the digital film festival, Resfest 2004, offers a section on 'Handheld Cinema': 'After years of hype, finally PDAs, mobile phones and portable entertainment devices can play short films . . . [T]here's already a group of inspired filmmakers pushing the boundaries and crafting unique moving images just right for the micro-screen' (*RES Magazine* 2004: 9). Whether these two instances herald a new form of art or whether they serve as further examples of the relentless incorporation of new cultural forms into commodities, they both deploy a do-it-yourself ethos that suggests that anybody can make a film, anybody can be a director. Does this portend the true democratisation of cinema – what we might call a cinematic punk new wave – or simply the extension of traditional Hollywood story-telling paradigms into new technologies? Is it possible to speak of the avant-garde today, when multinational companies like Samsung tout their new revolutionary digital phones in the pages of *Vogue* magazine?

New Punk Cinema explores these questions and others, tracing a tendency in cinema that owes some debt to the aesthetics and politics of 1970s' punk rock. Beginning in the mid 1990s, a series of films from around the world began to emerge that challenged, or at least radically revised, many of the narrative and aesthetic codes that governed mainstream Hollywood fare. The films included *Gummo* (1997), *Idioterne* (*The Idiots* [1998]), *The Celebration* (*Festen* [1998]), *Pi* (1998), *Lola rennt* (*Run Lola Run* [1998]), *julien donkey-boy* (1999), *The Blair Witch Project* (1999), *Fight Club* (1999), *Amores perros* (2000), *Dancer in the Dark* (2000), *Requiem for a Dream* (2000) and *Time Code* (2000). These films offered an often brutal mixture of underground, avant-garde technique and mainstream, genre-based story-telling that wove together cinematic traditions that included the French New Wave, Italian Neorealism and *cinéma vérité*. What is immediately clear is that these films were not all 'independent' – a term which has less value today when so many films are financed by complex and interrelated networks, when many of the major studios have their own supposedly 'indie' divisions, and when popular films, such as *The Passion of the Christ* (2004) and *Fahrenheit 9/11* (2004), blur the lines between Hollywood and indie films.

New punk cinema is animated by the same do-it-yourself approach that characterised 1970s' punk in the United States and in Britain. Digital cameras and desk-top editing have made it possible for a greater number of people than ever before to make films. Although we need to be sceptical of Utopian claims about the democratisation of film-making (especially claims that ignore the underlying economics that allow and deny access to these digital technologies), digital cinema has opened up striking alternatives to Hollywood's multimillion dollar productions, in the same way that 8 mm and 16 mm film had done in the past. Although the punk movement was not the first, nor the last, to exploit the do-it-yourself aesthetic for artistic means, its cultural stamp on film has been largely neglected. But it reveals itself in the remarks of film-makers such as Darren Aronofsky who described his film *Requiem for a Dream* as 'a punk movie' (Stark 2000: 3). It is also there in the comments of Jim Jarmusch who, referring to the punk music scene in New York in the 1970s, has said that if 'it hadn't been for that music scene we probably wouldn't be making films. Rock 'n' roll bands said, "Fuck virtuosity. We have something that we feel, and even if our expression of it is amateurish, it doesn't mean that our vision is." That helped me, and other people, to realize that even if we didn't have the budget or the production structure to make films, we could still make them, using Super 8 and 16 mm equipment, and scratching funds together' (Hertzberg 2001: 90).

New Punk Cinema maps the animating spirit of punk in contemporary cinema. As many who have written about punk have noted, punk's influence is far reaching and can be detected in many cultural forms not obviously associated with punk. According to Roger Sabin, 'punk was not an isolated, bounded phenomenon, but had an extensive impact on a variety of cultural and political fields' and 'it's hard to imagine a modern Europe and America not transformed by punk' (Sabin 1999a: 5). Tricia Henry has written that '[P]unk rock has been a significant factor in shaping Western aesthetic trends since the mid-1970s. It has influenced not only the evolution of performing arts but also of fashion, graphic arts, literature, film, and popular entertainment' (Henry 1989: 6). And in his book *Punk Productions*, Stacy Thompson notes that punk textuality cuts across many different cultural forms, including music, style, the printed word and cinema (Thompson 2004: 3). This book responds directly to Sabin's claim that there is 'a long way to go before its [punk's] contribution to other fields is properly recognized' (Sabin 1999a: 5). Yet this complex relationship between punk and other cultural forms, such as film, is not always clear, and we are sensitive to the dangers of reducing a complex, often contradictory, web of connections to a reductive cause-and-effect argument. For that reason, this book offers itself as an initial exploration of the relationship between punk and cinema, an exploration that we hope will spawn further inquiry and study, and even refutations of some of our claims. Like punk itself, we offer our hand to you, our readers, in a gesture of both community and defiance.

New Punk Cinema sketches a tendency in contemporary cinema, a tendency informed by the aesthetic sensibility of the punk movement in the United States and Britain in the 1970s. This is by no means a coherent, unified school of film, which is why we use the word 'tendency' as opposed to 'movement'. In our post-postmodern era, we are rightly suspicious of making grand claims about movements or schools that would serve to impose some rigid narrative structure on something as complex and contradictory as film. And yet we believe it is equally risky to avoid – out of fear of the inevitable exceptions and counter-arguments that can and should be raised about such an endeavour – naming and delineating the contours of such a tendency. To claim that a film is new punk does not mean that the film is not something else, too. In this sense, new punk films function much like film *noir* as described by Paul Schrader. Like film *noir*, new punk cinema coheres not around a genre – Schrader suggested that *noir* should not be defined as a genre, but rather by 'the more subtle qualities of tone and mood' (Schrader 1972: 53) – but rather around a loose affiliation of stylistic tendencies, narrative choices and production qualities that owe some debt to the punk sensibility.

Punk Rock

The term 'punk' itself is a notoriously contested term, resisted by some in the scene in the 1970s, embraced by others. While the animating spirit of punk can be traced back to many groups, including Bill Haley and his Comets, Question Mark and the Mysterians, early Beatles, early Who and others, its most direct influence was late-1960s' and early 1970s' bands centred for the most part in New York City, Detroit and Cleveland, such as The Velvet Underground, the MC5, The Stooges, The New York Dolls and The Modern Lovers. In the United States, punk emerged most strongly in New York City, where two clubs in particular – CBGB and OMFUG, which stands for Country Bluegrass, Blues and Other Music for Uplifting Gormandizers [CBGBs for short] and Max's Kansas City – became venues that very early on supported many of the bands that would become associated with punk, including Patti Smith, the Ramones, the Dead Boys, Television, Richard Hell and the Voidoids, the Dictators, and Suicide. In Britain, the scene developed at roughly the same time although, it can be argued, inflected with a more aggressive, less Pop-oriented sound, especially in groups such as the Sex Pistols, X-Ray Specs, and the Buzzcocks.

Fortunately, punk has been written about by some eloquent and daring writers who have helped to frame the music and its styles in essays and books, the approach and prose of which often capture the riskiness and danger of punk itself. Writers and artists including Lester Bangs, Nick Kent, Greil Marcus, Clinton Heylin, Richard Meltzer, David Laing, Jon Savage, Mary Harron, Nick Tosches, Robert Christgau and others have engaged punk in ways that recognised its contradictions. The most sustained and critical approaches include Dick Hebdige's *Subculture: Elements of a Style* (1979) which was among the first to treat from a cultural-studies approach the complex and uneasy negotiations between punk's subcultures and the mainstream. Greil Marcus's *Lipstick Traces: A Secret History of the Twentieth Century* (1989) is less a history than a relentless coupling of dada-ism, surrealism, and punk, suggesting a secret, beyond-reason affinity that flies in the face of typical studies of influence. In style and layout, the book performs its thesis, and remains a testament to creative scholarship. Jon Savage's *England's Dreaming: Anarchy, Sex Pistols, Punk Rock, and Beyond* (1992) provides a wealth of cultural detail in a kind of analysis that, like Hebdige's and Marcus's books, ignores the line between academic and popular writing. Most recently, Stacy Thompson's *Punk Productions: Unfinished Business* (2004) approaches punk from a materialist perspective, paying close attention to punk's resistance to capitalism's relentless push towards commodification.

One of the unique strengths of much writing on punk is that it rejects easy distinctions between academic and popular writing, often mixing theoretical insight with aphorisms and anecdotes. These writers – especially Hebdige, Marcus, and Bangs – approach punk as scholars writing with a rock critic's eye, or as rock critics writing with a scholar's eye. Their writing assumes an abiding intelligence and curiosity in their readers and benefited from the best strains of cultural studies which, in the spirit of Roland Barthes, Theodor Adorno, Marshall McLuhan, Susan Sontag, Pauline Kael, Andrew Sarris and others, approached popular culture in ways that moved beyond the measured safety of much academic writing. If their prose style often seemed outrageously designed to pick a fight, it was always in the service of an argument that made you believe that popular culture – whether film, television, photography, style, horoscopes, radio and so on – mattered enough to be brought under the fierce scrutiny of critique. In short, they made you believe that music was worth arguing about.

In addition to the critics and writers, those most closely associated with punk – the musicians themselves, the artists and writers who were part of the scene, record producers and others – have contributed what amounts to a deep (and often very funny) oral history of punk. Two books in particular stand out here: Clinton Heylin's *From the Velvets to the Voidoids: A Pre-Punk History for a Post-Punk World* (1993) and Legs McNeil's and Gillian McCain's *Please Kill Me: The Uncensored History of Punk* (1997). Our understanding of punk today is shaped not only by our own gut reaction to the music, but by these authors whose efforts to mythologise and demythologise punk have endowed it with a sort of ghost life. Simon Frith has written about what is perhaps the single most-important and overarching dimension of punk music: the uneasy tension between raw expression and self-consciousness. Frith suggests that punk 'queried the "naturalness" of musical language. Beginning from the assumption that all music is constructed, they sought to strip it down to its foundations; they juxtaposed the rules and regulations from different genres; listeners were invited to notice the musical presence of effects that were previously inaudible. These musicians valued the pop quality that rock fans most despised – artificiality' (Frith 1981: 162). Frith doesn't use the word 'artificiality' to dismiss or to trivialise punk but rather to acknowledge that punk was a product of post-modernism. Most of its practitioners came of age in the 1960s and 1970s, the era of television, of public access cable, of exploitation cinema, of multi-tentacled media that reproduced and replicated cultural forms so pervasively that, as Robert Ray has written, the previously invisible narrative structures became visible as distinctions between high and low culture began to collapse. In the post-Vietnam, post-Watergate, Andy Warhol era, an ironic – if not cynical – sensibility was not so much an affect but part and parcel of everyday cultural productions.

In fact, punk aimed to pierce through the cloak of 'authenticity' that characterised the progressive, serious, macho, arena-rock of Led Zeppelin, The Eagles and other supergroup bands for whom virtuosity had created a distancing effect between themselves and audiences. Whereas the supergroups played in massive arenas and stadiums, punk played itself on cramped stages in small clubs and bars, where there was ample opportunity for audiences to 'interact' with bands, pelting them with beer bottles and other objects, while band members could hurl insults, objects and often themselves into the crowds. As Scott Kempner has said of Iggy Pop's early performances, '[E]very single show involved actual fucking blood' (McNeil 1997: 66). Or, consider Bob Gruen's description of traveling with the Sex Pistols during their final 1978 tour: 'It wasn't only the band who were crazy – the people who were supporting them were worse. The Sex Pistols weren't violent people, but by shouting their boredom and rage with everything, they attracted the most bizarre reactions from every side' (ibid. p. 327). Clearly, mainstream arena rock and punk shared a keen sense of theatricality, but punk distinguished itself in its sheer intimacy – smaller crowds and stages – and in its sense that there was something more at stake in the performance than merely putting on a show.

Punk's other defining feature, especially in light of its influence on cinema, was its stripped-down minimalism, its return to 'the basics'. While it is not true that all bands associated with punk eschewed intricate, virtuoso musicianship – the intricate guitar play of Robert Quine in Richard Hell and the Voidoids or Richard Lloyd in Television come readily to mind – most bands actively cultivated the image of untrained, do-it-yourself amateurism. Ironically, this anti-aesthetic produced an aesthetic and a style that has outlived punk's brief moment. Bill Martin suggests that '[P]unk's rejection of musical technique is first of all a rejection of the orientation of the aesthete' (Martin 2002: 90), while Jim Curtis claims that '[T]he key attitude which conceptual art and punk have in common is their disdain for technique; only if technique is irrelevant does everybody have the chance to be creative' (Curtis 1997: 309). Much like the Dogma 95 movement, punk ended up delineating a very distinctive style by its very refusal of the tyrannies of style: the distinctive sound of, say, the Ramones was important, not so much for what they added to popular music, but to what they took away. This was the art of subtraction.

Punk in its 1970s' incarnation shares with new punk cinema a complex and contradictory set of reading codes. Indeed, there are many such contradictions about punk's meaning. On the one hand, punk was distinctly nostalgic, harking back to an earlier, 'purer', simpler sound reminiscent of early rock and roll. Craig Leon, who produced the Ramones' first album in 1976, noted that '[Q]uite honestly we thought we were creating a hit pop record. The Bay City Rollers, Herman's Hermits, and the Beatles were our competition in our minds' (Leon 2004). Nancy Spungen, Sid Vicious's girlfriend, described punk as 'just real basic fifties and early sixties rock' (McNeil 1997: 260). On the other hand, punk – especially its British strain – has come to be associated with anarchy and nihilism that vehemently rejected tradition and the past. This is particularly true of the Sex Pistols and the Dead Boys, both of whom embraced a sort of terminal, last-great-stand aesthetic that rejected both the past and the future.

There are numerous other contradictions, as well. The contradiction between irony and sincerity scrambled the codes that normally prompt audiences to respond emotionally in certain ways. Punk confused these codes. Media coverage, especially in Britain, grew in direct proportion to the punks' outrageous rejection of cultural norms. 'The "movement" had now developed, within six months,' writes Jon Savage of British punk in 1976, 'into a complex, ironic phenomenon containing a rich mixture of truth and hype. Most of those involved had always wanted to engage with the mass media, indeed sought self-justification by so doing, and they now had their wish' (Savage 1992: 231). Contradictions abounded in many punks' usage of symbols and icons associated with racism and death, such as the swastika. Were these symbols appropriated in a way that acknowledged the surface of all signs, or were they reflective of a deeper and more disturbing racist ideology? Writing in his 1979 essay 'The White Noise Supremacists' – an essay with a thesis that was denounced by many in the punk scene at the time – Lester Bangs wrote about the 'spiritual flatness' that characterised punk and noted that '[T]his scene and the punk stance in general are riddled with self-hate, which is always reflexive, and anytime you conclude that life stinks and the human race mostly amounts to a pile of shit, you've got the perfect breeding ground for fascism' (Bangs: 273, 275). Addressing the ambiguity of the punks' usage of symbols, such as the swastika, Roger Sabin has written that '[A]part from the Nazi material, other punk symbolism and lyrics were up for grabs. The Union Jack, for instance, also a ubiquitous fashion item, could be worn ironically (especially around the time of the Jubilee, e.g., the Pistols, Clash), could be a homage to the mod era (e.g. The Jam and their fans), or, much less commonly, could be a statement against American influence (and American punk)' (Sabin 1999b: 209–10).

Behind all this, however, was the animating spirit of punk: its fierce do-it-yourself ethic, its adventurous sense that music belonged not to the virtuosis but to regular kids. Part of the mystique of punk came from the belief that anybody could do it. Johnny Ramone recalls the bewilderment of some record executives when confronted with demos the band had made before signing a record contract: 'We didn't sound like all the groups out there. Also, we couldn't play – quote, unquote . . . I guess that's a pretty strange aesthetic to ask people to understand: that there's something more than musicianship involved here' (Heylin 1993: 178). That 'something more than musicianship' was a raw energy, humour and speed that were diametrically opposed to the slow, blues-inflected, self-serious, non ironic arena rock that had come to dominate the music scene and FM radio in the 1970s, epitomised by virtuoso macho bands such as Led Zeppelin or the Eagles. This was also an era dominated by the sensitive singer-songwriter. Despite their arguable merits, performers such as Jackson Browne, Cat Stevens, Linda Rondstadt and others epitomised to many the exhaustion and failure of the 1960s. The promises of the 'great society', the bitter Utopianism of folk-singers, ranging from Bob Dylan to Joan Baez, the politically engaged dimension of so much music in the 1960s, all these had given way in the 1970s to an unapologetic narcissism and non-ironic inward looking-ness.

In Britain and in the United States, punk emerged during a time of dwindling expectations and economic crisis. As Dick Hebdige has suggested, the punks in Britain in 1976 and 1977 were not simply reflecting the economic and social crisis, they were representing it, making art from it: 'In the same way, punks were not only directly responding to increasing joblessness, changing moral standards, the rediscovery of poverty, the Depression, etc., they were *dramatizing* what had come to be called "Britain's decline" by constructing a language which was, in contrast to the prevailing rhetoric of the Rock Establishment, unmistakably relevant and down to earth' (Hebdige 79: 87). Jon Savage notes that '[I]n June [1976], unemployment reached 1,501,976, 6.4 percent of the workforce, and the worst figure since 1940' (Savage 1992: 229).

In the United States, the punk scene developed during an era which had witnessed serious blows to the American ideals of progress, confidence and Utopianism. There had been the terrible assassinations of some of the nation's most idealistic leaders, including President John F. Kennedy in 1963, his brother Robert Kennedy in 1968, as well as Malcom X in 1965 and the Reverend Martin Luther King, Jr in 1968. The culture was increasingly saturated in images of violence, ranging from the Manson murders in 1969, the Watts and Detroit riots in which hundreds were killed, the beating of anti-war protesters by police outside the 1968 Chicago Democratic Convention, and increasingly graphic daily images of violence from Vietnam. In 1974, President Nixon resigned in the Watergate scandal, which implicated him in ordering the break-in of the Democratic National Headquarters. In 1975, the United States left Vietnam in defeat.

New York City, where punk's identity in the United States was solidified (although Cleveland and Detroit had important punk and pre-punk scenes), was in many ways the poster child for an America in crisis. The city was on the brink of economic bankruptcy in the mid 1970s, and was bailed out only at the last moment. '[Mayor] Beame Submits New Cuts Requiring added Layoffs Running into "Thousands"' ran a front-page headline in *The New York Times* in October 1975, followed by 'Mayor is Bitter'. The article is typical of the sort of news New Yorkers were reading every day: 'The exact layoff total will be decided in the next week, and unofficial estimates circulating among city administrators who coursed fretfully through City Hall was that the dismissals might total up to 8,000 beyond the 21,000 workers laid off thus far in the fiscal crisis. Police officials said up to 900 policemen would be laid off, and school officials predicted "several thousand" teachers and school workers would have to be let go' (Clines 1975: 1A). Entire sections of the city were abandoned by policy-makers whose idea for 'planned shrinkage' suggested that certain portions of the city be wilfully denied city services to help reduce and relocate the population. The rhetoric of a sort of economic social Darwinism was in the air. As historian Fred Siegel has written, '[N]ew York had bankrupted itself in pursuit of policies that both eroded the economic base and produced a poverty rate that when adjusted for price levels approached Mississippi's . . . Here was a failure of near-Soviet proportions' (Siegel 1997: 240).

While mainstream, radio-friendly progressive rock had absorbed these cultural shifts by falling back into languid self-doubt characterised by heavily produced tomes that fetishised the lead singer and a virtuoso solo guitar player (the Robert Plant / Jimmy Page model works this to near perfection), punk responded with short, fast and loud songs that more often than not contained no guitar solos. Rather than deploying the language of macho seduction ('hey hey mamma . . .'), punk offered more compact, self-effacing songs about the glories of doing nothing.

Punk Cinema

In an interview, film-maker Richard Baylor has said: 'I have always been interested in films, but never really thought about making my own until I was exposed to the work of Richard Kern, Nick Zedd, Lydia Lunch, and other "Cinema of Transgression" filmmakers. What captured my interest was their approach to the media. It was very much "punk film". The emphasis was on the content and the expression, not on the technical skills and budgets.' (Kerekes 1999: 74) Like the term 'punk' itself, punk cinema remains a contested term, especially in our era of high-alert scepticism about authorship, genre and periodisation. Among the earliest critics to write about punk cinema was J. Hoberman, whose 1979 *Village Voice* article 'No Wavelength: The Para-Punk Underground' set out some ideas that were developed in greater detail in the seminal book he co-authored with Jonathan Rosenbaum, *Midnight Movies*. In the section 'Punk', Hoberman writes that '[S]een strictly as a youth movement, punk was a kind of perverse, high-speed relay of the counterculture, complete with its own music, press, entrepreneurs, fellow travelers (including more than a few ex-hippies), and, ultimately, movies' (Hoberman and Rosenbaum 1983: 275). Hoberman discusses key films, such as Derek Jarman's *Jubilee* (1978), which he terms 'the first narrative feature to deal with punk' (ibid. p. 280). He also discusses the super-eight film-makers Eric Mitchell, Beth B and Scott B, James Nares and Vivienne Dick, 'closely linked to local art-punk, "no-wave" bands', whose films 'began to parallel the music's energy, iconography, and avowed anyone-can-do-it esthetic' (ibid. p. 283). Finally, Hoberman mentions *Rock 'n' Roll High School* (1979) starring the Ramones. And, although he doesn't discuss it in his chapter on punk, Hoberman might just as easily have included David Lynch's *Eraserhead* (1977) which, in a strange way, creates a time-warped punk universe slowed down to a crawl. One could imagine the nearly inarticulate black-and-white Henry, with his wild hair and skinny tie, bursting to life on the stage at CBGBs.

More recently, a handful of writers have begun to articulate the possible contours of punk cinema; among them Stacy Thompson, whose essay in this collection and whose book *Producing Punk* offer a map of punk cinema. In a previous essay, 'Punk Cinema', Thompson argues that punk cinema must be understood and interrogated in material terms: '[A]ny attempt to articulate the logic of punk cinema's aesthetic must therefore attend to the assumptions about – and commitments to – the particular modes of production that punk cinema bears.' He continues: '[F]or the term "punk cinema" to carry some weight, to describe something more than a consumable style, it must bear, aesthetically and economically, a filmic version of punk's democratizing dictum' (Thompson 2004a: 48). As Thompson sees it, the signature aesthetic marker of punk cinema is its self-awareness, its willingness to leave in, rather than erase, footprints of its own production: '[W]hen punk passes into film, it demands of film that it offer up material traces of its production, that it open itself up to its audience as an "open" text by pointing out how it came to be, rather than reifying its means of production and thereby folding in on itself as a "closed" text' (ibid. p. 49). While Thompson does not restrict himself to

1970s' and early 1980s' film-makers, many of the directors he discusses made their first films during this period, including Amos Poe (*Night Lunch* [1975] and *Blank Generation* [1976]), Don Letts (*The Punk Rock Movie* [1978]), Julien Temple (*The Great Rock 'n' Roll Swindle* [1979], Jack Hazan (*Rude Boy* [1980]), Lech Kowalski (*D.O.A.* [1981]) and Penelope Spheeris (*The Decline of Western Civilization 1* [1981]).

Jack Sargeant has also been instrumental in documenting and theorising the relationship between punk and the 'cinema of transgression' which critic Amy Taubin described in a 1979 essay in the *Soho Weekly News*. In *Deathtripping: The Cinema of Transgression*, Sargeant delineates the contours of this critically neglected movement, providing detail and perspective on its key film-makers, including Nick Zedd, who 'announced the launch of the Cinema of Transgression in his self-published "crudzine" *The Underground Film Bulletin*' (Sargeant 1995: 25, 27). Exploring connections between the 1970s' Cinema of Transgression and other related directors and movements, Sargeant notes the importance of Jack Smith and John Waters, who 'was a punk before punk existed' (ibid. pp. 11–12). He goes on to note the significance of punk in general on a generation of New York film-makers, including 'Amos Poe, Eric Mitchell, James Nares, Michael Oblowitz and Vivienne Dick. These filmmakers were inspired by the punk geist at clubs such as CBGBs, where the first generation of punk bands such as Television, the Ramones and Richard Hell and the Voidoids had delineated the "punk aesthetic"' (ibid. p. 14). This aesthetic – in large part defined by 'a sense of immediacy and "anyone-can-do-it" ontology' (ibid. p. 14) – is indeed what links punk and new punk cinema.

Others, such as Jim Jarmusch, who began making films during this period have recognised the importance of the punk scene on New York film-making in the 1970s. Jarmusch has noted that 'starting in like 76 or so, there was a really important spirit, especially in the music scene, because the spirit was that you didn't have to be a virtuoso musician to form a rock band. Instead, the spirit of the music was more important than any kind of technical expertise on the instrument, which of course was – in New York – first Patti Smith and Television and the Heartbreakers, the Ramones, Mink de Ville, Blondie, Talking Heads – all those bands. And that influenced a lot of people in other forms as well' (Hertzberg 2001: 27).

New Punk Cinema

Unlike the Cinema of Transgression or the New American Cinema, new punk cinema is not really a formal movement, but rather a tendency and an approach to film-making that share certain key gestures and approaches with punk. Like punk itself, it is not confined to one city, nor one nation – this in itself distinguishes it from many previous New Waves and film movements.

New punk cinema is global, including the work of directors from Denmark (Lars von Trier and others from the Dogma 95 movement), Germany (Tom Tykwer), Britain (Danny Boyle, Mike Figgis, Christopher Nolan), America (Harmony Korine, Darren Aronofsky) and others beyond the scope of this book. What links new punk films and directors together is a do-it-yourself sensibility, an almost romantic notion that anyone can create something that matters, a troubled desire for and yet a suspicion of authenticity and the Real, an approach to film-making that foregrounds the medium of film itself, and an interest in simplicity which, ironically, allows for great freedom and experimentation.

The rhetoric surrounding the rise of digital cameras and the Dogma 95 movement is deeply intertwined with the do-it-yourself discourse of the punk movement, as well as its claims of authenticity. Director Amos Poe, a contemporary of Jarmusch, notes in the DVD director's commentary for his film *The Foreigner* (1977) connections between his style of punk film-making and the Dogma 95 movement: 'This soundtrack, by the way, has no mix . . . When we hear music, there's no other sound, and when you hear dialogue there's no other music . . . It's just cut. Straight cut. This pre-dates the Danish school . . . of Lars von Trier . . . Dogma . . . this is the Dogma thing, twenty years before.' (Poe 2001) In both punk and Dogma, claims about creating something more 'authentic' or 'real' are of course predicated upon very complicated forms of technology. According to Simon Frith, '[Punk's] ideology may have been anti-technology, but the late 1970s rush of home-made records and independent labels was dependent, in fact, on the lower cost of good quality recording equipment' (Frith 2004: 117). Lars von Trier has said that '[T]he reason why I laid down the Dogma rules or put a camera on my shoulder was to get away from all this perfectionism and concentrate on something else' (Lumholdt 2003: 149). Indeed, technologies of production can never be separated from production itself. As Theodor Adorno noted some time ago in language which echoes the Dogma 95 manifesto:

> [F]ilm technology has developed a series of techniques which work against the realism inherent in the photographic process. Among these are soft-focus shots – a long outdated arty custom in photography – superimpositions, and also, frequently, flashbacks. It is about time to recognize the ludicrousness of such effects and get rid of them because these techniques are not grounded in the necessities of individual works but in mere convention . . . (Adorno 1966: 184)

Von Trier offers among the most Utopian defences of digital cameras; like the punks before him, he argues for simplicity: 'I think technology right now is great, because it makes filming so easy, you know. Early on, when I was young, everyone would say, No, you can't make films, it's too difficult to make films. Which was always a lie, it's always been a lie that it's difficult to make films. But now, nobody believes it anymore, because of the technology' (ibid. p. 155).

While it can be argued that the small, hand-held, digital cameras are merely more efficient means to replicate ideologies that formulate Hollywood moviemaking and realist cinema in general, the potential for alternative narrative and aesthetic approaches to film-making should not be underestimated. As Robert Ray has asked: do we in film studies want to keep finding the same bad ideologies over and over again? And what if audiences, raised in an ironic culture that has already taught them to be suspicious of master narratives, already see through the mystifications of the culture industry? In any case, while alternatives to the presentation of linear time in cinema are not unique to new punk films (Stanley Kubrick's *The Killing* [1956] is just one example), non-linear films have achieved a greater degree of public visibility, acceptance and comment recently, as they share the same grammar as their audiences.

Visually, new punk cinema is the product of the increasingly rapid-fire editing that owes much to MTV and, later, the Internet, where users jump-cut between images. As Maria Demopoulos suggests, film-makers and audiences have been deeply affected by the fast editing that characterises television commercials, promos, and – in its heyday – MTV:

> If viewers can now process cuts as brief as two frames, the equivalent of one- twelfth of a second, it's because MTV and its surrounding advertising-marketing complex have finely tuned our optic nerves, both promoting and portraying a more accelerated pace of daily life and, consequently, a new rhetoric of emotional and psychological fragmentation and disorder. More than a decade of translating music into visuals has yielded a new, self-taught, self-generated way to connect moving images. This highly mannered editorial aesthetic embodies the very essence of advertising: compression ... Where classical film editing melds transitions into seamless, gliding passages, New School editing slams images together in head-on collision. Rooted in rebellion, this aggressive, anarchic, fuck- the-line approach, landing you at your next edit faster, evokes the youth culture that spawned it. (Demopoulos 2000: 38)

The stylistic thread that connects films as diverse as *Pi, Requiem for a Dream, Run Lola Run, The Blair Witch Project, 28 Days Later* (2002) and other new punk films is a style of editing influenced by MTV. As Gus Van Sant has noted, 'I don't think 23 years ago we would have thought that MTV would have influenced the way movies are shot. But now, 90-to-100 percent of the films made are influenced by things that happened first – if not on MTV, MTV adopted them and used them the most' (Van Sant 2003: 1).

Additionally, non-linear story-telling has become one of the defining characteristics of new punk films, many of the directors of which came of age immersed in a post-modern media mix where media such as television, VHS tapes and DVDs, video games and the Internet scrambled past, present and future. In films ranging from *Pulp Fiction* (1994) to *Run Lola Run* to *Memento* (2000) to *Eternal Sunshine of the Spotless Mind* (2004), time is not presented as unfolding in a relentlessly forward direction. In a key article, Evan Smith uses the term 'thread structure' to describe recent films that weave together multiple storylines in ways that defy Hollywood's classical linear, three-act structure: '[W]hile most threads boast a recognizable beginning-middle-end (three-act development), others, brazenly, do not. Key plot points, even entire acts, are compressed, combined, or omitted altogether' (Smith 1999–2000: 88–9).

Gary Winick – co-founder of InDigEnt, a film production company devoted to digital films – has said that the recent InDigEnt film, *November*, directed by Greg Harrison and shot by Nancy Schreiber on a $2,800 Mini DV camera, was selected to be financed 'in *part* because he saw its "fragmented, nonlinear nature" as a good match for digital' (Peterson 2004: 64, 65). In an issue focused on 'Random Shuffle: Storytelling in the New Millennium', *RES Magazine* published a series of articles exploring new narrative possibilities in digital cinema. Acknowledging the contribution of Quentin Tarantino to the mainstreaming of non-linear commercial film, David Geffner writes that 'the chances he [Tarantino] took on the page a decade ago have made their mark: consider films like *American Splendor* [2003], *Swimming Pool* [2003], *21 Grams* [2003], and *Dogville* [2003] or television shows such as *24* [2001–current], *Carnivàle* [2003–current], and *Six Feet Under* [2001–current] which preen their fractured storylines like happy peacocks' (Geffner 2004: 45). In the essay, *21 Grams*, screenwriter Guillermo Arriaga notes that when 'people tell stories to each other, it's never in a linear way. They skip from point A to D back to B, because that's how life happens' (ibid. p. 45).

New punk aesthetics extend beyond alternatives to linear story-telling, however, and into the very notion of *auteur* director itself, as the small digital cameras can help, under the right circumstances, to call into question the very concept of the director. Like punk, fuelled by the poetics of anarchy and the loss of control despite its often fascistic iconography, new punk cinema explores the extremes of total control and total freedom. In this regard, *The Blair Witch Project* bears a strong resemblance to the Dogma 95 movement. Shot in eight days in 1997 for 'about as much as the price of a decent car' (Roddick 1999: 1), *Blair Witch* eschewed the concept of the director altogether, turning cameras over to its actors. According to co-director Daniel Myrick, '[W]e hooked the actors up with a little mini-film school before they went out into the woods, and we gave them the cameras, the batteries, the lights, the DAT machine' (Myrick 1999: 2). Other than information about where to go and which scene to act out, the actor/directors were given little or no instruction about how to shoot the scene, what camera angles to use, etc. 'We tried to give them as little information as possible', notes co-director Eduardo Sanchez. This raises interesting questions about control, authority, and expertise: who was the 'director' of *The Blair Witch Project*?

Like films of the Dogma 95 movement, which also exploited self-imposed limitation, *The Blair Witch Project* embraced simplicity in ways that generated its own degree of complexity. Joshua Leonard, one of the actors, has said that 'Sony could have $50 million and a sound stage and A-list actors and never make the same film. The constraints on this film became the essence of this film, became the power of this film' (Mannes 1999: 3). This constraint – a sort of anti-aesthetics that produces its own aesthetic – is similar to punk's rejection of complexity and elaborate, expert production. The digital camera evokes punk's dream of do-it-yourself autonomy with its point-and-shoot technology that promises to elevate the untrained amateur to film-maker. Of course, film theorists are rightly suspicious of such democratising claims, as they bring to the study of film an awareness of how technology is never neutral, but always is shaped by the economic forces that shape representations of reality. And yet it would be wise to bear in mind what Frith has said about punk's claims to more simple, authentic uses of technology to create their music: 'Technology, the shifting possibility of mechanical reproduction, has certainly been the necessary condition for the rise of the multinational entertainment business, for ever more sophisticated techniques of ideological manipulation, but technology has also made possible new forms of cultural democracy and new opportunities of individual and collective expression' (Frith 1986: 121). We risk overdetermining and foreclosing the possibility of change if we greet every innovation as just another permutation of the same oppressive ideology.

Several films of the Dogma 95 and Dogma 95-related school have also experimented with the displacement of the director. Like punk, which often depersonalised the 'star' performer (e.g. the Ramones in their look-alike street uniforms), new punk cinema often elaborates on the impersonal, documentary qualities of the camera eye. In Lars von Trier's *Dancer in the Dark*, 100 digital cameras were mounted so that various sequences could be captured from multiple angles. While this approach does eliminate the director, it focuses attention on to the technologies of directing and opens up possibilities for an emerging aesthetics of error and randomness. In this regard, new punk cinema shares with punk a high degree of self-awareness and self-consciousness that is somewhat embarrassed by the theatricality of performance, and thus calls attention to the mechanism of performance. As Lawrence Grossberg has noted, '[P]unk called into question the affective power of rock and roll; it attempted to incorporate its own possibility of incorporation . . . It tried to celebrate rock and roll even as it acknowledged its conceit' (Grossberg 1984: 331). In new punk cinema, this self-consciousness often takes the form a sort of realist-authenticity, marked by signature gestures such as shaky, hand-held cameras, degraded (out-of-focus, highly pixilated) film images, poor lighting, and occasionally the 'accidental' inclusion in the film frame of the film crew, as in von Trier's *The Idiots*, which periodically shows us von Trier with his camera, or a boom microphone, etc. This tendency towards a representation of a supposedly unvarnished reality has strong connections with the punk aesthetic. Ove Christensen writes that '[T]he search for a more ascetic aesthetics of film is not something unique to the brotherhood of Dogma 95 but has to be seen in relation to a much wider tendency within cinema as well as contemporary culture as such. The ugly and apparently amateurish look has for instance been a trend within advertising at least since the 80s. Punk aesthetics has had a great impact for the last twenty years' (Christensen 2000: 5).

These errors are often calculated; like the signature moments of the French New Wave, they constitute a stance. According to Peter Hjorth, Technical Director from *Dancer in the Dark* '[T]he 100 cameras was [sic] transferred to film with a cathode ray tube, like a big television . . . This CRT technique . . . is an older technique and has a very analogue feel to it that looks very . . . that has little errors that sort of work very well for the concept of the 100 cameras' (Hjorth: 2001). If at the heart of new punk cinema is the attempt to create something more 'authentic' than standard blockbuster material, it is an attempt shot through with a deep awareness that authenticity is itself a construct. In new punk cinema, this tension is foregrounded, as in the hand-held anarchy of *The Celebration* or *The Blair Witch Project*, or the beautifully degraded images in *28 Days Later*.

In a related sense, new punk cinema depends as much on the user as it does on the creator. Like punk audiences, who wanted to 'see through' the spectacle of rock and interact with the bands on a more personal, intimate level, new punk cinema is sustained by audiences who increasingly manipulate – rather than passively consume – films. Contemporary audiences inhabit an era when the codes and mechanics of film-making are no longer invisible, when the strategies of the classical Hollywood films have been demystified not only by the increasing availability and affordability of the tools of desk-top film-making, but also by the rise of film- and media-studies classes and tracks in colleges and universities, the multiple commentaries, bonus features; and ubiquitous 'behind-the-scenes' features on DVDs, in multiple popular print- and web-based film journals and magazines that critically examine the craft and technique of film-making, and finally in the ironic, post-modern self-puncturing sensibility of popular films such as *Scream* (1996) and *Not Another Teen Movie* (2001), where the 'rules' and previously invisible narrative codes of genre films are openly exposed and mocked. Whether these developments offer the possibility for critique or simply another mystification which provides the illusion of critique, new punk audiences are highly aware of the artifice that underlies the films they watch.

While the future of cinema, as something that exists in primary form on celluloid, is in question, the emergence of new digital and web-based forms in many ways extends the logic of punk even deeper into cinema. While it is too early in the evolution of digital cinema to predict what modes of distribution will supplant celluloid, there are new movements that seek to move beyond the worn-out 'mainstream vs independent cinema' paradigm, a paradigm which, as suggested earlier, is trickier to sustain now that 'indie' cinema has become a multi billion dollar industry. One new model – microcinema – is closely aligned with the do-it-yourself ethos that characterised punk. The website *microcinemascene.com*, for example, provides, among other things, a forum for digital filmmakers to post the films. 'Because of the do-it-yourself (DIY) mentality behind Microcinema productions', the site claims, 'the movies often lack technical polish, but excel when it comes to originality and vision.' (*'What is Microcinema?* 2004) Another site, *The New Venue*, not only provides a forum for posting films, but also detailed guidelines for the do-it-yourself film-maker who is just beginning to master the technologies of digital cameras and home editing systems. Like punk and like the Dogma 95 movement, which turned limitations and constraints to their advantage, *The New Venue* acknowledges the liberation that comes from limitation: 'The secret to making digital flicks is recognizing that the small image size, low frame rate, and pixilated artifacts are "generative constraints", rigid boundaries that evoke creative workarounds, like the restrictions a poet faces when composing a sonnet or haiku' ('Flicktips' 2004).

The importance of underground bulletins, journals and magazines cannot be underestimated in nurturing and documenting the new punk spirit in film. Of the many publications over the years that have helped nourish this sensibility, two are especially important. *Film Threat*, founded in Detroit in 1985 and published in paper form until 1997, covers 'cult films, underground shorts, alternative films and independent features' (*Film Threat*: 2004). In its current on-line incarnation, the magazine continues to offer a forum for film-makers to discuss their work in ways that are often theoretically informed. This is especially true of the regular 'DIY Filmmakers'' interviews, where no-budget and low-budget film-makers discuss their works.

The DIY punk moniker also extends to the DIY Convention, which hosts (among other events) the DIY Film Festival, which 'honors films from the growing field of cutting-edge, do-it-yourself storytelling' ('DIY Film Festival': 2004). Another journal giving relatively wide public exposure to independent film is *Filmmaker: The Magazine of Independent Film*, founded in 1992. Although, as its title suggests, *Filmmaker* is more mainstream in its orientation and coverage, it regularly gives exposure to alternative film-making, as in its spring 2004 focus on no-budget and micro-budget productions. Finally, there are magazines that, while their focus is not exclusively on cinema, are important venues for developing critical and theoretical approaches to punk culture. Of special note here are *Punk Planet*, which exists in print form and in an online version, and *Bad Subjects: Political Education for Everyday Life*, which features the work of Charles Bertsch, Joel Schalit, and others who write about punk history, politics and poetics in compelling ways.

It is our hope that this book spurs further study of new punk cinema. Perhaps a new revolutionary cinema is emerging on the web, which allows for the possibility not only for the creation of no-budget film-making, but its distribution as well. In this regard, new punk cinema of the future might be radically different from previous do-it-yourself movements, such as those associated with 8 mm and 16 mm film, which were limited in terms of performance and distribution to relatively small, localised audiences. Is it possible that the Samsung video phone – touted in advertisements as a lifestyle accessory of the beautiful – can be re-purposed for a new cinematic avant-garde? In *Subculture: The Meaning of Style*, Dick Hebdige wrote: 'The punk subculture, then, signified chaos at every level, but this was only possible because the style itself was so thoroughly ordered' (Hebdige 1979: 113). This tension between chaos and order, between resistance and commodification, between negation and creation remains at the contested heart of new punk cinema.

PART I

BACKGROUNDS AND CONTEXTS

1. PUNK CINEMA

Stacy Thompson

There is nothing sexy about materialist critique which is why it is often ignored in favour of ideological analysis or aesthetic evaluation. That said, it is precisely to materialist critique that I want to turn, as I propose a definition for 'punk cinema' in this essay. Two pieces of punk culture should prove instructive toward this end. The first is the famous set of diagrams, from a 1976 issue of the punk-zine, *Sideburns*, that demonstrates the proper tablature for three guitar chords – A, E, and G. Four short sentences accompany them: 'This is a chord. This is another. This is a third. Now form a band.'[1] This set of directions and blunt demand contain within themselves, in compressed form, the logic of punk and, by association and extension, that of punk cinema. Punk clearly has little to do with technical proficiency: the punk guitarist need only know three chords. Furthermore, as the diagrams suggest, punk is profoundly democratic: anyone should be able to play it. It is a socialised mode of music-making and performance in the sense that Walter Benjamin describes when he comments (on authorship) that 'what matters . . . is the exemplary character of production, which is able first to induce other producers to produce' (Benjamin 1978: 233). By by foregrounding its simplicity, punk produces producers. It propels potential producers over the gap between production and consumption, and it is this shift that socialises the music, which is not produced by an élite technocracy but by anyone who cares to create it. The best case in point is the 1992 Riot Grrrl convention in Washington DC, where, according to the authors of the Experience Music Project, 'it was not unusual for a band to play their first show the same week – or even the same day – that they first picked up their instruments' (Experience Music, 2004: n.p.).

This punk dictum has an essential, obverse, materialist component. On the first page of every issue of the fanzine *MaximumRockNRoll* (*MRR*), which has been in publication since 1982 and, within punk as a whole, is the most read, if also the most despised, arbiter of all things punk, appear the zine's 'Ad Criteria': 'We will not accept major label or related ads, or ads for comps or EPs that include major label bands' ('Ad Criteria' 2004: n.p.). Any music, zine or punk production of any kind that obtains corporate backing is no longer, by definition, punk. In other words, in defining punk, punks separate themselves from everything produced by the major record labels, or 'Big Five' which, in 2004, are the Universal Music Group, Sony Music Entertainment, the EMI Group, Warner Brothers Music, and BMG. For the past thirty-five years – all of punk's tenure – five or six major labels have controlled between 80 and 90 per cent of the global music market. Independent labels comprise the last 10 to 20 per cent of the market and, as I have argued elsewhere, punk productions account for less than 1 per cent of that market.[2] In other words, punks purposefully relegate their productions to the margins of the music industry, setting themselves up as enterprises or cottage industries and not corporations.

In sum, two vectors run through punk as a whole, aesthetics and economics. The history of punk is the history of the interplay between these two lines of force which find expression in and through one another. Within punk productions, the aesthetics always give voice to the underlying economics and vice versa. Consequently, there is no purely punk aesthetics or economics; neither can stand alone. The metal cover band that practises Slayer songs in your neighbour's garage is not a punk band simply by virtue of the fact that they have no corporate investors, and The F-UPs are not a punk band – despite the fact that they wear ripped jeans and T-shirts, two of their members sport mohawks, one looks suspiciously like Billy Joe Armstrong, the lead singer of Green Day, and the band's sound approximates early 1990s pop-punk – because their first album will be released on Capitol Records, a subsidiary of major label EMI. As the advertising criteria from *MRR* make clear, the punk position is uncompromising on the economic front. Aesthetics simply cannot be separated from economics. In the 1970s, punks learned this lesson the hard way, twice: once in New York City and once in London.

The history of punk is invaded and fundamentally reshaped by economics in 1976 and 1977, at the end of the first two punk scenes. In both cases, the major labels bought up the principal players in an early scene, thereby corporatising punk and denuding it of its economic resistance. In 1976, a first spate of independent, punk-label signings put the Ramones and other bands from the CBGBs, New York scene under contract. Shortly thereafter, the second wave of signings hit London, and the interested parties in this case were major labels. Among others, the Sex Pistols, the Clash and Generation X all signed. This corporatisation of punk set the historical stage for a major shift in punks' economic strategies, as well as preparing the ground for the definition of punk and punk cinema that I am proposing here.

This hard kernel, this uncompromising attention to economics, exemplified by the *MRR* advertising criteria, but also implicit within the *Sideburns* diagrams (you do not need venture capital to form a band), is the defining centre of punk, although this foregrounding of economics loses its popularity outside of punk itself, and here we have returned to the common analytical preference for aesthetic evaluation or ideological analysis instead of materialist critique. After all, who, upon setting out to read or write about music, expects to slog through economics to get there? But in no other musical genre does the economic context from which the music springs bulk so large. In jazz, for instance, it hardly matters that Warner Brothers releases Joshua Redman's albums or that Blue Note Records' parent company is EMI. These facts do not negate the fact that Redman's music or the Blue Note catalogue are jazz but, in the case of punk, they would do exactly that. In punk history, two of the most famous examples of sell-outs are Green Day and Chumbawamba. Both bands began as punk groups but, as soon as they signed with Reprise (which is owned by the Warner Music Group) and EMI, they became non-punk bands, regardless of the fact that their aesthetics had not, technically, changed. Their aesthetics *had* changed, though: to punks – if to no one else – these bands sounded different after, and because of, the corporate signings. There is a question of ethics at stake here that, I think, can be best explained through Marxist terms. Within the domain of punk, prices do not serve their properly capitalist function, which Marx describes as standing in for the labour that went into the commodity, equating it to money and hiding the qualitative nature of that labour. In Marx's words, a price is expressed as a sum of money, and '[s]ince money is the transformed shape of the commodity it does not reveal what has been transformed into it: whether conscience or virginity or horse dung' (Marx 1867: 1073). In contrast to this capitalist function, punks want to glance behind the price and look at the labour and the social relations in which it is situated, and, for punks, that labour is either non-corporate, ethical, and does not smell like horse dung, or it is corporate, unethical, and does smell, in which case it must be avoided.

But why bother resisting corporatisation? And how has that resistance inflected punk aesthetics? Punks resist the major labels because they grasp them as a synecdoche for capitalism as a whole, and punk's constant resistance to capitalism can be read in the song lyrics and zines of the past thirty years. From Crass's 'Do They Owe Us a Living?' ('Do they owe us a living? / Of course they fucking do!' [1978: n.p.]) to Fugazi's 'Merchandise' ('Merchandise keeps us in line / Common sense says it's by design' [1990: n.p.]) to the thousands of zines and webpages outlining, sometimes crudely and sometimes with great subtlety, the social, ecological and moral dangers of exploitation, commodification and corporatisation, punks have always opposed capitalism as a perceived evil. This anti-capitalism sentiment took on a new intensity in the late 1970s in reaction to the first major label incorporation of punk. In Walter Benjamin's terms, this event in punk history marks the moment when punks shifted from adopting a particular 'attitude' towards the capitalist mode of production to taking responsibility for their own position as producers within that mode of production (Benjamin 1978: 222). From the late 1970s on, punks have attempted to absent themselves from capitalism as much as possible, both in terms of their aesthetics and their economics. Aesthetically, punk emerged as an abrasive, non-commercial form of rock music centred around three instruments – the electric guitar, electric bass guitar and drum kit – and a vocalist who sang, chanted and screamed lyrics over the top of the simply structured, loud, racing instrumentation. When this initial sound became widely available from the Big Five, the punk aesthetics embarked upon a course of evasive action that has continued for the past three decades, arriving in the mid-1990s at a variety of hard-core punk forms (including Screamo, Power Violence and Grindcore) that the music industry has, in 2004, still failed to capitalise or corporatise. As a result, they are punk 'successes'. Economically, punks have engaged in self-sustaining enterprises and eschewed corporations, content to make music as, above all, a labour of love and politics, while maintaining a sharp suspicion of anyone out to make money selling punk.

Punk Cinema

With this definition of punk in mind, what can we say about punk cinema? I have argued that the term 'punk cinema' acquires a critical edge only if we maintain the underlying logic of punk itself.[3] In other words, punk as a project (which includes not only music but zines, clothing styles and film) brings the same demands to bear upon music and upon cinema, meaning that punk cinema, like punk rock, must resist capitalism through aesthetic and economic means. Just as a few major corporations dominate the music industry, an analogous group controls most film production in the United States. There is even some overlap between the music industry's Big Five and the film industry's Big Nine, namely Warner Brothers. In June 2004, 98 per cent of the US film industry's yearly revenue was generated by nine studios, all corporately controlled: Warner Brothers, Disney, Twentieth Century–Fox, Columbia, DreamWorks, Newmarket, Universal, Paramount, and Metro-Goldwyn-Mayer/United Artists. The independent studios are left to fight it out for the remaining 2 per cent of the market. These are only the current statistics, but the corporate structure of the film industry has changed little over the past thirty years although ownership of the studios today is concentrated in even fewer hands than it might appear to be. For instance, the Time Warner parent company owns not only Warner Brothers but also New Line Studios, meaning that Time Warner alone accounts for roughly 20 per cent of the total US film market. In keeping with the logic of punk economics, punk cinema must be produced without backing from the major studios. Again, because punks consciously situate their productions in an antagonistic relationship to the capitalist mode of production, 98 per cent of US films can be categorically disqualified from the domain of punk cinema, based upon their corporate backing.

But aesthetics must also play a role in punk cinema as it does in punk rock. It seems logical to assume that punk cinema's aesthetics would parallel punk rock's, in which case we might expect punk films to be fast paced, elliptically edited and calculated to offend bourgeois notions of taste and morality. Independently produced versions of *Natural Born Killers* (1994), *Fight Club* or *Memento* might fit the bill. But these assumptions would hold up only if films that employed such an aesthetics could thereby resist Hollywood (commercial-corporate-capitalist) aesthetic norms. Hollywood films, however, have been narrative driven and fast paced for decades. In fact, if a Hollywood writer or director wishes to produce a film that will immediately be embraced as edgy and avant-garde, he or she merely needs to abandon the clearly structured narrative form that has heretofore dominated Hollywood hitherto. Even films that merely rearrange the narrative in interesting ways (*Memento*, *Mulholland Drive*, *Pulp Fiction*) tend to be heralded as boldly experimental.

But the punk cinema aesthetics is, in fact, the antithesis of what we might expect. Instead of fast-moving narratives, numerous cuts both within and between shots, innumerable scenes, and frequent jump cuts, punk film-makers do just the opposite. To resist the easy commodification of their films, they slow their narrative pace to a crawl, scarcely move the camera, make infrequent cuts and, in general, forego most of the techniques that would lend their films commercial viability. Examples of these aesthetics include Ulli Lommel's *Blank Generation* (1979), Jack Hazan and David Mingay's *Rude Boy* (1980) and Penelope Spheeris's *Suburbia* (1984).[4] For this chapter, I want to examine two films as examples of the definition of punk cinema that I am proposing: one film from the initial flowering of punk cinema and a more recent movie that could easily be mistaken for a punk film. Because my claim, here, is not only that punk cinema carries out a particular economic and aesthetic programme but that the punk cinema project remains ongoing.

Now Make a Film

In 1977, Amos Poe, one of punk cinema's most prolific film-makers, wrote, produced, and directed *The Foreigner*, an exemplary text within the subgenre. In a simple but brilliant punk cinema move, Poe includes, as the film's final credit, the price tag: 'This film was made possible by a $5,000 personal loan from the Merchants Bank of New York'. Commenting on the finances for the film, Poe explains that he asked for a loan to finance a film but the bank agent told him that the bank didn't give loans for films, so Poe had to take out a $5,000 car loan instead. Even considering inflation, $5,000 is an incredibly small budget for a feature-length film (the movie is ninety-five minutes long). Additionally, Poe takes pains to inform the audience of the film's budget and how the money was obtained, an uncommon practice for film-makers, thereby highlighting the fact that film-making is well within the economic reach of anyone who can obtain an car loan. Popular independent film-maker, Jim Jarmusch, saw *The Foreigner* before he made his first film and comments, '*The Foreigner*, which to me was a really important film because when I first saw it – it was before I made *Permanent Vacation* – and when I saw that he [Poe] made a feature film for, like, six thousand, I knew that I could make a film too' (quoted in Poe, 2001: n.p.). In short, Poe's explicit attention to the film's material means of possibility both reveals that making a film doesn't require corporate backing (while also expressing pride in that fact) and encourages potential film-makers to bridge the divide between audience member and film-maker. (Another material condition of the film's production rendered obvious in the credits is how few people were needed to make the film. The movie's full cast and crew amount to thirty-eight people, several of whom act in the film and work on the crew.)

Not unlike *The Foreigner*'s material conditions of possibility and its attention to them, the film's punk aesthetics serve two ends. The film positions itself against Hollywood aesthetics and is an object lesson in how little a film-maker needs to know about the craft of film-making before exposing film. Although the film has never had a major box-office opening, it was recently screened in Philadelphia and several critics commented on it. In a brief, dismissive review, Sam Adams describes it as 'an unholy marriage of Andy Warhol and *Alphaville* that starts with endless shots of bottle-blond foreign spy Max Menace (Eric Mitchell) walking the streets, and ends with endless shots of him running through the streets. This is progress?' (Adams 2003) Slightly more willing than Adams to grant Poe the benefit of the doubt, Matt Prigge nevertheless gripes that *The Foreigner* 'isn't an easy sit', adding that 'Poe is comfortable shooting Warholian long-takes of characters watching TV on hotel beds. And good luck following the plot: On the disc's commentary, he admits even he has no idea what one dominatrix-dressed character's function is supposed to be' (Prigge 2003). Prigge also notes that the film is '[d]efiantly unfocused and sloppy' (ibid.), but it is his insight into *Blank Generation*, the film that Poe made two years before *The Foreigner*, that is instructive. Reacting to the earlier film's aesthetics, which are very similar to the latter's, Prigge writes, 'The film is grainy, black-and-white, anxiously handheld, thrown together and frankly ugly. In other words, pretty darned punk' (ibid.).

Several of the above reviewers' observations bear closer analysis in relation to *The Foreigner*'s content and form. Adams describes Max Menace as a 'foreign spy' and Prigge labels him a 'German agent – on some unnamed operation' (ibid.). Poe himself has identified Menace as a European terrorist. Based on the plot, all of these options seem plausible although, in the film, Eric Mitchell has little to no discernible German or European accent that might lead the viewer to presume his nationality, nor does the spectator know where the flight originated that has apparently brought him to the John F. Kennedy International Airport as the movie begins. Not only in the beginning of the film, but throughout it, the audience is never granted even the most basic information about who Max Menace is. Nor does the audience ever learn why he came to Manhattan nor what he is trying to do, apart from obtain some kind of aid (information? shelter? money?) from the people whom he encounters.

The basic narrative building blocks or causal chain that might establish some curiosity, some desire to know, for the spectator are also notably missing. First, little happens in the movie in terms of traditional plotting. Max arrives at Kennedy (presumably, at least – the audience first sees him walking down empty corridors in the terminal but it is not immediately clear that he has just arrived), takes a cab, driven by a punk, into Manhattan, watches part of a television documentary on punk in his Chelsea Hotel room, meets a number of people from whom he unsuccessfully attempts to solicit aid of an unspecified sort, and is shot to death in Battery Park by two men in black suits. In the final shots of the film, a group of punks find Max dead in the park, cluster around his corpse, and then disperse.

The inclusion of the punks in the film seems particularly extraneous. Although Poe has commented that they belong to a (fictional) group, called the Bags, that enjoy meeting tourists at the airport and terrorising them, it is difficult for the spectator to arrive at this conclusion unaided. The punk who drives Max from the airport to Manhattan drops him off, steps into a phone box, and has a cryptic telephone conversation with another punk, who might or might not be the leader of the Bags. Occasionally, one of the punks passes Max on a Manhattan street and glowers at him a little, and one of them is clearly following him for a time. A group of four punks (played by the non-fictional band The Cramps) in CBGBs attacks Max in the bar and in the bar's bathroom, cutting his chest with a knife and beating him up. And the Bags, finally, gather to look at his dead body (it is hard to say where they came from or how they knew that Max was in Battery Park). All in all, the Bags are an odd supplement to the film, a part of it that sticks out and does not gel with the rest. The most excessive moment of this supplementarity occurs during a scene in which the audience observes the punks in their lair, crammed together on a sofa, talking about power drills, coffee stains, spots, another character named Fili Harlow, and, occasionally, 'the foreigner' whom they plan to trail and watch. Near the end of the scene, a direct cut connects a shot of all six Bags on the couch to a close-up of a doll being electrocuted in a doll-sized electric chair. Another direct cut and we observe two of the Bags sitting on the couch behind the doll and chair. It is unclear where the other Bags have gone or whether any time has passed. There is another direct cut and the camera shows us a close-up of a firecracker in a punk's belt loop. The firecracker explodes and the scene is over. It is difficult to conceive of a logical reason for including it, apart from the fact that there is no reason. The scene's refusal to make sense in corporate terms opens up the possibility that the film aims at something besides profit. If Poe can 'waste' film – every second of film shot is an index of some amount of money spent – on a scene that neither forwards the plot nor develops characters and cannot be contained within the film's narrative, then this is because he is not solely out to make money. In other words, if the logic of the commercial film is that it turns a profit, then the extraneousness of the punks and their scenes suggests a supplemental reason for making film, a reason not governed by money. Even if that reason is never made explicit – although it is not difficult to imagine possibilities: to make a political point, for art's sake, for pleasure – the film's excesses nonetheless invoke it as a possibility.

Compare *The Foreigner*'s plot with movies from the same year: *Star Wars, Annie Hall, Saturday Night Fever, Smokey and the Bandit, Close Encounters of the Third Kind*. Although *Close Encounters* was oddly contemplative, almost elegiac, for a science fiction film, its teleology was nevertheless clear. In short, apropos of content, Poe refuses to provide even the bare bones of character and plot that Hollywood cinema demands. These aesthetic choices alone situate *The Foreigner* in opposition to the dominant commercial-corporate model of film. Further aesthetic elements, such as its lack of closure, guarantee that the film will never be mistaken for a commercial product. Even corporately produced films that seem to forego a readily digestible conclusion usually allow one to slip in the back door.

Lost in Translation (2003, distributed by Focus Films, a subsidiary of Universal) is an interesting example. In the conclusion, just before the two main characters part, possibly forever, Bob Harris (Bill Murray) leans close to Charlotte (Scarlett Johansson) and whispers something in her ear to which the audience is not privy. What did he say? Have we been left without a conclusion, without closure? But a quick run through the repertoire of lines Bob could have said reveals how inadequate any of them would have been: 'I love you.' 'What's your e-mail address'? 'Same time next year.' In each case, we would have been given too much information, too much closure. What looks like a gap, a lack of closure, is, in fact, precisely the proper amount of it. Another word or two and we would feel that the film had become overly obvious, didactic, clichéd. The film's driving tension, the element that keeps us watching, is not the sexual tension that arises when Bob and Charlotte lie together, clothed, on top of the bed covers and talk, or, rather, what drives us is not the desire to see their relationship consummated sexually but the fear that this will happen, that the sexual tension will be channelled into familiar forms. In short, our interest grows out of the possibility that some sort of 'new relationship' is possible between a married woman in her early twenties and a married man in his late fifties, a relationship not defined by the obvious choices of an affair or a friendship. For this reason, it is with anxiety that we watch Bob put a drunk Charlotte to bed one night, because we fear that the tension between them – the interest – is about to collapse into sex and an affair. In a sense, what we have here is a film structured, like language, around a constitutive gap. To come too close to that gap is to recognise it for what it is: in Lacanian terms, the Real, the impossible fulfilment of desire. And to come too close to the *objet petit a* that sits in the gap, that marks it as a gap without filling it in, is to find only another affair, only another friendship, only a partial fulfilment, not that new, promised Thing. So it is with relief that the audience watches the film conclude as it should, with, the gap, and the film's pleasurable and simultaneous flirtation with and maintenance it, of still in place. Approaching the gap is pleasurable; definitively arriving at it disappointing.

The observation worth making here is that when a corporately funded film refuses closure, it does so only because it must. In this case, it is the only satisfying closure possible. Furthermore, the corporate film undergoes a different process of leaving the gap than *The Foreigner* or a punk film. In Hollywood, there must be no doubt about the gap's gap-ness, for instance. The pure gap does not stick out, anamorphically, the way that *Lost in Translation*'s does. This film announces its gap; it situates it carefully (at the end of the film – a privileged position) and marks it on all sides. It becomes impossible to ignore. In short, the lack of closure in a Hollywood film demands that the audience take it into account as such, which is another way of containing it within the narrative after all. The film's cordoning off of the space lays an injunction upon the audience: 'Here comes a meaningful elision. Make it signify something.' The audience recognises that the film, with painful deliberateness, constructs for itself and resists shedding light upon a final space of mystery, but it marks the mystery as such. We know it as unknowable and, in that sense, it is known after all.

A pure gap surprises us and starts us thinking; dozens of 'Bridge Closed' signs haven't been posted around it to forewarn us. At the end of *The Foreigner*, for instance, Max Menace emerges from the bar in which he has been beaten by The Cramps and runs, in an extreme long-shot, towards the camera. He runs for a solid two or three minutes, finally arriving at the camera and running past it. The camera then tracks slowly with him as he spends the final several minutes of the film also running, at last making his way to Battery Park on the southernmost tip of Manhattan. As he descends a set of steps towards a railing overlooking the Hudson River, two men who have been waiting on either side of the stairs, step out and shoot him repeatedly, then leave. Max staggers to the railing and slumps against it, his back to the camera. He remains motionless for the rest of the film, caught in a long-shot as the punks circle him and disperse, and a yacht eventually passes behind him. The gaps abound. Who was Max Menace? What did he want in New York City? Who was he working for? Who was working against him? Who killed him? What does his death mean? Does it mean anything? Why make a film about Max to begin with? The camera's refusal to track or zoom any closer to Max in the final shot denies the spectator even the possibility of observing Max's response to his own death. His face remained impassive as he ran through the park, so perhaps it remained equally unfazed in death, but the camera maintains a polite distance, and the audience remains at a remove. In the end, we are as lost as the punks who have troubled Max to no real end but, finally, bear witness to his death, as the audience does, without understanding why he died or what it means. It is difficult to imagine a corporately funded film concluding (so to speak) with more gaps than it began with, and this fact alone sets *The Foreigner* outside the domain of Hollywood cinema.

The Foreigner's filmic techniques, or lack thereof, further establish it as a punk film. Commenting on a scene between Doll (a dominatrix in real life and in the film) and Fili Harlow in which the camera's placement shifts randomly between shots, Poe remarks, 'We had no idea about the 180 degree rule or any rule at this point' (Poe 2001: n.p.). Poe also notes the 'campy dialogue and delivery' in the same scene and explains that he was imitating Andy Warhol's aesthetics. During his commentary on the DVD version of the film, Poe watches the film as the spectator does and muses over his influences: Jean-Luc Godard's *Alphaville* (1965), John Cassavetes's *Shadows*, and Andy Warhol's films in general.[5] Both of these observations of Poe's underscore the punk-ness of his film's aesthetics. First, his inattention to, and ignorance of, continuity editing throughout the film demonstrate, like the economic (as well as the other aesthetic) components of the film, that a film-maker need not be well versed in the technique of film-making before committing his or her work to celluloid. The film's sound reinforces this point: Poe used no mix, opting instead for cheaper, one-track recording. Consequently, music accompanies dialogue in the film only when it happens to occur diagetically within the scene, during the scenes in CBGBs, for instance. When non-diagetic music plays, there is no dialogue. The simplicity and availability of this technique become apparent in an early scene in which Max meets a contact of some sort at a building site. We view the meeting in an extreme long-shot, yet their conversation is clearly audible. It is obvious that Poe has made no attempt to synchronise the men's discussion with the words on the sound-track; rather, we get the impression that the image and dialogue were recorded separately and then one was simply laid over the other, which is, in fact, what happened.

In sum, punk cinema producers encourage viewers, through a particular set of economic and aesthetic means, to make films. Punk cinema says, 'You can do this. You should do this.' At the same time, however, again through economic and aesthetic means, it resists capitalism and corporatisation and the dominant economic and aesthetic models associated with them.

Punk Critique

Punk is not, finally, an aesthetic, which is to say that it has always been more than an aesthetic. Just as punk rockers took evasive action in the late 1970s and early 1980s, retooling their economics and aesthetics to distance their fashion and music from ever-encroaching corporate control, the initial wave of punk film-makers did likewise. In 2004, punk cinema continues as contemporary film-makers introduce new anti-capitalist aesthetics into film, while cleaving to a punk economics that has not changed. Like the films that preceded it, today's punk cinema encompasses independently produced films that attack the dominant, capitalist economic and aesthetic models for producing films, while socialising the means of production. Finally, punk offers us a method for critiquing film from a materialist perspective because, in the end, punks concern themselves with how films make material interventions in the world. An interesting film to look at through punk critique's lens is Jean-Luc Godard's recent film, *In Praise of Love* (*Éloge de l'Amour*) (2001), because much of Godard's work could be misconstrued as punk if his aesthetics alone were the basis for judgement.

But first things first, which, for punk rock or cinema after 1979, means economics. For the production and distribution costs of *In Praise of Love*, Godard cobbled together backing from no fewer than seven production companies[6] and four distributors.[7] But the sticking point for a punk critique is the inclusion of the French arm of the Canal+ Groupe as a source of funding because this production company is a subsidiary of Vivendi/Universal, one of the Big Nine major studios. Consequently, Godard's film is not punk. Perhaps the case could be made that Godard steals more from Vivendi than they steal from him because historically, he has rarely pleased his producers or catered to their desires, but punks do not allow for wiggle room. *Pecunia olet*: money smells of its source. In some small way, Godard is helping Universal accrue capital with which it can expand its corporate reach.

Why might Godard's aesthetics be mistakenly characterised as punk then? Wheeler Winston Dixon writes that '[u]nlike the films of most contemporary directors, Godard's cinema disregards the realities of the marketplace' (Dixon 2003: n.p.). It is tempting to argue just the opposite, though: far from disregarding the commodity market-place, Godard deliberately opposes it. In his own words, 'out of principle, I've always chosen to do what others aren't doing. "No one does that, so it remains to be done, let's try it." If it's already being done, there's no point in me doing it as well' (Godard, 2001: n.p.). Still, Godard's aesthetics might not initially strike one as punk. No doubt *In Praise of Love*'s leisurely pace and elegiac mood seem far removed from most people's conception of punk. A couple of useful cues from punk rock can guide us here. After the New York and London punk sounds and sartorial styles became commercially viable, hard-core punk emerged in the United States and has, for the past twenty-five years, mutated in response to the market-place, always one step ahead, or outside, of that market. In the early 1980s, for instance, after hard-core had become famous for rapid-fire tempios and ultra-short haircuts and both were beginning to obtain a modicum of economic viability, bands like Flipper slowed their sound down, inching through their dirges, while the members of Black Flag grew their hair. As I have mentioned regarding *The Foreigner*, the aesthetics of punk cinema undertook evasive action as well, not disregarding the market but opposing it as Godard does. As in punk rock, tempo became important, and *In Praise of Love*, like *The Foreigner*, maintains a languid pace.

In terms of plot points, little happens in the film. It is split into two halves, one set in the present and shot in black and white and the other set two years earlier and shot in colour. The order and coloration of the film's halves are surprising, with the present preceding the past and shot in black and white (which, conventionally, suggests the past). The first half is shot on 35 mm and the second on digital video. The half set in the present concerns the attempts of a film director, Edgar, to cast the roles of four couples who will represent the 'four stages of love' in one of his films. The second half centres around Edgar's visit, two years earlier, to a couple living in Brittany who served in the French Resistance during World War II. In the latter half (chronologically first) Edgar is attempting to write a cantata based on the work of Simone Weil and, while researching it, visits the former Resistance members who are in the process of selling the story of their experiences to Steven Spielberg and Associates. Edgar and their granddaughter, referred to as 'Elle' in the credits, both happen to sit in on the elderly couple's negotiations with the Spielberg representatives, and Elle impresses Edgar with her caustic remarks and questions about the representatives' cultural imperialist intentions. Elle is the bridge that links the two halves of the film: the first chronicles the first time that Edgar meets her, and the second his attempts to cast her in his new work. In the present of the film, he eventually locates her cleaning railway carriages in Paris, and, although they enjoy a lengthy, wide-ranging discussion, he cannot convince her to undertake the project which, at the end of the first half (and the chronological end of the film), he abandons. In short, the film is about a man who does not write a cantata and then proceeds, two years later, to not to cast a film.

Of course, the spectator looking for a tightly constructed narrative should not turn first to Godard's films, in which plot is never really the point. Dixon writes that Godard's film-making 'strategy is in direct contradiction with the Hollywood model in which the script always comes first, to be followed by casting, choosing a director, director of photography, set designer, and so on. Godard works from instinct, instinctively choosing the path that goes against the grain of conventional cinema practice' (Dixon 2003: n.p.). Like punk rock, Godard's early films, such as *Breathless* (1960), *Une Femme est une Femme* (*A Woman is a Woman* [1961]), and *Vivre sa Vie* (*My Life to Live* [1962]), all of which preceded punk by about fifteen years, introduced a frenetic, cut-and-paste, elliptical aesthetics that directly opposed the Hollywood pacing and craft of the time, perfectly embodied in Alfred Hitchcock and Douglas Sirk films (*North by Northwest* [1959], *Imitation of Life* [1959]), enslaved as they were to continuity editing with its establishing and master-shots, 180-degree rule, eyeline matches, and so forth. But the New Hollywood of the 1960s and 1970s caught up with Godard's aesthetics, which changed accordingly. I do not propose to sketch the historical progression of Godard's work, here; rather, I want to note that, in 2001, Godard arrives at a contemporary formula for resistant cinema: slow paced, concerned with politico-philosophical questions, esoteric.

The difficulty of Godard's films, which might be expected to prohibit filmmaking rather than encourage it, diminishes with the introduction of one essential factor: his movies need to be approached as questions rather than answers. They are thought problems, and, as such, they militate against attempts to bind them into contained, easily consumable commodities. They are less statements than provocations that, when successful, start their audiences thinking by structuring a space for thought, bracketing off the time that we spend experiencing them as time devoted to ideation, the characters' and the viewers'. As Dixon writes,

> Godard . . . asks his viewers to do a considerable amount of work when watching his films, something that contemporary audiences are apparently loath to do . . . [T]he cinema viewer of today seeks, above all, safety, cohesion, and the certainty of closure that the genre cinema provides . . . [N]o one wants the viewer to be confused, after all. (Dixon 2003: n.p.)

But *In Praise of Love*, like *The Foreigner*, sets out to, among other things, risk confusing the audience because confusion demands thought. Confusion is a blockage or knot in the movement of thought that must be lingered over and that we try to separate out into its threads, and that attempt is valuable even if we do not wholly succeed. Perhaps the most obvious moment for thinking occurs near the midway point of *In Praise of Love*. Edgar and Elle stand in front of a low wall overlooking a railway line. Godard catches them in a medium shot, facing away from the camera and positioned to the right of centre. For about three minutes, the spectator stares at their backs as they talk about time, history, and how Americans lack the latter and, consequently, try to buy other nations' histories. It is time for thought, in which we think along with Edgar and Elle.

But what about the punk axiom, 'Now form a band', the demand that a punk production should encourage others to produce? Can a Godard film really be said to encourage production, particularly among spectators who are not skilled technicians? Surely his films' obscurantism, philosophy and opacity, in addition to his technical expertise, prevent rather than promote further film-making? Yet, who else do film-makers cite so frequently as an influence? From Amos Poe (who subtitled *Unmade Beds* [1976] 'un homage du Jean Luc Godard et les nouvelle vague Francaise' [sic]), to Quentin Tarantino (whose production company is called A Band Apart, after Godard's 1964 film of the same name), to Hal Hartley, to the Dogma 95 'brethren', to countless others. I suspect that, although Godard's films can, in fact, be interpreted as cohesive units,[8] it is precisely because they suspend so many Hollywood film conventions and techniques that they open up a space for other, and others', experiments. Even if Godard's suspension obeys a logic of its own, if the rules are broken in a consistent fashion, the suspension nevertheless serves, within each film, as material proof that a film can be produced in which realistic acting, chronological and causally structured narratives (or narrative at all, for that matter) and continuity editing can be abandoned in favour of other possibilities. That abandonment has proven liberating for innumerable directors, both commercial and non-commercial.

In terms of content, Godard's films have no doubt inspired film-makers to rework, loosen or reject conventional narrative structures in favour of lengthy philosophical, literary or political diatribes and citations. It is the rare Godard film that does not include citations from his favourite artists, literary figures, philosophers and film-makers; often quotations are read straight from a book by a character in the film. *In Praise of Love* includes citations from Pablo Picasso, Henri Bergson, Max Ophüls, and a line from Robert Bresson's film, *Pickpocket* (1959), among many others. The film concludes with a lengthy shot of an image of Edgar's head, seen from behind and resting against the headrest of a car seat. This shot is superimposed on another of the sun setting behind some rocks jutting out from the sea. The saturated colour of the image fills the eye, as Edgar muses over the impossibility of seeing or knowing any image in itself, free from mediation, how every image can be seen or understood as an image only because of other images which it is not. In short, Edgar brings the assumption that language is structured by difference to bear upon images, suggesting that they must be grasped as a language. An image can never be seen or known in itself; it can be grasped only as a negative term through the ways in which it differs from other images.

Although I find Godard's suggestion that film is structured like a language provocative, the point is not, finally, whether or not his film encourages genuine, as opposed to pseudo-philosophising but that it expands the parameters of what can be included in a film. Walter Benjamin asserts that socialising the means of production, in this case expanding the number of film-makers, means that a medium gains 'in breadth what it loses in depth' (Benjamin 1978: 225). In short, the ability to increase the number of people who control and have access to the means of producing film outweighs the likelihood that the resulting films will not obey conventional notions of quality. More important than bourgeois aesthetic or intellectual evaluations is the fact that Godard's movies demonstrate that film can contain practically anything, if the film-maker is not concerned with money as an end rather than as a means.

Like Godard's inclusion of theory, the heavy-handedness of Godard's editing might initially seem calculated to discourage future film-making, particularly by non-technicians, rather than open it up. After all, doesn't a Godard film leave the spectator thinking, 'I don't even understand how this film was edited, let alone imagine that I could create something similar myself'. Richard Dienst argues the obverse of this conclusion:

> With Godard, making images looks so easy. Each of his films, no matter what else it does, offers an extensive demonstration of technique, as if it wants to be more than merely 'reflexive' about itself – instead, it sets out to teach you how it was made. Making a film is to be treated as a practical extension of watching films – it seems to be nothing more than a matter of learning how to use a camera, finding some people who want to act, and coming up with a story as you go along. (Dienst 2000: 23)

In other words, Godard's deliberately, obviously unconventional use of formal elements serves the same end as the broad scope of his films' content. First, again by suspending the rules, Godard's films open up on the possibility of editing a film however you like, as Amos Poe did with *The Foreigner*, without regard for the 180-degree rule or continuity editing. Furthermore, even if a potential film-maker fails to grasp the logic of Godard's idiosyncratic techniques, the flouting of the rules speaks for itself.

Godard punctuates the film with long sections of black leader, sometimes adorned with a few words but often not. These insertions emphasise particular lines or images within the film. More importantly, though, these moments of black screen seem only sometimes calculated to create particular effects. Often, their occurrence strikes the viewer as deliberately random reminders that the film is being edited. In short, these long blinks emphasise not only lines of dialogue and images but also the fact that Godard can include them whenever and wherever he pleases. It is as if Godard is flaunting the arbitrariness of his editing choices and simultaneously revealing how little it matters where or when he ends a shot or begins another. Similarly, the sound in a scene often ends in mid-sentence, before the scene itself ends, leaving a few seconds of silence without even ambient noise. Again, this technique does not simply emphasise the sound occurring just prior to the silence but opens up the possibility of ending sound arbitrarily, or wherever one wishes to place an emphasis. Similarly, Godard introduces music as punctuation. Snatches of a recurring piece of simple, mournful piano music can be heard sporadically throughout the film, sometimes beginning in the middle of a shot and half-obscuring the voices for a few seconds, sometimes connecting two scenes with a sound bridge, but usually accompanying the images contrapuntally.

Despite *In Praise of Love*'s provocations to produce, it remains a difficult nut to crack for many audience members. Godard makes no apology for this fact, remarking, instead, that '[i]n films, you have to give, but first of all you have to receive. Audiences no longer give because with television you stop giving. There's only the receiving end' (Godard 2001: n.p.). Responding to Alain Robbe-Grillet's *The Voyeur* (1958), Tony Bennett writes that the *nouvel roman* calls 'into question the fixed division of labour between writer and reader which the traditional novel proposes' and exposes 'the conventions whereby the relationship between the roles of writer (the issuing source of meaning) and the reader (the passive recipient of the offered meaning) is constructed' (Bennett 1979: 52). In parallel fashion, Godard's cinema socialises the means of producing knowledge about his films. As viewers, we produce them, because they come to us unfinished, incomplete, full of gaps.

To sum up, all the elements of *In Praise of Love*'s aesthetics agree with a punk cinema aesthetics. Yet, because punk critique is first and foremost materialist critique, the first and last question to ask is, 'Who benefits, materially, from this film?' In spite of the socialising impulses at work in it, the movie ultimately makes money for Vivendi/Universal, which is trying to monopolise, not socialise, the means of production. And punks refuse to suffer this contradiction. Within the logic of punk, the proper attitude toward capitalism, by itself, unattached to an anti-capitalist economics, will never suffice to render a cultural production authentically punk. In other words, it is impossible to rage against the machine when you are a part of it; you only wind up making it stronger.

Last Sounds

The obvious protest to my line of argument is that I have left little or no room for aesthetic evaluation or that I have conflated economic considerations with aesthetic ones. After all, must we condone every film that socialises the means of production, not only of film but also of knowledge? Is a film necessarily good just because its economics and aesthetics encourage further production? What about quality and beauty? Won't a materialist model of assessing film force us to approve of a host of aesthetically horrific films? After all, isn't *The Foreigner*, in truth, a bad, ugly film? Isn't *In Praise of Love*, finally, hopelessly dull? But these are precisely the questions over which punk rock and punk cinema refuse to compromise. Punk film-makers, like punk musicians, are, in a sense, out to create beautiful, aesthetically pleasing work, but not in the usual bourgeois sense. One of the greatest hard-core punk songs, Minor Threat's 'Minor Threat', is two minutes long and, in the conventional terms of music appreciation, consists of little more than frantically played rock instruments in competition with hoarsely shouted lyrics. But in punk's terms, it is certainly beautiful. The radical assumption or move at stake here is the possibility of an ethical aesthetic. Marx writes that tasting the bread will not tell us who grew the wheat. Punk tells us that we need to know who grew it and under what circumstances, and, as Marx would no doubt agree, that knowledge will affect the taste.

Notes

1   For a reprint of the diagrams and text, refer to Savage (1992: 80).
2   See Thompson (2001).
3   See Thompson (2004a).
4   For the purposes of this chapter, I am differentiating between fictional, feature-length punk cinema and documentary punk cinema because two different aesthetics are at work here. Documentaries in this subgenre would include films such as Amos Poe's *The Blank Generation* (1976), Don Letts's *The Punk Rock Movie* (1978), and Penelope Spheeris's *The Decline of Western Civilization* (1981).
5   Even the DVD commentary to *The Foreigner* cleaves to punk aesthetics. Poe is the only commentator, and he is clearly speaking on the fly, often lapsing into silence for

a minute or two, leaving the viewer to watch the film in complete silence (the soundtrack is inaudible). At one point, Poe's voice fades as he moves away from the microphone to find a cigarette. After he finds one, his voice gradually grows louder as he returns to the microphone and the viewer hears his seat scrape the floor as he resettles himself before the scratch of a match is heard, followed by deep inhalation.

6 The production companies were: Avventura Films (fr), Le Studio Canal+ (fr), Les Films Alain Sarde (fr), Périphéria (fr), Télévision Suisse Romande (TSR) (ch), Vega Film AG (ch), and Arte France Cinéma (ft).

7 The distributors were: ARP Sélection (fr), Manhattan Pictures International, Optimum Releasing (gb), and Revolver SRL (it).

8 Kaja Silverman and Harun Farocki's *Speaking About Godard* offers several compelling readings of Godard films that bind the smallest details of narrative, editing, and *mise-en-scène* into meaningful wholes.

2. ITALIAN NEO-REALIST INFLUENCES

Jay McRoy

CONTESTING REALITIES

In the United States, punk cinema, like the sonic and cultural matrix from which it arose, has long been defined by a 'do-it-yourself' aesthetic. Employing a myriad of relatively inexpensive film-making techniques, from location-shooting with amateur performers to cut-rate special effects and rudimentary editing, talented visionaries, such as Nick Zedd, Beth B and Richard Kern, created a multitude of challenging works. Revelling in film's materiality and artifice, these visual artists critiqued the dominant culture's economic, social and political logics. Consequently, in their distinctly counter-cinematic structure, a narrative and visual style marked by the 'desire to play unrestrained within the terrain of the visual, free from the political, social, cultural, and financial constraints of dominant cinema' (Sargeant 1999: 9), many of the earliest cinematic productions linked with the US punk rock scene resemble the films of Jean-Luc Godard and other prominent 'New Wave' and avant-garde directors of the 1960s. This freedom from, and at times outright rejection of, commercial film-making practices allowed for the exploration of previously 'taboo' subjects and images, frequently culminating in visually arresting reconsiderations of conservative notions of 'obscenity' and 'taste'.

Not all of punk cinema's foundational texts fall exclusively within the domain of the 'experimental' or avant-garde, however. Several of this cinematic tradition's offerings mobilise familiar documentary and *cinéma vérité* aesthetics to present fictional and ostensibly 'non-fictional' accounts of marginalised identities and stigmatised subcultural practices. Of the numerous directors to apply an overtly verist aesthetic, Penelope Spheeris is perhaps one of the most widely known. In her 1981 documentary, *The Decline of Western Civilization*, for example, Spheeris mixes carefully edited interviews with members of bands such as X, Black Flag and The Germs with strategically selected testimonies from club owners, fringe journalists and seemingly random attendees of punk rock performances. The resulting text provides a glimpse into the early 1980s' Los Angeles punk rock scene, albeit through Spheeris's inevitably subjective lens. Likewise, Spheeris's *Suburbia*, though a work of fiction, endeavours to depict the southern California punk rock scene in an accurate light. Working primarily with amateur actors culled from local punk rock clubs, and filming the majority of her scenes within actual abandoned housing developments and dingy, exhaust-shrouded streets, Spheeris fashions a film that, despite its occasional hyperbole, evokes the works of Italian neo-realist directors, such as Roberto Rossellini and Vittorio De Sica in its apparently social realist agenda. While not a documentary in the strictest sense of the term, through the use of hand-held cameras, available lighting and diaegetic sound, Spheeris's *Suburbia*, offers viewers a work of 'critical realism' that, in the words of the Italian film theorist, Guido Aristarco, aims to 'reveal the dynamic causes of social change through exemplary situations and figures' (Stam 2000: 74).

In recent years, four controversial directors – Harmony Korine, Larry Clark, Edward Lachman and Gus Van Sant – have surfaced in the wake of the above-mentioned artists, deploying both traditionally formalist and conventionally verist film-making practices to startling effect. In the pages that follow, this chapter examines Korine's *Gummo*, Clark and Lachman's *Ken Park* (2002), and Van Sant's *Elephant* (2003) as works of new punk cinema that at once draw upon and subvert the fertile tensions between realist 'fact' and creative fiction. In the process, these directors have forged powerful visions that, like Spheeris's works, build upon filmic conceits that can be traced back to the Italian neo-realist movement. Taking the daily lives of disaffected and alienated American teenagers as their films' primary subjects, Korine, Clark, Lachman and Van Sant use documentary and *cinéma vérité* techniques to craft visceral, episodic narratives that not only raise vital questions about the social conditions that continue to plague suburban youth but also interrogate the ideologies and voyeuristic impulses that inform the film-making process and the politics of film spectatorship.

Of course, when embarking upon a project such as this, one must note that the meaning of terms such as 'fact' and 'fiction', or 'realist' and 'formalist', are nebulous and provisional at best; critics who use them tread on perilous ground, flailing about in a semantic mosh pit while trying to avoid the treacherous out stretched leg of reductionist thinking. As Neil P. Hurley writes in *The Reel Revolution: A Film Primer on Liberation*, 'movies at their artistic best are . . . humanistic achievements. While the camera is neutral, its use is not' (Hurley 1978: 14). Thus, before beginning our consideration of how Korine, Clark, Lachman and Van Sant rework Italian neorealist aesthetics, it is important to revisit and re-assess the Italian neo-realist movement as a filmic renaissance that, along with the French New Wave, has had the most profound impact upon post-war cinema.

Real to Reel: New Chords or the Same Old Song?

Since cinema's earliest days, film theorists from André Bazin and Rudolf Arnheim to Cesare Zavattini and Christian Metz have advanced compelling, if disparate, arguments concerning film's importance as a mechanism for accurately representing 'reality'. Even the style and content of the art-form's earliest practitioners illustrate the emerging medium's visual and narrative diversity. For instance, though created contemporaneously, the works of the Lumière brothers, two of cinema's initial documentary film-makers, and the screen fantasies of the pioneering special-effects' 'magician', George Méliès, remain telling markers of film's potential both to convey information to mass audiences and to fabricate intricate lies for entertainment purposes. The locomotive immortalised in the Lumière brothers' short, *L'arrivée d'un train en gare* (*The Arrival of the Train at the Station*, [1895]), is every bit as illusory as Méliès's rocket in *Le voyage dans la lune* (*The Trip to the Moon*, [1902]); likewise, the fin-bedecked woman of Méliès's *La Sirène* (*The Mermaid*, [1904]) is as 'real' as the homeward-bound labourers in the Lumière brothers' *La sortiedes ouvriers de l'usine Lumière* (*Workers Leaving the Factory* [1895]). As Robert Stam points out, the emergence of sound, only complicated already thorny theoretical deliberations concerning filmic representations of 'reality', exacerbating conflicts 'between the "formative" theorists who thought the artistic specificity of cinema consisted in its radical differences from reality, and the "realists" who thought film's artistic specificity (and its social *raison d'être*) was to relay truthful representations of everyday life' (Stam 2000: 72).

At the core of these discussions reside ideological concerns about the social responsibility of artists, as well as philosophical debates regarding subjectivity and the (im)possibility of designating a stable chain of signification in a culture of simulation. For this chapter's purposes, however, it is perhaps most important to remember that 'reality' and 'realism' (or the act of embracing a 'realist' aesthetic) are not synonymous. One can posit that *all* films, regardless of their content and style, arise from a shared physical reality. At the same time, any attempt to represent that physical reality on film – or, in the case of many contemporary directors, on digital video – is immediately compromised by the artificial perimeters and parameters imposed by the simple act of pointing a camera in a given direction at a given moment while using a particular lens, film stock or amount of light. Thus, when the figures whose works embody the Italian neo-realist tradition began wielding cameras in Italy's rural countryside, or in the rubble-filled streets of its major cities during the waning years of World War II, they faced similar challenges to those encountered by the Soviet directors of the 1920s and the French poetic realist film-makers of the 1930s. Namely, they had to find a way to balance the aspiration to tell a story with the desire to depict, through *mise-en-scène* and the use of available technology, the daily lives and struggles of the nation's populace.

Although the term 'neo-realism' was not coined until Umberto Barbaro employed it in a 1943 document bemoaning the decline of an attitude of progressive social awareness in Italy's film industry, Italian neo-realism as a cinematic tradition began in earnest in 1942, with the release of Luchino Visconti's *Ossessione*, a gritty adaptation of American writer James M. Cain's hard-boiled crime novel, *The Postman Always Rings Twice*. Barbaro, however, was not the only Italian cultural theorist calling for a cinematic infusion of social realism. In his mammoth work, *A History of Narrative Film*, David A. Cook locates Cesare Zavattini as 'the theoretical founder of Italian neorealism', citing the screenwriter's calls 'for a new Italian film – one that would abolish contrived plots, do away with professional actors, and take to the streets for its material in order to establish a direct contact with contemporary social reality' (Cook 1996: 424). In a gesture that recalls the democratic spirit of Dziga Vertov and the Soviet directors he inspired, Zavattini advocated a cinema of and for the people that, 'in the name of solidarity' (Stam 2000: 73), focused on the everyday struggles of Italians endeavouring to come to terms with a radically changing social and political environment.

As Guido Aristarco suggests in response to Zavattini's call for a purely contemporary and 'reality'-based cinema, a strict adherence to such guidelines is perhaps an easier notion to contemplate than to realise, especially on a consistent basis. Although the movement was accompanied by a marked rise in the use of non-professional actors as protagonists, some directors chose to use such amateurs strategically. For example, in Roberto Rossellini's *Roma città aperta* (*Rome: Open City* [1945]), a film often cited as Italian neo-realism's most famous text, professional actors played leading roles. Furthermore, as Rossellini scholar Peter Bondanella notes, *Rome: Open City* also broke from Zavattini's tenets in its use of dubbed sound, as well as its appeal to stereotypes by having 'Nazis embody unmitigated evil with no redeeming virtues whatsoever' (Bondanella 1993: 50). Thus, the extent to which major Italian neo-realist directors, such as Roberto Rossellini, Vittorio De Sica and Luchino Visconti, absolutely heeded Zavattini's call for a new, truly democratic cinema is open to question. While the daily lives of ordinary people became a central concern for neo-realist directors, a more accurate assessment of the tradition's aesthetics and politics may be found in Roy Armes's assertion that the neo-realist director 'is not a man who simply uses a movie camera to record reality: he is, in Nathalie Sarraute's words, one who, above all . . . "seiz[es] with all the sincerity of which he is capable . . . [and] . . . scrutinize[s] as far as his sharpness of vision will permit him to see, what appears to him to be reality"' (Armes 1971: 204).

Nevertheless, it is possible to locate certain crucial recurring features that contribute to Italian neo-realism's status as a pivotal and highly influential tradition in post-war world cinema. In addition to employing non-professional actors frequently and shooting almost exclusively on location, often with very little in the way of artificial lighting, neo-realist directors generally favoured loosely plotted or episodic narratives, a documentary visual style that avoided 'slick' Hollywood-style editing, and scripts containing dialogue composed and eventually performed in an attempt to portray accurately the way people conversed in everyday verbal interchanges. These stylistic elements culminated in films that emphasised emotion rather than abstract ideas; nevertheless, careful viewers will detect an ideological *mélange* of Christian and Marxist Humanism. To this day, over sixty years after the cinematic tradition's origin, Italian neo-realism continues to influence film-makers around the globe. In the pages to follow, this chapter explores Italian neorealism's impact on some of the more recent and controversial texts of new punk cinema, as well as how the film-makers behind these powerful narrative and visual compositions deviate in important ways from neo-realist aesthetics, pushing cinema in vital new directions.

Life is Great, Without it you'd be Dead: Harmony Korine's *Gummo*

> You never can make anyone trust you. You have to somehow appeal to them, I guess. I don't know. A lot of people don't want to be in a movie. It really depends on your rapport with the person. If they can see that you're not wanting to make fun of them, necessarily. For me, it's never exciting, or I never have any interest in making fun of someone. It's very easy to do that, to film someone and look down on them or belittle them. But I've always had a curiosity for all my characters. It's something I want [to] stare at and want to see and examine. So I guess if you're earnest in that way, a lot of times they're inclined to give you their trust. (Harmony Korine on establishing trust with the non-professional actors during the filming of *Gummo* ([Sato 2001: para. 25])

Since its release in 1997, Harmony Korine's *Gummo* has regularly elicited severe, often polarised, reactions from its viewers. Lauded for its originality by legendary film-makers such as Werner Herzog and Bernardo Bertolucci, and famously derided as exploitative and voyeuristic by critics, such as Janet Maslin and David Walsh (the latter labelled the film a 'libel against humanity' [Walsh 1997a]), Korine's *Gummo* echoes earlier marginalised filmic curiosities such as Tod Browning's *Freaks* (1932) both in its overtly episodic narrative structure constellated about a story of revenge, and in its presentation of what Benjamin Halligan refers to as 'a questionable voyeuristic experience masquerading as an *exposé*' (Halligan 2002: 153). In addition, like Browning's infamous 'behind the scenes' peek at the daily lives of circus performers, Korine's fusion of the melodramatic, the comedic and the grotesque conflates documentary conceits with conventional fiction film-making strategies to evoke a pestilential collage adorned by moments of almost Bressonian transcendentalism. One could posit that, as a fictional record of life in a town devastated by catastrophes beyond the humble residents' control, Korine's film could have been titled *Xenia, Ohio: Open City*, for, like Rossellini's *Rome: Open City*, *Gummo* shares an obvious pretence towards photographic realism and verist authenticity, while ultimately adhering to an overriding formalism.

Framed by, among other disparate images, stock footage of tornadoes that at once calls to mind such American Midwest-based fantasies as *The Wizard of Oz* and prefigures the film's meandering, chaotic trajectory, *Gummo*'s plot presents a glimpse into the economically depressed lives of the residents of Xenia, Ohio, focusing primarily on events surrounding the daily struggles of five main protagonists: Solomon – the film's sometimes narrator – and Tummler, who ride through the town's desolate streets on their rickety bikes in search of stray cats to stock the kitchen of a local Chinese restaurant, and three slender blonde-haired sisters, Darby, Dot and Helen, who, over the course of the film's first forty-five minutes, learn that their cat is pregnant, and then spend the remainder of the film searching for their pet when it suddenly goes missing. Conflicts arise when Solomon and Tummler learn that a frail, effeminate local boy has encroached upon their money-making scheme by devising a more effective way of collecting the corpses of renegade felines, and the three sisters are temporarily abducted by a lecherous gossip-columnist claiming to be *Chico and the Man* star, Freddie Prinze's, brother. But unlike works of mainstream Hollywood directors, texts that provide audiences with the kind of closure they have come to expect, *Gummo*'s central story-lines lack conventional resolutions. As the film concludes, the cat-meat industry remains competitive; Solomon and Tummler, in a strangely tender scene, turn off the ventilator keeping their competition's bedridden grandmother alive; the pregnant cat is never found.

Telling a coherent story in *Gummo*, however, is less important to Korine than capturing something 'honest' and 'true' (Hack 1999). Furthermore, in discussions of his aesthetic vision, Korine repeatedly voices scepticism regarding the value of traditional narrative structure in cinema, preferring a filmmaking style that mimics the fragmentary, non-holistic way that the human mind processes experience. If this methodology sounds strangely reminiscent of Godard's famous claim that films may very well consist of a beginning, middle, and end, but that these parts do not necessarily have to come in that order, such a comparison is not altogether inaccurate. Like Godard, Korine's cinema is founded on what Peter Wollen describes as a counter-cinematic mode of narrative intransitivity in which 'digressions' compromise the illusion of order to a degree that 'the basic story, as much of it as remains, does not have any recognizable sequence, but is more like a series of intermittent flashes' that rupture 'the emotional spell of the narrative and thus forces the spectator, by interrupting the narrative flow, to reconcentrate and refocus his attention' (Wollen 1972: 75).

Thus, although capturing something 'real' is a priority for Korine who, in a practice that evokes the works of neo-realist film-makers, largely populates *Gummo*'s decaying Ohio town with non-professional actors (indie icons Linda Manz, of Dennis Hopper's *Out of the Blue* [1980], and Chloë Sevigny, of Larry Clark's *Kids* [1995], are notable exceptions), the film's ' "attention-deficiency" impressionism' disallows 'an evocation of the world in a mimetic fashion' (Halligan 2002: 156–7). The film's 'look' and 'feel' derives from a schizophrenic collage of multiple film stocks – from scratchy Super 8 mm to jumpy hand-held video to extended 35 mm steady cam and tracking shots – that variously have an impact on the audience's experience of the text's 'ethnographic authenticity' while consistently disrupting the film's diaegesis. As Benjamin Halligan correctly notes, *Gummo* is by turns 'a coming-of-age narrative . . . Godard-like performing/improvising for the camera; a Neo-Realist-like investigation of the world of the film; abstract video art; and even, at one point, a cable dating service (an albino waitress talks about Patrick Swayze as the ideal man and dances around her car)' (Halligan 2002: 157). Additionally, voice-overs – some clearly attributable to Solomon or Tummler, others left deliberately ambiguous – variably complement or compromise the images they accompany.

Consider, for instance, two consecutive sequences from Korine's film, the first of which aurally introduces the audience to murderous brothers who may or may not be the shaven-headed twins displayed, and the second of which relates a first-person account of incest as we watch an anonymous pre-pubescent girl playing near a large, muddy puddle filled with assorted floating litter and the skeletal frame of a discarded bicycle. In the first sequence, the muscular twins who lean up against a sports car, playfully wrestle with a Rottweiller, vigorously pump weights and, lastly, engage in a profanity-filled bare-knuckled brawl within the tight confines of their kitchen, bear little resemblance to the brothers described in the voice-over as Jehovah's Witnesses who always came to school with clean shirts and their hair combed. Korine further amplifies this apparent semiotic rupture in the film's very next scene. As a female voice relates a narrative of sexual abuse suffered at the hands of her father, the pre-pubescent girl playing by the aforementioned puddle looks up at the camera that films her from a high angle (emphasising her powerlessness) and, at one point, apparently says something to the person filming. Shot on hand-held video, the image of the girl by the puddle conveys the authenticity of a home movie. As with the brothers depicted in the previous sequence, however, the relationship between what we hear and what we see remains ambiguous at best. Viewers must actively connect the speaker's voice with the image, a process that *Gummo*'s narrative incessantly undermines with its loosely constructed story-line and frenetic collage of image, sound and motion.

Thus, the residents of Xenia, Ohio, are relegated to the status of characters and caricatures. Defined almost exclusively by their physical and class-based traits, they are fictional 'grotesques' in the literary and most overtly exploitative sense of the term. Like the eponymous 'freaks' of Tod Browning's film, the residents of Xenia, Ohio, are fictions. In addition to the albino waitress, a representative cross-section of the town's populace includes: developmentally disabled teenage girls, one of whom is coerced into prostitution by her brother; a gay African-American dwarf; mullet-haircut-bedecked racists lounging in a semicircle of rusting lawn-chairs; adult identical twins bathing each other in a tub; a scab-speckled child using a framed family portrait to crush the multitude of cockroaches swarming over his living room wall; a large, angry man wrestling with a kitchen table and chairs; and a young boy in a pair of rabbit ears who urinates off a flyover, plays an accordion while sitting in a filthy lavatory cubicle and skateboards through the streets before, in one of the film's final images, making out with Darby and Dot in a swimming pool during a storm. Indeed, given the presentation of the film's eclectic personages, it seems strangely appropriate that Nick Sutton, who plays Tummler, was cast by Korine after the director saw him on a daytime chat show dedicated to glue-sniffing teenagers. The daytime chat show, with its propensity for serving as an arena for social trends, is, after all, a post-modern revision of the side-show exhibition, as well as a forum for the most extroverted of exhibitionists. Indeed, the lengthy quote that opens this section, in which Harmony Korine confesses to the spectatorial pleasures he receives from wanting to 'stare at', 'see' and 'examine' his characters – while not making fun of them, '*necessarily*' [emphasis mine] – reveals the extent to which *Gummo*'s working-class and underemployed characters are objectified for our entertainment and contemplation. Korine invites us to peer into their lives, but with the understanding that we, like Korine himself, are outsiders invested with, and ultimately *defined by*, a critical, ironic distance.

Given cinema's voyeuristic economy of spectator and spectacle, in which the viewer assumes the privileged position of an observer behind a one-way mirror, the process of 'watching a film' is inherently invested with an imbalance of power. This disparity is enhanced by the film's *mise-en-scène*, which privileges medium- and long-shots (often from high angles that amplify the character's objectification) while shunning point-of-view (POV) shots and saving close-ups for moments when the perceived proximity of the actor's face provides an opportunity for Korine's audience to 'step right up' and take a closer look at the estranging physiognomies on display. Furthermore, although the characters may occasionally draw upon our sympathies, allowing us to forge temporary affinities with them, their position as objects for our curiosity ensures their ultimately insurmountable 'difference'. *Gummo*'s audience is denied a character with which to identify. This crisis in identification occurs as a result, not only of the film's style – its narrative intransitivity – but also because the 'norm', like the assemblage of grotesques on display and the simulacral borough they inhabit, does not really exist except in the viewer's, and Korine's, imagination.

Dislocated Vision and the Promiscuous Gaze in *Ken Park*

With a cast composed largely of non-professional actors and a visual style that draws upon a *cinéma vérité* aesthetic reminiscent of Italian neo-realism, Larry Clark and Edward Lachman's controversial film, *Ken Park*, confounds the narrative and visual logics that have come to define much of contemporary cinema, presenting an episodic, slice-of-life foray into the lives of six teenagers from Visalia, California. Based on a screenplay by Harmony Korine, *Ken Park* is a work that, according to film critic Michael Rechtshaffen, vacillates between 'insightful' social commentary and the film-makers' desire to 'incite' (Rechtshaffen 2002). As such, Clark and Lachman convey their images in an energetic, new punk visual style that blends traditional documentary film-making techniques with 'hard-core' depictions of non-simulated sex and carefully composed set pieces that are ultimately far more elegiac than exploitative. Additionally, through the creation and frequent interjection of a promiscuously non-aligned perspective, a conspicuously dislocated yet voyeuristic perspective emerges. Informed by a visual rhetoric of both immediacy and flexibility, this process of visual displacement appeals to multiple viewing/subject positions simultaneously, providing for the construction of a pluralistic gaze too often disavowed within contemporary film-making practices.

Famously banned in Australia and not released in the United States until September 2004 (two full years after its completion), *Ken Park* consists of a narrative and visual logic that provides a corrective for the plethora of conventional Hollywood films depicting the lives of young people in clichéd and phallocentric ways. Accompanied by the rhythms of a punk rock-laden sound-track, the troubled lives of Ken Park, Claude, Shawn, Peaches and Tate differ greatly from the lives of teenagers populating the vast majority of formulaic motion pictures, from the popular *American Pie* films and the comic melodramas of John Hughes, to cautionary moralistic tales disguised as 'social problem films', such as Catherine Hardwicke's *Thirteen* (2003) and Larry Clark's own controversial début feature, *Kids* (1995). Furthermore, *Ken Park*'s narrative differs from the dominant cinematic paradigm in which teenagers occupy a world seemingly void of parents, or in which the parents that the audiences do see are depicted as either bumbling, clueless and ineffectual oafs, or as abusive autocrats. Clark and Lachman's troubled teenagers share screen time with their equally troubled and emotionally complex parents. In this sense, Clark's film continues within the Italian neo-realist tradition by presenting the lives of everyday people struggling just to get by in a collapsing economic landscape. Claude's sexist, alcoholic and abusive stepfather, for example, is an emotionally weak and broken man whose excessive masculinist posturing eventually slips away as he makes drunken sexual advances towards his stepson. Likewise, Claude's mother (played by Amanda Plummer, one of the film's handful of professional actors) is a complicated figure who, trapped by pregnancy and economic pressures, wavers between maternal desires to protect her son, the fear of losing her husband, and a fleeting sexual desire for her offspring – a yearning illustrated by a carefully composed point-of-view shot that lingers on Claude's boxers as they puff out from his jeans' sagging waistline, followed by a reverse-shot medium close-up of Claude's mother's face sporting a momentarily lascivious expression.

Similar complexities and character flaws define the other parental figures that populate the narrative. Peaches's religious father is a man who, heart-broken and mourning the death of his wife (whom Peaches closely resembles), fixates upon his daughter's purity to such an extent that he beats her and her boyfriend when he discovers that she is sexually active, finally forcing his daughter to don her deceased mother's wedding gown and take part in an impromptu marriage ceremony with himself as the groom. Rhonda, the mother of Shawn's girlfriend, seduces Shawn to prove to herself that, although married and aging, she still possesses the ability to entice young men. Tate's elderly grandparents, a seemingly loving couple, try their best to raise their grandson despite the substantial generation gap separating them from Tate and his misdirected hostility. Thus, although the behaviours exhibited by the parental figures in *Ken Park* are, with the possible exception of Tate's grandparents, variably disturbing, they are not incomprehensible. Similarly, the teenagers at the core of Clark and Lachman's film are multi-faceted and thoughtful personages, contributing to the film's verisimilitude; unlike the eponymous 'kids' of Clark's debut feature, the trio of Shawn, Claude and Peaches, though the target of abuse by parental figures, nevertheless function more as a promise for the future than as a threat to the present. Ironically, this dynamic is perhaps best illustrated by the scene many viewers locate as the film's most controversial: a tender and meditative *ménage à trois* that, while depicting 'realistic', non-simulated sex between the ostensibly under-age protagonists, provides perhaps the film's most optimistic moment. This is especially evident when one takes into account the directors' use of soft, yellowish-brown lighting and the scene's non-linearity. The sexual encounter, though taboo by the standards of conventional cinema, provides a euphoric, almost Utopian period of warmth and affection in an otherwise violent and unsettling film. In this sense, though the sequence's multiple couplings and re-couplings replicate, at times, a traditionally 'pornographic' *mise-en-scène*, the tone of altruistic sensuality, in conjunction with repeated cuts to moments of gentle post-coital reflection, redeploy the pornographic aesthetic in a way that disallows readings of the allegedly 'offensive' scene as exploitative, gratuitous or, considering the balanced apportioning of sex acts, as privileging a specifically masculinist visual logic.

Given not only Larry Clark's background as a photo-essayist concerned with immortalising gritty, 'realistic' representations of desperate, disenfranchised youth trapped at society's margins (see, for instance, his books *Tulsa* [1971] and *Teenage Lust* [1997]), but also Edward Lachman's expansive career as a cinematographer for celebrated independently minded directors like Todd Haynes (*Far From Heaven* [2002]), Steven Soderbergh (*The Limey* [1999]), and *Erin Brockovich* [2000]) and Paul Schrader (*Touch* [1997]), the ease with which *Ken Park* carefully vacillates between documentary and formalist visual motifs should come as no surprise. Clark and Lachman not only borrow cinematic conceits from neo-realist film-making, but also rework them in important and innovative ways. Particularly, Clark and Lachman infuse their text with a mobile, promiscuous perspective that disrupts traditional continuity editing's reliance upon a visual rhetoric of shot–reverse shot. The result of this deliberate economy of dislocation is a momentary fracturing of the film's diaegesis that interrupts viewer identification with the characters. This rupturing occurs through the abrupt imposition of a long shot, often lensed from behind foregrounded objects, or through the sudden application of an overtly fluid, often hand-held panning shot that results in the spectator's gaze literally drifting unmoored within the scene.

Such departures from conventional editing practices compel viewers to reconsider the politics of spectatorship, particularly in terms of the viewer's emotional alignment. This is achieved by removing the audience from the immediacy of the action and placing them, if only for an instant, either at a perceived spatial distance from the characters through long-shots, or at an abrupt psychic distance through the camera's suddenly restless mobility. These disruptions at once complement and contribute to *Ken Park*'s loosely plotted/episodic structure and *vérité* style, both trappings familiar to viewers of Italian neo-realist cinema. Iit would be a mistake, however, to understand Clark and Lachman's film as intended to impose a sense of objectivity towards the events transpiring on screen. Though the directors periodically force viewers to observe an intimate or intense exchange from a sudden distance, or impose a metaphorical 'wandering eye' that obliges the audience to consider the details of the characters' surroundings as merely fragments of a larger collection of critical details, viewers are not placed at an objective remove from the action but, rather, assume a differently voyeuristic relationship to the filmed image. What the audience sees, in other words, may appear to be what Dziga Vertov would describe as 'life caught unawares', but their vision is ultimately proscribed and restricted in ways that disavow the possibility of understanding what they see as objective.

Consider, for example, the following sequence from *Ken Park*, in which Clark and Lachman alternate between external long shots of Claude practising tricks on his skateboard and close-ups of Claude's stepfather watching his stepson through the kitchen window and guzzling a beer. A single shot from Claude's stepfather's point of view breaks the order of this sequence, aligning viewers – at least momentarily – with the stepfather's gaze. By repeating the long shots of Claude and the close-ups of Claude's stepfather three times, Clark and Lachman establish a stable geometry from which viewers understand not only the events transpiring on screen, but their spatial relationship, as spectators, to the *mise-en-scène*. The camera then follows Claude's stepfather as he walks outside to confront his stepson. In an extreme close-up, he breaks Claude's skateboard and, in subsequent free-floating medium shots, physically abuses Claude. Clark and Lachman employ a series of rapid edits to depict the violence of this confrontation. These quick cuts heighten the jumpiness of the hand-held photography, adding a palpable sense of verisimilitude to the scene. The intensity of the action, coupled with the shots' variation, would ordinarily be enough to convey the scene effectively. Intercut throughout this violent altercation, however, are three new long-shots that differ from those mentioned above. Although the original long-shots capture enough of the environment to allow the directors to establish location (the position of a car in the driveway provides a critical visual anchor), the latter shots are lensed from a noticeably different geographical position. Hence, though these new long-shots capture the scene's action from a comparable distance, the exact location of the camera in relation to the conflict is not immediately clear. Further complicating these new, disorientating long-shots is the increasing intrusion of foliage dangling down from the frame's upper edge and, on several crucial occasions, obscuring Claude and his stepfather's bodies to such an extent that one can only speculate as to the action transpiring behind the leaves. Such foregrounding of the tree's branches prohibits the illusion of objectivity through the imposition of a visual signifier (sight-obscuring branches and leaves) linked almost exclusively with subjective vision in general and voyeurism in particular. In short, Clark and Lachman's manipulation of the audience's gaze consistently reminds the viewers that everything they see, despite how seemingly authentic or 'realistic', is nevertheless proscribed and restricted in ways that prevent a neutral or omniscient perspective. Therefore, while this visual dislocation constructs a plurality of potential viewing positions, it does so in a way that disallows even an illusory neo-realist 'objectivity'. The result is the creation of a hyper-voyeuristic cinema, a cinema of uncomfortable intimacy and radical dislocation, of clinical gazes and prurient leers.

Shooting What We See: Gus Van Sant's *Elephant*

Amid the deluge of reviews, interviews and essays following the awarding of the prestigious *Palm d'or* at the 2003 Cannes Film Festival to US director Gus Van Sant's *Elephant*, two distinct narratives regarding the origin of the film's title emerged. The most frequently cited explanation locates the film's title as a homage to Alan Clarke's short film about youth violence in Northern Ireland, a docudrama also named *Elephant*. According to Van Sant, the title of Clarke's film, refer to an expression that illustrates people's willingness to ignore difficult problems rather than face the assorted and potentially unpleasant reasons behind them: '[I]t [Clarke's film] was about the *Elephant* in the living room that no one could mention' (Taubin 2004: 29). In a *Film Comment* interview with Amy Taubin, however, Van Sant responded to a question about the relationship between his film and the infamous 1999 massacre of thirteen people at Columbine High School in Littleton, Colorado, with the following statement:

> It [Van Sant's *Elephant*] has elements of Columbine. But we never really tried to get at who those people were. We sort of invented our own. There are profiles of kids who bring guns to school and kill other kids. Were they too alone? Were they secretly tortured? Were they abused? Did they play too many video games? Did they see too many violent movies? Did they torture animals? You know, what are the things that caused it to happen? And one of the reasons it's called *Elephant* – besides the fact that it's named after an Alan Clarke movie – is that it's hard to tell. You know, for five blind men the *Elephant* is like a wall to one, a

rope to another, a tree to another, a snake to the fourth one . . . it's an unanswerable question. (Taubin 2004: 27–9)

That these two justifications for the title of Van Sant's film arise concurrently seems particularly appropriate, especially given the multiple narratives woven throughout the film, as well as the visual style the director and his cinematographer, Harris Savides, apply to convey them. Van Sant's *Elephant* is a meditation on the limits of 'seeing' and the impossibility of 'knowing'; inspired by 'real-life' events, it is a text concerned with revealing a moment in time from a seemingly objective distance that, paradoxically, welcomes only a plurality of ultimately circumscribed perspectives. Like *Gummo* and *Ken Park*, *Elephant* never escapes the formalist impulses that permeate not only Italian neo-realism, but all attempts at verist film-making. Indeed, spectacle may be the film's very point, and it is finally the audience's role as spectator that is, both literally and figuratively, 'in the line of fire'.

Heavily indebted to the masterful camera manipulations of Hungarian director, Béla Tarr, especially his *Werkmeister Harmüniák* (2000) and *Sátántangü* (1994), Van Sant and Savides's compositions are meticulous and yet, at times, sporadically 'open' or 'loose'. In some instances, the camera seems to linger on a given environment – like a cafeteria or athletic field – as *Elephant*'s young, non-professional actors drift in and out of the frame. These moments create the illusion of objectivity, as do the copious tracking shots for which the film is most frequently remembered. Lensed from some distance behind the actors, these tracking shots follow the film's characters as they wind their way through the Portland, Oregon high school's eerily anonymous and labyrinthian corridors. As the critic Kent Jones notes, this perspective, allows viewers to feel 'not so much' like they are 'observing the students as hovering in their midst', wandering 'without apparent purpose or ambition' (Jones 2004: 28). As such, even though the camera follows certain protagonists (introduced via title cards) through a fraction of their daily activities, conventional systems of sympathetic alignment between audience and characters are conspicuously eschewed. Rather than allowing viewers to form emotional attachments to the protagonists, or to perceive what the characters perceive, Van Sant instead limits the audience to observing the characters as the characters observe – or remain hopelessly oblivious to – the world in which they exist.

Given this conceit, it is tempting to equate the camera's observational 'hovering' with the kind of 'fly-on-the-wall' objectivity commonly assigned to filmic documents that purport to take viewers 'behind the scenes' or to follow an individual as s/he goes through a 'typical' day; even *Elephant*'s strapline – 'An ordinary high school day. Only that it's not' – locates the film as gesturing towards a kind of neo-realist authenticity. Such a reading of the film's dominant *mise-en-scène*, however, disregards the extent to which Van Sant deploys blatantly formalist strategies, including a myriad of mechanical distortions, to create and sustain a tone of impending menace. Van Sant's use of sound, for example, varies from the naturalistic (overlapping dialogue, voices captured 'off-mic') to the surreal (layered voices and ambient sounds morph into vaguely animalistic howling and screeching). Such sonic occlusions and gradations create a dissonance that allows viewers to experience an outsider's paranoia and alienation. This effect is most notable when the white noise of a high school cafeteria swells to an almost predatory roar, or when individual, clearly articulated words ('loser', for instance) emerge from the cacophony. Similarly, Van Sant strategically uses natural lighting early in the film to establish an almost documentary verisimilitude before switching, as the film progresses, to a more overtly controlled system of illumination designed to impact on how audiences understand what they see. During the film's denouement, for example, the sunlight that floods through the school's plate-glass windows does not merely create shadows or cast bodies into silhouette, but transforms the back-lit physiognomies into almost spectral figures and, in some cases, obliterates any recognisable form.

Elephant, then, is a film about spectacle. It is a work concerned with the power of the filmed (or photographed) image and the risks one takes when one either imposes dogmatic systems of signification upon visual signs, or mechanically embraces hyper-mediated images that have been virtually de-contextualised through their repetition and incorporation into popular culture. Like Eli, the photography student who fittingly aims his camera as the killers, Eric and Alex, raise their weapons, Van Sant (like all film-makers) is obsessed with images: capturing them, developing them, analysing them, and then redeveloping them until they convey what he wants them to express. As a result, the Nazi-themed documentary at *Elephant*'s core – a thoughtful extension of the film-within-a-film motif – provides valuable insight into the text's preoccupation with notions of spectatorship and the power that audiences and film-makers alike assign to cinematic images. Designed to emulate the many stock-footage-laden World War II documentaries airing daily on cable television, the programme Eric and Alex watch while awaiting the arrival of an automatic rifle via tomorrow's post describes how film-makers can manipulate images to sway public perception and have an impact upon cultural memory. 'From now on', the documentary's narrator explains as footage of hand-held wartime cameras and Nazi rallies flashes across the television screen, 'the German people will know only what their leaders want them to know'. Furthermore, the programme's narrator explains how Nazi culture functioned as a culture of appropriation and evacuation, transforming numerous images, culled from a plurality of cultures, into a simplistic iconography for a media culture that, like the one that exists in the United

States at the dawn of the new millennium, is predicated largely upon slogans and sound bites.

This is not to suggest that the shooting spree that concludes Van Sant's film is motivated within the film's diaegesis by a preoccupation with Nazi culture. Indeed, given *Elephant*'s narrative and visual logic, such a reading is exactly the type of reductionist response to tragic events that ensures their incomprehensibility, if not their recurrence. The same teenagers that gun down their class-mates not only lack the historical and cultural perspective necessary to recognise the image of Adolph Hitler, but are also shown as involved in a variety of other activities, including playing Beethoven on the piano, drinking milk and orange juice, and quoting Shakespeare. As Van Sant explains, the film's audience encounters a large quantity of information, including:

> . . . a video game, a spitball thrown, a Nazi war documentary, a kiss, a Satan car freshener. Things that ask you to think about the piece of information and what it means . . . [The teenagers responsible for the massacre at Columbine High School] were humans and not demons. They were not outside the community – they are you and me. They are not to be demonized by any one piece of information. And if you are a person who would demonize the two kids . . . then you are the type of person who would probably carry a sign [outside of Columbine High School] saying 'Fags did this'. (Taubin 2004: 32)

What the inclusion of the documentary on Nazi war propaganda does suggest, especially when understood within the film's larger motif of photography-as-(un)reality and the malleability of the visual image, is that in a culture saturated with images, oppression may arise when people endeavour to force inflexible meaning on to what they see; similarly, when historically coded images are decontextualised to the point of mere spectacle, people not only open themselves up to manipulation by those who possess the resources to re-invest images with whatever meanings they wish, but they also turn the very act of living into a repetitive performance void of insight or critical reflection. In other words, audiences risk wandering endlessly down the same pathways through which they have meandered countless times before, confusing objectivity with subjectivity and passing off opinions as 'truth'.

It is during *Elephant*'s bloody climactic moments, however, that Van Sant advances perhaps his most compelling, if initially perplexing, critique of the politics of film spectatorship. As Eric and Alex roam the halls, picking off their fellow students with an imposing arsenal of automatic and semi-automatic weapons, the audience is introduced to Benny, one of the film's few African-American characters. Seemingly obliged to discover the origin of the bursts of gunfire and random explosions echoing throughout the school, he calmly wanders towards his inevitable death, his expression stoic as panicked teenagers race past him searching for an exit. In this sense, Benny represents the sado-masochistic impulse underlying the voyeuristic practice of film spectatorship, the desire to 'view' and 'understand' despite the possibility that what there is to see may be disturbing, unpleasant or frustratingly impenetrable. Additionally, Benny's ill-fated sojourn to discover the 'method behind', or the 'cause of', the film's 'madness' is emblematic of Van Sant's intellectual and aesthetic project in *Elephant*. Members of Van Sant's audience journey through a narrative that twists, turns and doubles back on itself; at times, the narrative presents spectators with the very same scenes viewed from multiple angles. Furthermore, like Benny, whose race denotes an 'outsider status' even as his yellow shirt recalls the very first student whom audiences meet (and with whom they are temporarily invited to identify), viewers attempt to excavate 'meaning' or 'answers' from Van Sant's film at their own risk. Indeed, spectators must consider *Elephant* as a work that was never intended or designed to reveal such information in the first place. It is a film that, though deploying a visual grammar that seemingly suggests a kind of objectivity, ultimately illustrates the impossibility of truly *knowing* anyone or anything. There is no simple answer to the cinematic riddle that is *Elephant*; nor, Van Sant implies, are there easy solutions to the multitude of political and ontological dilemmas that inform our daily lives.

3. THE FRENCH NEW WAVE: NEW AGAIN

Timothy Dugdale

The great Spanish director Luis Buñuel loved his Martinis. 'Today I'm as old as the century and rarely go out at all', he wrote in his charming autobiography, *My Last Sigh*, 'but all alone, during the sacrosanct cocktail hour, in the small room where my bottles are kept, I still amuse myself by remembering the bars I've loved.' (Buñuel 1983: 16)

Ah, yes. The bar. The cocktail. Buñuel liked to sip away in sustained quiet but there are times when juke-box music is in order. Alas, the juke-box, like the Martini, is under siege. Rare is the bar that keeps a good juke-box loaded with an idiosyncratic selection of music that reflects the owner's tastes and not some trash hit parade from the rental company.

One bar I know, perhaps too intimately, has a great machine, lodged at the back of the room. The other day I noticed a couple of new selections. One of them was *Couleur Café* by Serge Gainsbourg, the legendary French singer. The record is pure kitsch now but, in the early 1960s, nobody was more happening than Gainsbourg. The cover has the baggy-eyed swinger staring down the camera while a cheroot smoulders between his raised fingers. In the brothel-red background a pair of Latin gentlemen work over some bongos.

Why does Serge look so defiantly blasé? Is it a pose? Or a *stance*? The difference is very important. In fact, stance is the essence of this essay. A stance is an individual way of confronting the indifference of the world, of making sense of life while imposing yourself upon it. Stance is the essence of existence and the keynote of cool. Cool isn't a given; it's achieved through the vigilant manifestation of your stance. That's not to say that you can't have fun while you're at it. And that is where it is perhaps best to begin a discussion of the influence of the French New Wave on new punk cinema.

The French New Wave: New Again

The New Wave: In the Street, On the Screen

The critic John Simon suggests that the French New Wave was a *ménage à trois*, consisting of Alain Resnais with Jean-Luc Godard and François Truffaut. The breakthrough year was 1959 when Truffaut and Resnais offered *The 400 Blows* and *Hiroshima, Mon Amour* respectively. Godard followed shortly thereafter with *Breathless*.

Of the three, *Breathless* is the splashiest. The plot isn't much – a small-time crook steals a car, shoots a cop and then escapes to Paris where he tries to lie low while pestering a number of erstwhile paramours who are wise to all his moves but give in nonetheless. The real star of the film is Paris. Godard and his cinematographer, Raoul Coutard, didn't have much money but they did have a new, portable 16 mm camera and a wheelchair, a perfect combination for guerilla film-making.

I was fifteen when I first saw *Breathless*. It was a revelation of the highest order. Everything about it was stunning – the hand-held camera-work in the sexy streets of 'Gay Paree', the jazzy score, the insouciant mischief-making of Jean-Paul Belmondo, the blonde *naïveté* of Jean Seberg and, of course, the stylistic cheek of the director himself. The film was all energy, from start to finish, breaking all the conventions of Western cinema, which hitherto had been condemned to the sound stage. Condemned is perhaps not the best word because it was in the interests of all concerned – the actors, the technicians and the studio heads – to have maximum control over the aesthetic elements of the film. The assembly-line nature of the studio product allowed for endless tinkering with sound and image and performance. By going into the streets and cafés and apartments of Paris, Godard thumbed his nose at such practices. *Breathless* was an accident waiting to happen, gloriously so; Godard knew how to steer into the skid.

At times the ambient noise is so loud, you have to strain to hear the actors speaking. Sometimes Godard throws in a squall of bebop jazz further to complicate things. Likewise, Godard eschews visual continuity. The camera is playfully skittish, jerking away to follow something else that it's glimpsed out of the corner of its eye. The viewer is never sure if it will return but then again, who cares?

At one point, Belmondo's crook comes upon a cinema showing an old Bogart picture. The villain imitates Bogie's signature gesture of running his thumb across his lip, an iconic, defiant gesture of thought and indifference. We never get to know this character, but how could we? He is a cartoon, created by cinema for cinema. Simon called Godard the 'sick mother' of French New cinema for perhaps this very reason. As Godard moved on through the 1960s, 'we carry away the technical tricks and the atmosphere of nihilism that gradually yielded to anticinematic Maoist agitprop foolishness' (Simon 1983:163).

The advances in portable cinema technology made the New Wave possible. The lightweight camera allowed artists to articulate their world-views in ways that questioned the very idea of a coherent world-view. Two works of the New Wave illuminate this point beautifully. Chris Marker's *Le Joli Mai* (1962) is little more than a travelogue through the streets of Paris at a moment when it seemed blessed with good weather and good collective vibrations. But the film is hardly a valentine to the city; it is a meditation on perception and the mercurial effect of emotion on the processes of perception. *Night and Fog* (1961) by Alain Resnais is a cunningly short 'documentary' that mixes archival footage taken in the concentration camps of the Holocaust and contemporary images of the abandoned grounds of Auschwitz, the buildings and the railway lines that served those buildings now silent, empty and in reclamation to nature. It is probably the best film about the Holocaust because it is almost Zen in its worship of absence. (The cut-aways of the sky in Gus Van Sant's *Elephant* serve the same purpose.) Critically acclaimed documentaries such as *Shoah* (1985) and *Hotel Terminus* (1988), scream their intention to record, to document as a guarantee against forgetting those who lived the horror. Resnais gives us an elegy to the evidence on which we depend so much to sustain memory.

The genius of Marker and Resnais in these two early films was to foreground the *subjectivity* of the film-maker. There could be no Michael Moore without Marker and Resnais. Their films are more tone poems or meditations than documentaries; fragmented, elliptical narratives backed up with slow motion, freeze frames, jump cuts and asynchronous sound. Marker has gone on to make the cinematic meditation a singular art-form, best realised in *Sans Soleil* (1982). A fictitious film-maker sends letters to an unseen friend detailing his quest for 'things that quicken the heart'. Principal destinations are hyperdeveloped Tokyo and chronically under-developed Africa, at that time a hotbed of despotic client states of the Cold War. Marker's traveller also visits San Francisco where he retraces the tortured steps of James Stewart's smitten detective in *Vertigo* (1958). Marker can't help slipping in a reference to his own film, *Le Jetée* (1963), that mystic science fiction short told entirely with still images, which also tipped its hat to *Vertigo* (hint: the giant tree trunk). The early New Wave had the audacity to question the very nature of cinema while being playful and charming enough to make that challenge an enjoyable experience.

The Punks: The Revolt and The Revenue

Popular culture relies very often on its own mythology for oxygen. The punks of Britain survived for a relatively short period of time as a strong, if incoherent, cultural force. In fact, incoherence was their principal strength.

As Dick Hebdige notes in his seminal work, *Subculture: The Meaning of Style*, the punk movement that blazed onto the front pages of the disapproving tabloids of London in late 1975 was a glorious mess. Britain was a less inspiring one. The social safety net of health and welfare services was fraying, leaving the working classes with less stability and more anger. The mass media monolith of the BBC was tempered in acid by the street culture of the housing estate, the pub and the night-club. When Johnny Rotten of The Sex Pistols spat out the words 'No Future', he was more likely referring to the system, rather than to himself (financed by the Pistols' continuing lucre, he now luxuriates in a massive pile somewhere in Los Angeles).

Malcolm McLaren, the Svengali of the Sex Pistols, visited America in the early 1970s. He was exposed to the music and more importantly to the postures of such glam rock outfits as Lou Reed, the Stooges, the New York Dolls and Patti Smith. In America, these acts had little shock value. McLaren understood that Britain was more fertile ground for scaring the straights. Thus, the Sex Pistols were launched from the clothing shop of McLaren's paramour, a gritty boutique that featured all kinds of leather goods usually reserved for the boudoir.

Forget music. Noise was their claim to fame; and a call to arms among the sweaty, reedy youth that filled squats and basements to hear the Pistols thrash away on their instruments. Knowing how to play was beside the point. In fact, energy trumped expertise as a hallmark of commitment.

By 1978, the punks were finished. The Sex Pistols broke up, ironically, after a disastrous tour of the United States which included stops in some of the most conservative and, hence inhospitable, locales of the South, birthplace of the blues and rock 'n' roll. Punk never really had any theoretical underpinnings to carry it through after the music industry commodified its sign system; it was a collective improvisation fuelled by cheek and frustration, realised in real time. Hebdige (1979) marvels at the punks' aptitude for *bricolage* – finding things in your immediate environment that are good to think with. The punks were oh so young and poor. Thus, this improvisation involved taking household objects, such as the safety-pin and rethinking their use in shocking and disruptive ways. The do-it-yourself aesthetic celebrated the provisional nature not just of shocking the straights, but making do with meagre means. Hebdige suggests that the punks transformed reality into an alternative reality that contained within it both a critique of convention and a parody of that critique.

In this light, the American connection to punk is particularly important to the study of cinema. While the punks were shaking up Britain with their music, John Waters was trying to do the same to America with his cinema. It is only appropriate that in the very first issue of the now legendary magazine, *Punk*, Tommy Ramone described the audiences at CBGBs as 'something out of *Pink Flamingos* ('Ramones' 1976). In his home town of Baltimore, beginning in the late 1960s, Waters and a stock cast of nutters, junkies and sexual weirdos culled from skid row and drug circles began to make crude extrapolations on the overheated melodramas of Douglas Sirk. Waters makes no bones about his admiration for past masters of shoe-string budget trash such as Russ Meyer, an old World War II photographer who was able to churn out soft-core porno biker-chick movies year after year.

Aesthetically, Waters's 'better' works, such as *Pink Flamingos* (1972) and *Female Trouble* (1974), look and sound terrible. Waters couldn't afford work prints so he had to cut directly from the negative; the films were shot on the cheap with a rickety 16 mm camera under guerilla conditions. Waters has always argued that to read his films as camp or trash misses the point. White and upper middle class, Waters could be accused of being a dilettante except for the fact that he is openly gay. Sex and class in America had always been a taboo, hidden by and for polite society. When you see the 135-kilogram transvestite, Divine, in full drag-queen regalia, descend from a dilapidated trailer home on to a desolate carpet of mud, you have a hard time seeing where the documentary aspect is. And yet it's right there. Waters was articulating a political *stance* – taking the refuse of America, human and material, and reconfiguring it into a terrible spectacle.

By 1981, when he released *Polyester*, Waters was, as so many are, a victim of his own success. His shock value now belonged primarily to his distributor, New Line Cinema. *Polyester* was a failure precisely because even though it had all the hallmarks of a Waters production – dreadful acting, depressing suburban sets, hyperventilating dialogue – it all looked too clean, too well put together. You didn't have the feeling of conspiracy, of receiving a communiqué from that dark side of Baltimore where truth trawls the gutter.

A good parallel to this can be found in the blaxploitation genre of the early 1970s. A film such as *Sweet Sweetback's Baad Asssss Song* (1971) laid out an explosive political agenda packed tightly with the dynamite of race and sex. The film exudes an irascible negritude through the shabby, often inept deployment of various aesthetic tropes of the New Wave. The result is a feral and ultimately mystical work that articulates an inarticulate rage. As the blaxploitation genre caught on and was caught up in the studio machine, the mercurial do-it-yourself aesthetic of *Sweet Sweetback*'s was reduced to clichés.

As Hebdige notes in *Hiding in the Light* (1988), his elegiac ode to the study of subcultures, oppositional art has limited staying-power – once the secret codes are cracked and sold on the open market, the gig is up. The entertainment industries, with increasingly ruthless precision, neutralise subcultures through commodification of their sign systems. They buy low and sell high. And what they bring to market is often junk.

THE FRENCH NEW WAVE: NEW AGAIN

THE NEW WAVE BECOMES OLD: LEGACIES AND LIBELS

Ah, *Breathless*. All these years I've waited once again to live that exquisite feeling. All these years my hopes have been dashed by the ascendancy of big-budget black-box nonsense such as *Star Wars* (1977), *Wild Wild West* (1999) and *The Matrix*, among countless others. So imagine my delight as I sat watching *Run Lola Run* and my skin began tingling with goose-pimples. Girl with flaming red hair and *La Femme Nikita* (1990) attitude takes phone call from frantic boyfriend – girl hits the pavement running – girl keeps running until clock strikes 12 or the techno music drops out. Repeat three times. As the cheeky security guard suggests in the title sequence, film is like a soccer match – a ball and 90 minutes. That's it.

Indeed, never before has the Luddite aspect of cinema been so pronounced. As is their wont, critics have tried to saddle the film with various forms of cultural *gravitas*. To wit: Here is the new post-Wall, MTV Germany in all its vibrant Day-Glo iconoclasm, on full display as opposed to the dour black-and-white humanism of Berlin *circa Wings of Desire* (1987).

Or here is hipster existential *Angst*, as seen in *Go* (1999) and *Sliding Doors* (1998), at its smartest. True, in each of the three repetitions of the same vignette, Tykwer changes minute parts of the plot and, thus, the whole changes. But does this leave us pondering the profound caprices of life while we sip lattes at a coffee house as Jewel wails earnestly in the background? No dice. *Lola* is nothing more and nothing less than a formalist exercise in old-school montage. Director Tom Tykwer has incorporated a bit of multimedia trickery – favoured by Oliver Stone (see *Natural Born Killers* [1994] and *Nixon* [1995]) – such as animation, 35 mm stills and video-camcorder cutaways, but they're brief and well-timed. And timing is everything in a film that lasts no longer than eighty-one minutes.

Yet, how time flies. Indeed, even though the film is scored with frenetic techno-trance music that drives Lola onward, Tykwer occasionally closes everything down until we are left with an extreme close-up of her face, bouncing hypnotically in the frame, as she whispers to the waiting boyfriend that she's on the way. One is reminded of the magnificent title sequence of *Marathon Man* (1976) in which double Olympic marathon champion, Abebe Bikila, scampers along to nothing more than the sound of his preternaturally calm breathing.

It seems only yesterday that all praises were being sung for young Richard Rodriguez who had sold his body for medical experiments to finance *El Mariachi* (1992). Shot on the Mexico-America border with an antique 16 mm camera and non-synchronised sound, *El Mariachi* was a *tour de force* if for no other reason than that Rodriguez could shoot only one-minute takes, and had to do a lot of cutting and pasting to make his film move. Necessity is the mother of invention, after all. Warner Bros spent close to $1 million tweaking the sound and picture to make it palatable to a commercial audience conditioned to Dolby and 35 mm. Then they spent more money to make another version more in keeping with the Hollywood aesthetic.

Running away from convention makes for good press. It always has. Look no further than the much-ballyhooed works of Quentin Tarantino. While toiling in a video rental shop for years, Tarantino produced a massive 1,000-page plus script that was eventually broken down to produce a number of films. His breakthrough work, *Reservoir Dogs* (1992), clearly shows what he learned behind the counter – an almost encyclopedic knowledge of genre cinema. *Reservoir Dogs* is ostensibly a movie about armed robbery – a group of small-time crooks are assembled by an older small-time crook to rob a jewellery shop. The robbery goes badly and the surviving members of the group limp home to the designated rendezvous, the reservoir where the 'dogs' have at each other.

This film delights in the sense of *déjà vu* it throws off in every frame. Kubrick's *The Killing* here, a John Woo movie there, then a motif lifted from Kurasowa. In the Tarantino funhouse, you've seen it all before yet never in such quicksilver and audacious assembly. Tarantino rubs your nose in the fact that the characters are constructs – we see Mr Orange, the undercover agent, actually practising his speech that will convince the other crooks he's bona fide. At the same time, Tarantino employs a novelistic approach to the narrative structure. Each character is shown 'on the path' to the moment of truth. This is a device with very limited novelty, however; Tarantino tries the same sort of thing in *Jackie Brown* (1997) but because the action is much less kinetic and the character's perspectives are far less disparate, the trick fails to thrill.

Tarantino understands his audience very well – Generations X and Y, youths raised on television and the VCR in homes often rife with domestic turmoil. Pop culture was no longer fiction; it was a lifeboat. In no Tarantino film are emotional demands made on the audience, except for self-congratulation in catching all the cinematic allusions and artifice of emotional intensity. That's not to say that clichés can't be moving. As Umberto Eco notes in his seminal essay on *Casablanca* (1942), precisely because *all* the archetypes are here, precisely because *Casablanca* cites countless other films, and each actor repeats a part played on other occasions, 'the resonance of intertextuality plays upon the spectator' (Eco 1985: 38). But in the cinema of Tarantino, the characters are emotionally crippled ciphers, yammering away about pop culture arcana, foot massages and such. Even in *Jackie Brown*, where you have two genuinely wounded adults trying to make a go of it in shady Los Angeles, the romance is deadened by the director's skittish devotion to imitation and citation. Indeed, if Tarantino is a genius of anything, it is taxidermy. For all the violence and gore and tough-guy gush of Tarantino, he's playing in a sand-box. And he invites you to join him. I am reminded here of the great French gangster film, *Touchez Pas au Grisbi* (1954). Arguably the good father of *Breathless*, it is also ostensibly an armed robbery movie – a suave yet aging gangster, Max (the legendary Jean Gabin), is sitting on a nice pile of loot that he and his crew lifted from a bank but when his rather dim best friend gets embroiled with a rival gangster, the money is once again hot. Truffaut remarked that the film's real subject is 'turning 50'.

So perhaps the real value of Tarantino has been the opportunity for other directors, better directors, to use genre conventions to create intriguing character studies of faded or fading gentlemen of ill repute. Steven Soderbergh's *The Limey* (1999), Jonathan Glazer's *Sexy Beast* (2000), and John Frankenheimer's *Ronin* (1998) are three terrific examples. *The Limey* and *Sexy Beast* put the viewer in the head-space of the lead characters, both old gangsters working at redemption yet facing one last trial by fire. Not one sound, one camera move, one visual trick is unmotivated, particularly in *The Limey*. Soderbergh purposely throws the viewer off-balance in the opening sequence; in a mosaic of images flashing forwards and backwards, we see the weathered geezer (Terence Stamp) arriving in Los Angeles from Britain, the worse for wear.

Ronin is the best riposte yet to the Tarantino *œuvre*. Helmed by veteran director John Frankenheimer and written by that master of stoic verbal acid, David Mamet, *Ronin* takes the narrative keynote of *Pulp Fiction* – a mysterious briefcase with unknown contents – and re-contextualises it in a gritty heist caper framed by post-Cold War geo-politics. The two leads, Robert de Niro and Jean Reno, are tired hired guns searching for something to do for *themselves* now that the old causes have become defunct. They are the samurai without masters of the title. There is almost no character exposition – only action, action and more action. And yet, by the end of the film, when we still don't know what was in the case for which they so valiantly sought, the two operatives have our sympathies as they sit in the same Parisian café where they first met. They played the 'game' and played it well.

Perhaps the apogee of this 'cinema as game' moment is found in the minimalist movement called Dogma 95, perpetrated by Lars von Trier. Before he took his cinematic 'vows of chastity' von Trier gave us *Zentropa* (1991), the most sophisticated film, aesthetically speaking, to come out of Europe in the last decade. *Zentropa* was a laboratory for von Trier's coming attractions. Here he débuts his favourite character tropes – the duplicitous damsel in distress and the hapless and callow young man who falls for her charms after he has fallen for the less sultry charms of an ideologically corrupt society. In the film's climax, the callow young man (Jean Marc Barr) drowns literally in the rancid history of World War II. This visually stunning film has a frozen emotional centre. Von Trier plays you, much like Hitchcock, the obvious inspiration for the film.

Along with his partner in crime, Thomas Vinterberg (*The Celebration*), von Trier promised to make films as impersonal as possible with minimum input and creativity from the director. It is as if he has chosen a New Wave made of ice crystals. To be fair, there could a method to this madness. Like the punks, von Trier challenges the audience to lean forward into his work, to try to make sense of material purposefully resistant to coherence. At times you feel as if the director has had a few cocktails before shooting an early rehearsal of scenes from the completed film you are allegedly watching. *Breaking the Waves* (1996) and *Dancer in the Dark* are often maddening experiences because you imagine von Trier chuckling as he delights in your struggle to stay in your seat. Cinema as a game of chicken?

The question is: will tying a hand behind the back of a talented director make better films? Remember, this is much the same question we ask at the other end of the spectrum: do special-effects and computer-editing software, such as Final Cut Pro, help middling directors produce better films? One can call minimalism a throwback, but what does it signal? Is the cupboard of novelty bare? Is the audience so jaded that it has managed to work up, by sheer fatigue, a thirst for entertainment free of the snake oil of technology and hype?

The Blair Witch Project deserved attention for its ability to keep irony at bay. We never see the killer, leaving us and the so-called 'researchers' to let our imaginations run wild, a very rare luxury in a mass-mediated culture intent on setting your agenda 24/7/365. *Blair Witch* has, to borrow from artspeak, a lot of negative space. The film is one long POV shot, articulating the panic and the desperation of the characters as they move closer and closer to abject terror. You are there, in the woods, flipping out. Rather than attempting irony on screen, the *Blair Witch* directors have taken into account the irony obsession that lives in the intended audience, early twenty-somethings addicted to 'The X-Files' and Wicca Lite. The 'mockumentary' format of the film allows the directors to treat the spastic images as 'found footage' of the missing witch-hunters. That's the horror element that is allegedly so spellbinding. Sometimes less really is less.

Advertising, as it does with almost everything, has taken the aesthetic tropes of *Blair Witch* and quickly rendered them tiresome clichés cast adrift in the fetid waters of the cathode-ray sea. Like it or not, we become jaded to the tricks that seemed so powerful yesterday. Moreover, *Blair Witch* was an unexpected, albeit welcome, reprieve in the inevitable slide from *Nightmare on Elm Street* (1984) to *Scary Movie* (2000).

A Close Reading of a Far-out Narrative

I offer you a *close reading* – an analysis that makes no attempt to hide my idiosyncratic likes and dislikes – of a new punk film that I think exemplifies the legacy of the New Wave at its best. *Y Tu Mamá También* (2001) rejects the overheated, 'crazy-love' narratives of a number of other youth-oriented films such as *Requiem for a Dream* or *Amores perros*, preferring the more contemplative, hesitant mood of films by Kar Wai Wong (*Happy Together* [1997], *In the Mood for Love* [2000]).

Directed by Alfonso Cuarón, *Y Tu Mamá También* was released in Mexico in late 2001 and was almost instantly a target of conservatives who wanted to prevent teenagers from seeing a film that is really all about them. Only after a massive protest campaign did authorities relent; the film was a box-office smash. 'And your mother too' – so comes the final salvo of macho brinkmanship between two Mexican teenagers tippling immodestly at a cantina on an Oaxacan beach. Each has confessed to having sex with the other's girlfriend. Now, their friendship in ruins, the gloves are really off. Fuelled by mescal and testosterone, they try to outdo one another with boasts of sexual mischief and toasts to those boasts. Looking on (and egging them on) is Luisa, the Spanish-born erstwhile wife of one of the boy's cousins, a vainglorious upper-middle-class man addicted to cheating on her and then whining about it.

Y Tu Mamá También begins as one might expect – with sex. Two teenagers are engaged in it in a comfortable-looking bedroom under a poster for the film, *Harold and Maude* (1971). Between thrusts, the boy demands to know if the girl, leaving for a summer on the Continent, promises not to get it on with a variety of clichés torn from a European youth hostel – the French gay, the white American backpacker and of course, the smelly Mexican selling bracelets in the street. Seemingly used to this kind of talk, she provides cheeky additions to his litany as she moves on top. The ante has been raised. A half-hearted promise of fidelity is made. As the camera pulls away from the lovers, an unseen narrator divulges that, while the girl's mother, a French divorcee, doesn't mind her daughter sleeping with her boyfriend, Tenoch, his friend Julio has less luck. His girlfriend has a paediatrician and a Lacanian analyst for parents. The camera moves to their living-room, a joyless sterile place where the father nervously feigns reading the newspaper as the wife hovers behind the sofa where Julio sips a juice. The narrator tells us the parents are divided about Julio – the mother sees their relationship as innocent, the father disapproves. Upstairs, Cici can't find her passport. With the mother's blessing, Julio is dispatched. By now Cici has found her passport and lost her track-suit bottoms as she demands that Julio should shut the door and give her a sweet going-away present. Their coupling is a self-parody. The mother appears at the door. Cici throws Julio off the bed but he comes up smiling, passport in hand.

We move to the airport where the boys and girls are saying farewell. Tenoch confesses to Julio that he 'can't stand this goodbye bullshit. Why don't they just go?' Meanwhile, the girls express their own desire to get to Europe already, albeit with more finesse. Ana's father appears. The narrator confides that he is a journalist who has begun dabbling in politics with Mexico's main opposition party. The father likes Tenoch but calls him the 'preppie' when his daughter isn't around. As we hear this, we see the father take a call on his mobilel phone.

The boys are now left to their own devices. They drive around in Tenoch's saloon car, provided by his father under the condition that he take economics at university. We join them at Tenoch's luxurious house for a joint and a few laughs with their guru/dealer/partner-in-crime, Saba. The narrator reveals that Tenoch's father is some sort of bigwig in the ruling party. Overcome with patriotic fervour at the birth of his son, Tenoch was named after an Aztec emperor. Tenoch's mother arrives home, beautifully coiffured and resplendent in a flowing track-suit. She has the air of a New-Age devotee, a suspicion confirmed in an aside from the narrator. After chiding the boys for smoking, she invites Julio to a family wedding that will allegedly be attended by the president of the country. Tellingly, she cautions Julio that he must be very well dressed for the occasion.

It is at the wedding we meet the film's other crucial character. The boys quickly get high on clandestine *cuba libres* and start counting contemptuously the ridiculous number of bodyguards all the guests have brought with them. While Tenoch's father launches into a purple, self-serving toast to the president, the boys set their sights on a beautiful woman enjoying a quiet wine. Their mission is delayed by Tenoch's cousin, Jano, who tries to caution Tenoch about the burden of becoming a writer. Quickly tiring of his pretentious tripe, the boys conspire to send him packing. Julio spills a glass of wine on the bore's suit. Jano is led away by a fawning aunt. The boys move in for the kill. They chat up Luisa, telling her about a glorious beach called Boca de Cielo – Heaven's Mouth – that they are planning to visit. Does she want to come along?

No she doesn't. At least not until she takes a call from her husband who is at some academic conference. He tearfully confesses his infidelity. Unable to endure his confession, she hangs up. The next day she rings Tenoch, asking if the trip is still on. Taken by surprise, the boy leads her on. Sure, we'll pick you up. Tenoch rings Julio. They secure the use of a beaten-up estate car from Julio's sister (who was intending to take humanitarian aid to the rebels of Chapas), make a quick trip to a hypermarket to stock up on provisions (including, of course, condoms) and fetch Luisa.

If I have been overly descriptive, it is to point out the highly schematic structure of the film's 'identity' politics. The boys are happy idiots, obsessed with performing for themselves and for girls. In existential terms, they are pups frolicking in a well-padded incommensurability. Parents are either zombified bourgeoisie, invisible or, in the case of Ana's father, sell-outs. And the narrator, in all his Godardian (Cuarón has admitted his admiration for *Masculin/Féminin* [1966]) glory, directs the viewer to facile, left-leaning observations, intended to add resonance to the action.

Indeed, the narrator, with his detached tone and omniscience, seems at first sight to be the voice of good faith, revealing truths that the characters refuse to acknowledge or simply cannot know. He is a surrogate, to paraphrase Camus, of 'the absurd that may strike a man in the face at any street corner'. The characters are locked in their little dramas; the narrator locates them in the larger, unforgiving context of the absurd. Moreover, the narrator is the director's agent of discontent, the voice of a man at the edge of middle age looking back at the portal of adulthood with mixed emotions. 'I wish I had known . . . but to what cause?'

Julio and Tenoch are on the cusp of adulthood in Mexico, a country on the cusp of adulthood. The boys are on a journey with their country. But as much as this film is a coming-of-age tale, it is also a road movie. The existential crisis of the characters and the larger existential crisis of national 'development' in a globalised economy are best articulated on the road between Mexico City and the Oaxacan beach.

One morning, early into the trip, Tenoch enters Luisa's room to borrow some shampoo. She's crying but, perhaps thankful for his presence, she asks him to remove his towel. Is she seducing him or taunting him? He willingly rises to her challenge but, in his haste to ravish her, he ejaculates quickly. Meanwhile, Julio broods in the motel's pool. The narrator announces that the last time Julio felt like this was when he witnessed his godfather having it off with his mother. To fight back against his pal's good fortune, Julio tells Tenoch that he had an encounter with Tenoch's girl. The game is on. That night, the boys stage an inquisition, with Tenoch demanding every sordid detail from his pal and Julio, as the narrator reveals, keeps talking until the truth disappears. Or rather the possibility of truth disappears. After Julio has his own disastrous encounter, in the back seat of the estate car with Luisa, who seems to be trying to recalibrate the boy's friendship, Tenoch confesses to an indiscretion with Julio's moll.

'Truth exists' wrote Kierkegaard 'only as the individual himself produces it in action.' The lies that Julio and Tenoch tell each other about having sex with the other's girlfriend are devastating to their friendship. Sartre's maxim that 'hell is other people' is even more piquant among friends; if your friend is ultimately unknowable, at least friendship offers a tacit agreement of non-aggression and empathy. Without fraternity, hedonism puts you in the spotlight of existential isolation and keeps you there. A number of times, Tenoch and Julio exchange epithets – preppie, white trash – that invoke both national and international class warfare. How can these guys be true mates if history won't let them? But then again, fraternity may be the last refuge of psychic autonomy against the 'divide and conquer' strategies of global capitalism as it plunders and commodifies national youth cultures. Fraternity is refusal. To Marx. To McDonald's.

The boys' very shaky postures of machismo prevent them from seeing that they've been had by their own fantasies. To say that Luisa is some sort of *femme fatale* is wrong. In Truffaut's *Jules and Jim* (1962), the struggle for the lady is the linchpin of the film. Here it is a Trojan Horse; Luisa will have neither of the boys. We know she has their number from the very beginning, the way she invites their outrageous come-ons and then parries with salacious questions that force them to reveal their sexual callowness. When they gleefully recite their 'astral cowboy manifesto' – a sort of Ten Commandments for teenage Mexican guys who love drugs, soccer and girls – she feigns surprise and interest. It's a ploy of good faith though. She's trying to keep her tour-guides amused as she searches for her answers to the 'groundlessness' that's been thrust upon her. The world she had constructed for herself has revealed its lack of foundation. Like Mersault in Camus's *The Stranger*, she is making an eleventh-hour fight for freedom. Her life has been spent in the service of others. Unlike Mersault, she has lived a moral life, a moral life achieved through good works. Now she must live for herself.

The parched Mexican countryside is much more than a metaphor for the existential distress of the characters. Antonioni was a master of using the emptiness of city spaces and architecture to articulate the isolation of the individual and the capitulation of the individual into the ennui that the open spaces invited. And who can forget the final shot of *The Passenger* (1975) when the desert hotel where Jack Nicholson's *doppelgänger* meets his demise in the blazing midday sun is shown in quiet repose at twilight. Alfonso Cuarón uses the Mexican landscape with equal aplomb. Oaxaca is, in fact, the inconvenient Mexico that sits between the boys' pampered niche in the city and the bourgeois fantasy of the virgin beach. The countryside is all too real. At one point, the camera offers a point-of-view shot as the car drives through some dreary small town, the streets lined with cantinas and scrap-yards. A woozy melancholic Brian Eno song plays on the sound-track. Then the radio stutters and dies. Culture is being sapped of its comforting energies by the forces of nature. The music that the boys have used to keep their jocularity on track is suddenly gone. Moments later, we see Tenoch making the unhappy connection between his own life and the fleeting glimpse of a sign marking the town from which his nanny came to tend to his every whim. Suddenly, he is in the moment, in the landscape, in the history of the country. Then, the car breaks down.

Bye Bye Brazil (1981), a film by Carlos Diegues, used the same road-movie premise to discuss the impact of television on rural communities in northern Brazil, and the displacement and provisional reintegration of older communication technologies and practices under the cathode ray tube regime. As a ragtag vaudeville troupe crosses the Brazilian outback in search of an audience untouched by television, they realise the battle is lost. No place is safe from the glowing beast; the troupe breaks up and scatters. At one point in *También*, Luisa places a call from a phone-box in a dusty roadside bar. The camera cuts to her well-kept apartment where her message fills the empty rooms. She is saying goodbye to her husband but she is also saying goodbye to the false promise of communication technology – that human connections are inevitable and stable regardless of distance. They are not and the further the characters in this film move into the Mexican landscape, the less they can rely on communication technologies to 'solve' the absurd. No music can drown out their isolation. No device can plug them into a world revealed to be a fraud.

Diegues infuses *Bye Bye Brazil* with a *Breathless*-like curiosity about the life and work going around the main characters and events. This is in pointed contrast to the American road pictures of Hope and Crosby in which the bumbling duo visited Brazil yet saw nothing of it. Brazil, like all of Latin America for so long, was backdrop exotica for Hollywood. In contrast, Diegues presents Brazilian small-town life to be full of community spirit and folk wisdom that resist and then integrate the forces of progress to their own ends.

Cuarón is equally curious. Luisa exclaims to the boys, 'Mexico is teeming with life'. Indeed. As the boys joust with Luisa in a small-town restaurant, the camera leaves them to follow an old woman walking into the kitchen. She stops in an adjacent nook, downs a glass of firewater and does an impromptu soft-shoe number to a *ranchero* playing on the juke-box. Then onward to the kitchen itself where a group of women are joyously cooking. Earlier, at the society wedding, the camera tracks with waiters and maids as they deliver food to bodyguards minding the limos idling out in the car-park.

This film was made shortly before the 9/11 tragedy, a moment that put paid to 'The End of History' as it was pronounced by various neo-con/neo-liberal theorists at the fall of the Berlin Wall a decade before. The much ballyhooed Clinton/Blair 'third way' of government – driven by policies that were socially liberal, fiscally conservative – proved wanting. The film constantly makes mocking reference to the sclerotic ruling party of Mexico, the PRI, a symbol of everything the third way was meant to obliterate: cronyism, social inequality and that particular supercilious sense of *noblesse oblige* that middling bureaucrats exude when they gain use of a chauffeured limousine. And yet, at the time of writing the government of Vincente Fox has stumbled and the PRI are still a force to be reckoned with in Mexican politics.

As is often the case, the fantasies of a faster, more mobile (a.k.a. better) world are no match for the realities of the world in its present state. People are so busy marching forward that they can't smell the dug on their shoes. The Oaxacan countryside is not only chronically underdeveloped; it resists development. The police are everywhere, hassling *campesinos* while the boys blithely worry about getting caught with their stash. The countryside confounds the fetish of progress, so crucial to the globalisation project. Luisa feels a deep kinship with Dona Lucia, an old woman she meets at a roadside flea market precisely because the old woman has happily stayed put. The small stuffed animal we see hanging from the estate car's rear mirror, the narrator remarks, once belonged to the old woman's granddaughter who died trying to cross illegally into the United States. The mirage is not worth it.

Nor, it would seem, is the beach. Exhausted after fightinh it out with Tenoch while convincing Luisa not to abandon the journey, Julio turns down a dirt road and promptly gets the car sticl in a sand trap. The next morning, Luisa awakes and discovers that they have arrived at a beach as deserted as it is beautiful. She walks in a knowing daze towards the water and wades in, lost to the ecstasy of the moment. One might expect Julio and Tenoch to mend fences. Luisa is now off limits. She has also debased them of the notion that their girlfriends are being faithful to them. But they keep their distance from one each other, even when a local fisherman offers to take them on his fishing boat to an idyllic beach miraculously called Heaven's Mouth.

The narrator tells us that Chuy, the jovial fisherman, will lose his boat to a tourism consortium from Acapulco and, in two years, he will be forced to work as a janitor in a resort hotel. The noble savage will be in chains and his idyll overrun with refugees from the city. The boys are the first conquerors of this paradise, even if that conquest was a trashy improvisation. Hundreds of beaches around the world have been colonised by intrepid libidos and then further colonised by larger interests. The leisure industries of the global economy need the beach desperately. It functions as a psychic escape-hatch, promising a primal connection with nature mitigated by the creature comforts of consumer culture. *Tambien* clearly delights in Barthes's idea that the history is often naturalised, unhappily so; to know about the fate of Chuy diminishes our pleasure watching the boys and Luisa enjoying sun and surf. Their lack of a sense of privilege and their self-involvement are elemental to a larger political problem of the global leisure industries.

Tambien cuts against the clichés of the 'coming-of-age' genre to suggest that the characters are not only changed by their experience, they are ruined by it.

Many psychoanalytic screeds are sure to be written about the final night that Julio and Tenoch spend with Luisa in a beach cantina, throwing back beers and egging each other on to more and more outlandish confessions of sexual transgression, including Julio's having Tenoch's New-Age socialite mother. The trio retire to a cabana where a heavy threesome ensues. The next morning the boys wake up almost in each other's arms. Deeply hung over from shame and booze, Julio and Tenoch gingerly prepare to return home. Luisa is going to stay behind to tour more of the beaches with Chuy and his family. She wins? They lose?

An epilogue follows. Almost a year later, Tenoch and Julio meet by chance on the street. The narrator intimates that they have retreated into their own worlds, circumscribed by class and material resources. One is at university, the other at community college. Each is dating girls from their neighbourhoods. Over a very awkward cup of coffee, Tenoch reveals what the director has hinted at throughout the film – Luisa was dying and expired a month after the trip, that glorious body they so desired riddled with cancer. Clearly Tenoch and Julio have no idea what to do with this information. Its voodoo qualities are overpowering. Death is out there, circling in the water beyond the safety-net of adolescence. The film ends with Tenoch excusing himself to meet his new girlfriend. Julio, left alone in a massive sun-blasted diner, chokes on his words as he asks for the bill. The ground has finally fallen out from beneath him. Everything is up for grabs.

The film has a happy ending after all.

4. SINCERITY AND IRONY

Nicholas Rombes

> But you see, I think the Sex Pistols and the other groups would be quite acceptable if they seemed more ironic to people. But I think they're not perceived as ironic and once they are perhaps that will be their form of domestication. Then it will be perfectly all right. (Susan Sontag, quoted in Bockris 1998: 80)

New punk cinema developed during a time when irony became a mainstay in popular culture in the post-1970s era. As such, the moments of intense emotion and melodrama in key films, *Magnolia*, *The Idiots*, *Breaking the Waves*, *Fight Club*, and *Blair Witch Project* can be read through conflicting registers that blur the boundaries of sincerity, irony and camp. In his 1993 essay 'E Unibus Pluram: Television and U.S. Fiction', David Foster Wallace offers one of the more challenging and insightful readings of the commodification of irony in post-war US culture, especially as it is expressed in literary fiction (notably metafiction) and television. For Wallace, the first wave of post-war irony – being shown the difference between the way things appear to be and the way things are – worked to expose the 'absurd contradictions' (Wallace 1993: 35) and hypocrisies of American culture. Television – with its ubiquity, repetition of images and ability to 'repeat' shows over and over again – is for Wallace the ultimate ironic medium, because it has helped to transform us into *knowledgeable* viewers, that is, viewers who can see through the very narratives that constitute television. Wallace points to a host of advertisements on television in the 1980s that openly mocked the fact that they were ads, including the Joe Isuzu ads for Isuzu, which featured a creepy car salesman: 'The ads succeeded as parodies of how oily and Satanic car commercials are. They invited viewers to congratulate themselves for getting the joke, and to congratulate Isuzu Inc. for being 'fearless' and 'irreverent' enough to acknowledge that car ads are ridiculous and that the Audience is dumb enough to believe them' (ibid., p. 61).

This is the same sensibility that characterises many of the graphic novels which became popular in the wake of Art Spiegelman's *Maus* (1986), including Chris Ware's *Jimmy Corrigan* (2000) and Daniel Clowes's *David Boring* (2000) and *Ghost World* (1997), drawn in a 'bluish-green tint that suggests a TV on the blink – exactly right for these lives in which much of the color has been drained by a crippling irony and hyper self-awareness' (McGrath 2004: 33). Robert Ray has written that the very medium of television itself helped to create an ironic audience.

> [I]n the spring of 1963, for example, a television viewer could watch as network videotapes of the Birmingham race riots led directly into 'Cheyenne', 'Laramie', 'Mr. Ed', 'Ozzie and Harriet', or 'Wagon Train', depending on the network and the night. Inevitably, that viewer's attitude toward conventional versions of America's mythology became increasingly ironic. (Ray 1985: 266)

We could say that post-1960 media, no matter what its content, is ironic in the sense that it was made and consumed by people for whom the governing mythologies and narratives were relentlessly exposed and undermined by the very technologies of media. Jay David Bolter and Richard Grusin have noted that television 'acknowledges its mediation more explicitly and readily than film does' (Bolter and Grusin 1999: 186). Or, to get back to the One who sits at the fount of all this theorising, Marshall McLuhan, '[People] don't see movies on TV; they see TV' (McLuhan 1995: 294).

Recent technologies have further demystified the stories offered by film and television, as home playback systems make it possible to manipulate the previously fixed temporal order of film. Writing in 1993, before the advent of DVDs, critic Anne Friedberg noted that VCRs 'allow for time-shifting and playback of rental tapes' (Friedberg 1993: 136). She went on to argue that the VCR 'becomes a privatized museum of past moments, of different genres, different times all reduced to uniform, interchangeable, equally accessible units. The videocassette transforms the size and accessibility of film experience, markets it as a booksized, readily available commodity' (ibid. p. 139). This is pushed even further by DVDs, which accelerate the user's ability to manipulate a film's narrative and, with multiple options and commentaries, radically destabilises the aura of a primary, fixed film. As Graeme Harper has suggested, 'DVDs promote and develop the idea of film as a "game". No longer do audiences simply enter a text expecting to follow its narrative from

Point A through to Point Z' (Harper 2001: 24). The implications of these recent home-based technologies of viewing had and continue to have enormous impact on the emergence of an ever-increasingly ironic audience. The emblematic scene here is in *Scream*, when the teenagers (some soon to be victims) are watching John Carpenter's *Halloween* (1979) on the VCR. One of them stops the tape, and gives a professorial crash course in the not-so invisible narrative codes that structure slasher films:

> Don't you know the rules? There are certain rules that one must abide by in order to successfully survive a horror movie. For instance, Number One, you can never have sex. Big no-no. Big no-no. Sex equals death. Okay, Number Two, you can never drink, or do drugs. The sin factor. It's a sin, it's an extension of Number One. And Number Three, never, ever, ever, under any circumstances say, 'I'll be right back,' because you won't be back. (*Scream*)

As Jean-Pierre Geuens has noted, '[L]iterally everyone today, audiences as well as filmmakers, knows too much about making movies' (Geuens 2001: 193). According to Wallace, irony involves an emotional distancing and remoteness: 'All U.S. irony is based on an implicit "I don't really mean what I'm saying"', or '"How totally *banal* of you to ask what I really mean"' (Wallace 1993: 67–8). Conditioned to see through everything, 'the most frightening prospect, for the well-conditioned viewer, becomes leaving oneself open to others' ridicule by betraying passe expectations of value, emotion, or vulnerability' (ibid. p. 63).

What distinguishes and links many of the disparate films of new punk cinema is their ability to do both: to evoke a sincere emotional response while, at the same time, to create the possibilities for the audience to see through the very mechanisms that elicit this response. While this strategy is not necessarily unique to new punk film – one could argue that an eighteenth-century book such as Lawrence Sterne's *Tristram Shandy* similarly invites the reader into the same sort of narrative – what is unique is the self-consciousness of filmmakers and of audiences regarding the visibility of the narrative structures that underlie these films.

This awareness has been fuelled by the do-it-yourself aesthetic articulated in punk music from the 1970s, which demystified music by suggesting that it was simple and that it could be hand made by anybody with a desire to do so. Thus, in the 1977 documentary *Punking Out*, the Dead Boys at CBGBs could proudly proclaim that 'the Sex Pistols don't even know how to play their instruments' (*Punking Out*). Punk itself was created by a generation brought up on television, a generation for whom pop culture – television, comics, advertising, FM radio – was a part of 'reality' in an unprecedented way. The punk movement's – especially the American punk movement's – appropriation of pop culture was fraught with all the contradictions that Wallace identified in his essay, specifically in terms of irony. As Dick Hebdige – whose book *Subculture: Elements of a Style* remains among the most eloquent and perceptive readings of punk – has noted, 'the sensibility which punk style embodied was essentially dislocated, ironic, and self-aware' (Hebdige 1979: 123). Two groups in particular – Blondie and the Ramones – were open to this double reading: what level of irony was involved in their use of more innocent 1950s' and '60s' sounds? It is tempting to read as ironic Blondie's 1976 song 'X Offender', the lyrics of which about a sex offender are set against a very sweet, lush, 'girl-group' 1960s' sound, as ironic. The song opens with dramatic, spoken-word lyrics by Debbie Harry: 'I saw you standing on the corner, you looked so big and fine. / I *really* wanted to go out with you, so when you smiled, / I laid my heart on the line' ('X Offender'). While the song clearly evokes the 1964 Shangri-Las' song 'Leader of the Pack' – which also opens with a spoken-word section that includes 'Is she *really* going out with him? Well there she is, let's ask her' – what is less clear is the relationship Blondie stakes out between her song and that of the Shangri-Las. For one thing, 'X Offender' quickly moves into lyrical territory that would have been unlikely in 1964, with lines like 'You had to admit you wanted the love of a sex offender'. The lush, romantic, wall of sound of the Blondie song argues against its own explicit lyrics, however, raising all sorts of questions about how to read the song. Is it a sincere homage to 1960s girl groups, a send-up or a bit of both? Is the song ironic, or is it we, as listeners, who hear the girl-group opening and think that, of course, this must be ironic? Perhaps, instead of Wallace's 'I don't really mean what I'm saying', this song suggests 'I don't really mean how I'm sounding'.

The Ramones take this even further, especially on their 1976 self-titled début album which, in many ways, defined punk's sound. Amid the brutally fast and aggressive songs, such as 'Blitzkrieg Bop', 'Now I Wanna Sniff Some Glue' and 'Beat on the Brat', are a few like 'I Wanna Be Your Boyfriend', a slower, melodic tune that appears to be a straight-ahead love song. Taken in the context of the entire album, however, one wonders about the ironic possibilities: is the song a send-up of the perceived innocence of early 1960s' music, or is it a sincere love song in its own right?

The answer is: both. And it is this manoeuvre – creating worlds that both acknowledge and deconstruct pop-culture narratives – that is punk's enduring legacy. For one really could listen to *Ramones* as a brutal, nihilistic record, or one really could listen to *Ramones* as a Beatles-esque pop record of fun and innocence. The ability to sustain both readings is a tendency shared by new punk cinema which, like punk, often relies on a hand-made, do-it-yourself ethos that is as interested in investigating the way stories get told as much as the stories themselves.

The uneasy and contradictory codes of new punk cinema – codes that can be read as both ironic and sincere – are part of a broader trend that extends beyond cinema and into television, literature and the web itself. One noteworthy example – someone whose work has generated intense reactions from those who read it as indicative of post-modern irony and those who, on the contrary, read it as sincere – is Dave Eggers. His book, *A Heartbreaking Work of Staggering Genius*, was published in 2000 during a time of American soul searching about 'the state of the culture' that surrounded the anxieties concerning the millennium. The previous year, Jedediah Purdy's book, *For Common Things: .Irony, Trust, and Commitment in America Today*, was attacked in many quarters as offering a narrowly moralistic and nostalgic critique of contemporary American culture. Arguing that 'irony is powered by a suspicion that everything is derivative' (Purdy 1999: 14), Purdy raised many of the same points that Wallace had but, whereas Wallace was immunised from charges of moralism because he himself was considered ironic, Purdy approached his topic with transparent sincerity, and was pilloried. Indeed, Eggers's book was hailed by some as an inventive masterpiece that fused the memoir and the novel forms while being dismissed by others as the culmination of post-modern irony and cynicism. The book's reception – and Eggers's career – remain an important signal of the uneasiness regarding works that attempt to create emotionally involving (even melodramatic) stories while simultaneously commenting on the very process of narrative making. This isn't metafiction exactly, at least not as practised by William Gaddis, John Barthes and others, for its supposedly autobiographical strain is too strong. Is the very title an example of irony, a disjunction between what is said and what is meant? Is the book sincerely proclaiming to be a heart-breaking work of staggering genius, or is the title poking fun at itself as a title that would dare to proclaim itself as a heart-breaking work of staggering genius? Or, is the title a reference to the outrageous, overheated claims of many book reviews, offering what Linda Hutcheon calls an 'exaggerated signal' (Hutcheon 1994: 157)?

The much commented-on, extensive, self-conscious editorial apparatus that frames the book, especially the paperback version released in 2001, seems at first to be of the clever meta-commentary sort that had become a kind of clichéd indicator of post-modern smirkiness. But much like the film *Adaptation* (2002), which is also concerned with the extensive framing devices that go into the telling of any story, *A Heartbreaking Work* refuses to let its self-aware meta-commentary undercut the emotional core of the story. In the printed-upside-down section included in the paperback version, 'Mistakes We Knew We Were Making: Notes, Corrections, Clarifications, Apologies, Addenda', Eggers directly confronts those readers and critics who suggested that the book was ironic. I would like to dwell on this section for a little while because I think Eggers's comments here suggest a new, after-post-modern understanding of the relationship between sincerity, irony, and emotion that characterises not only his work, but the work of many new punk writers and directors, including Paul Thomas Anderson, Lars von Trier, Spike Jonze and Charlie Kaufman. Defining irony as 'the use of words to express something different from and often opposite to their literal meaning', Eggers resolutely denies that his book is ironic, and devotes much of his time specifically defending his use of various narrative frames in the book, including appendices, footnotes, etc.

> 11. Appendices are not ironic. 12. Having characters break out of character is not ironic . . . Still, we have reached a point, with a certain group of venally impatient and yet startlingly lazy cultural bystanders, wherein everything in the world falls into two categories: the Earnest and the Ironic. And neither, it seems, is acceptable. Everything is either glib and shallow, or maudlin and boring. (Eggers 2001: 35)

Under the heading 'People, please: Trust the motives and hearts of the makers of things', Eggers continues:

> See here: I do not live in a postmodern time. I did not live in a time when something *new* was called *modern*, so for me there is no such thing as *modern*, and thus there cannot be anything *postmodern*. For me, where I am standing, it is all New. The world, everyday, is New . . . These labels are slothful and dismissive, and so contradict what we already know about the world, and our daily lives. We know that in each day we laugh, and we are serious. We do *both*, in the *same* day, *every day*. But in our art, we expect clear distinction between the two. We expect a movie to be a *comedy* or a *drama*. We expect writing to be *serious writing* or *humorous writing*. (ibid. pp. 34–5)

Is there something – if not ironic then disingenuous – about an author of such a critically praised book, that was itself a profitable national best-seller, defending the book as if he were some sort of victim? Perhaps, but I think Eggers expresses an aesthetic point of view here that is similar to that of his new punk colleagues who also find themselves 'misread' by readers, viewers and critics who equate digression, humour and self-reflexivity with postmodern glibness and shallowness.

Nowhere is this more evident than in the collaborative work of writer Charlie Kaufman and director Spike Jonze who, between them, have either written or directed *Being John Malkovich*, *Human Nature*, *Confessions of a Dangerous Mind*, *Adaptation*, and *Eternal Sunshine of the Spotless Mind*. *Adaptation*, in particular, was subject to the same extremes of praise and contempt from viewers and critics who either saw it as a heartfelt, inventive masterpiece or as yet another example of post-modern narcissism that reflects the poverty of ideas in our recycled age. This is something that writer Susan Orlean, whose book *The Orchid Thief* was 'adapted' into the film, has herself commented on, noting that Kaufman's screenplay was about 'the ongoing, exasperating battle between looking at the world ironically and looking at it sentimentally' (Orlean 2002: ix). Beyond that, *Adaptation* is an exemplary new punk film, not because it must choose between these (irony and sentiment) but rather because it recognises that post-modern audiences *already know* that a movie is just a 'movie'. Kaufman recognises that it is no longer a trick or a post-modern stunt to tell a serious story while, at the same time, telling the story of how that story was made. Robert McKee, the legendary teacher of screen-writing who is played by Brian Cox, notes that 'Kaufman understands deconstructive rhetoric. He knows that we know film is ritual. To involve ourselves we must accept the conventions of the art' (McKee 2002: 134). This is no more a trick than lighting a scene is a trick: all films are tricks, whether they admit to it or not, because all story-telling is a trick, a trick accepted by the audience as the price they pay to lose themselves in the story.

Adaptation is structured around emotional reversals that invite the audience to identify with the characters in brief moments of emotional sincerity quickly followed by narrative re-framings that make us question our emotional attachments to these characters. Consider the scene where Kaufman lies in his bed at night, frustrated at how to adapt Orleans's book into a movie:

> Kaufman switches on a lamp, pulls *The Orchid Thief* from his bag, flips through it. There are now many yellow hi-lited passages. He reads one.
>
> ORLEAN (VOICE-OVER)
> There are too many ideas and things and people. Too many directions to go. I was starting to believe the reason it matters to care passionately about something is that it whittles the world down to a more manageable size.
>
> KAUFMAN
> Such sweet, sad insights. So true.
>
> Kaufman flips to the growing, smiling author photo.
>
> KAUFMAN (CONT.)
> I like looking at you.
>
> He stares at the photo. Its smile broadens. It talks.

ORLEAN
I like looking at you, too, Charlie.

The photo smiles warmly at him. Kaufman closes his eyes, begins to jerk-off. (Kaufman 2002: 54–5)

Such reversals lie at the heart of *Adaptation*, even more so than its much-discussed story-within-a-story-within-a-story structure. Because what these moments of intense sincerity, reversed by scenes where our emotional attachment is undercut by the 'bad' behaviour, do is cause us to question the very sincerity of those supposedly sincere moments. To return to David Foster Wallace: 'the most frightening prospect, for the well-conditioned viewer, becomes leaving oneself open to others' ridicule by betraying passé expressions of value, emotion, or vulnerability' (Wallace 1993: 63).

This disjunction is raised on a larger scale when the end of the movie becomes precisely the sort of film that Kaufman disdains and resists writing. As he tells Valerie from the film company for whom he is writing the script, 'I don't want to cram in sex or guns or car chases. You know? Or characters learning profound life lessons' (Kaufman 2002: 5). And yet this is precisely what happens at the end of the movie, when Susan Orlean actually enlists the help of Laroche to murder screenwriter Kaufman because he might 'write about this' in his screen-play (ibid. p. 88). Even though the film has gone through great pains to elaborate on how hollow and clichéd most Hollywood action films are, however, we are caught up enough in the story to go along with it. Is the 'action' ending ironical – an example of what David Foster Wallace calls the irony of 'I don't really mean what I'm saying?' (Wallace 1993: 67) – or is the ending something that we are really meant to care about? The movie has already pointed out and resisted the narrative syntax of mainstream Hollywood films, only to deploy it in the end.

If the 'invisible style' of classic Hollywood cinema perfected intricate codes and patterns for hiding the fact that a film was a film, and if various avant-gardes have gone to the other extreme by offering no pretense of mirroring bourgeois reality, then new punk film has emerged from, and absorbed the logic of, both these approaches in part because audiences are accustomed to both extremes, as well as hybrids in the form of television commercials and especially music videos, which borrow heavily from the practices and aesthetics of avant-garde film-making.

New punk cinema is the inheritor of the destruction of the invisible code, and is made by, and belongs to, a generation for whom the dethroning of master narratives is no longer a radical gesture but a fact of everyday life. Peter Lurie, writing in the online journal *CTheory*, notes that web 'surfing mimics a postmodern, deconstructionist perspective by undermining the authority of texts. Anyone who has spent a lot of time online, particularly the very young, will find themselves thinking about content – articles, texts, pictures – in ways that would be familiar to any deconstructionist critic' (Lurie 2003: 2). So, too, this generation of film-makers, raised in some weird variation of Marshall McLuhan's global village, has been so immersed, not only in narrative codes, but in the deconstruction of those codes, that it's not simple irony when, in their work, we see exposed the disjunction between the world 'of the film' and the world that made the film. For what is a film like *Memento* if not an object lesson in film-making itself by means of a narrative that continually asks us to consider the way in which the narrative was made? Paul Thomas Anderson, discussing his film *Magnolia*, has said:

> I'm a film geek; I was raised on movies. And there come these times in life when you just get to a spot when you feel like movies are betraying you. Where you're right in the middle of true, painful life. Like, say, somebody could be sitting in a room somewhere, watching their father die of cancer, and all of a sudden it's like, no this isn't really happening, this is something I saw in *Terms of Endearment*. (Anderson 2000: 205)

Whether this is an astonishing confession of shallowness or a profound, Baudrillardian insight into our simulacra, Anderson's comment points to the self-consciousness that characterises new punk cinema and which informs it on every level, from plot to technique to marketing. If such self-reflexivity and self-consciousness was once confined to 'new waves' (such as Godard films) or to 'art films' (such as Fellini's *8* , which was itself a film about making a film) or to avant-garde or experimental films, what distinguishes new punk cinema is the easy incorporation of this self-consciousness into popular, mainstream films themselves.

In *Magnolia*, the narrator says that '[T]hese are stories of coincidence and chance and intersections and strange things and which is which and who is who only knows . . . and we generally say, "Well if that was in a movie I wouldn't believe it" ' (ibid. pp. 189–90). In an earlier era, this sort of narrative commentary would have been taken as coolly ironic in a kind of Godardian way, reminding us that, of course, what we are watching is just a set of contrived narrative conventions. Yet there doesn't seem to be much debunking or unmasking going on in *Magnolia*; unlike Godard, Anderson isn't investigating the form to offer any sort of critique or even homage. As Graeme Harper notes elsewhere in this book, and as I have suggested in 'Professor DVD' (2002), DVD itself – with its relentless supplementary material that displaces the 'master' narrative of the feature film as well as the opportunity it affords viewers to navigate the film in segments rather than as a linear whole – fosters an ironic stance towards cinema, the previously invisible workings of which are now demystified. To return to Dave Eggers by way of example: issue number 11 of *McSweeney's Quarterly* – a literary journal he publishes and edits – comes packaged with a DVD of the authors of that issue reading and performing their work. The sections on the DVD include: 'Deleted Scenes', 'Extra-Deleted Scenes', 'Behind the Scenes of the Deleted Scenes and Extra-Deleted Scenes', and 'Outtakes from the Deleted Scenes, Extra-Deleted Scenes, and from Behind the Scenes of the Deleted Scenes and Extra-Deleted Scenes' (*McSweeney's Quarterly* 2003). The DVD promotes the idea of the Famous Author, even as it mocks the very mechanisms that promote such celebrity. The deconstruction of celebrity becomes the very strategy for making celebrity.

Dogma and Irony

Dogma's Vow of Chastity has been variously praised on the one hand as revolutionary and, on the other as a cynical publicity stunt. In truth, it is both. As Thomas Vinterberg has said, 'I think . . . Dogma is in the area between a very solemn thing and deep irony' (MacKenzie 2003: 54). And Peter Schepelern notes that what at first appeared to be an ironic gesture turned out to be something more serious: 'The Dogma manifesto . . . as well as the happening in the Odean theatre [where von Trier publicly announced the Vow of Chastity in 1995] were received as a humorous provocation, an ironic event *à la* Trier. But the best part of the joke was that Trier and Vinterberg were in ernest' (Schepelern 2001: 2).

The films of von Trier – especially *Breaking the Waves*, *The Idiots* and *Dancer in the Dark* – while distinct from camp, offer a profound awareness of film traditions and dramas. In one important sense, they share what Sontag refers to as 'the sensibility of failed seriousness, of the theatricalization of experience. Camp refuses both the harmonies of traditional seriousness, and the risks of fully identifying with extreme states of feeling' (Sontag 1966: 287). Even more significantly, Sontag identifies in camp a tendency that is shared by many new punk films, especially those by von Trier and others working in the spirit of Dogma 95: 'The traditional means for going beyond straight seriousness – irony, satire – seem feeble today, inadequate to the oversaturated medium in which contemporary sensibility is schooled. Camp introduces a new standard: artifice as an ideal, theatricality' (ibid. p. 288).

The Idiots is about a group of people who pretend, in public, to be mentally disabled. This activity – spassing – essentially tricks unwary strangers into emotional feeling for the spassers. One in particular, Karen, shows great concern over Stoffer, who has been brought to an expensive restaurant by his cohorts, where he proceeds to create a scene (to put it mildly). In a gesture of sympathy, she walks with him out of the restaurant, only to be laughed at and ridiculed by the spassers once they reveal to her their con. Out of curiosity, loneliness and the sense of identity and community that this group offers, Karen stays with them, an accomplice who eventually turns to spassing by the end. The film's plot – which seems outrageous – in fact, enacts the very mechanics of audience identification that we all experience each time we watch a movie. For what is a fictional film other than a group of people pretending to be someone else (spassing) in such a way that tricks us into entering into the film's world and suspending our disbelief long enough to be moved by the emotional cues offered to us?

Tim Walters has suggested that there might be a direct connection between spassing, with its formal rules and defiant reshaping of the social world, and the very rules of the Vow of Chasity. He notes that the 'charismatic and, arguably, brilliant Stoffer should then be considered as a more-or-less direct representation of von Trier himself, someone who experiences great frustration as he tries to passionately coax his fellow malcontents to reconsider the way they function in opposition to a system they find abhorrent' (Walters 2004: 48). One scene, in particular, strongly suggests actors debriefing after a performance or, to extend Walters's argument, a director chiding his performers on the day's work. After their visit to the Rockwool factory, the spassers return to the country house and, in a college all-night-talk-session-like scene, sit on the floor in a room lit by candles and discuss the day. At one point, Stoffer says: 'Jeppe copped out right in the middle and it pisses me off.' Other characters either agree with Stoffer or else defend Jeppe regarding the quality and believability of his spassing at the factory, with lines like 'I thought Jeppe was good', and 'Where the hell was Jeppe good?' On one level, we are invited to read this as a part of the fictional world of the movie into which we have entered. On another level, the scene reminds us that the characters are not only talking about their 'performance' in the Rockwool factory for the factory manager, but also that they are talking about the quality of their performance as actors who are playing the role of spassers in a film called *The Idiots*. In this regard, Stoffer's criticism of Jeppe's performance comes not from Stoffer, the fictional character who is leader of the spassers, but from Stoffer as a sort of theatre director who is evaluating the work of his actors that day. Or, the scene evokes a connection between Stoffer and von Trier: both are 'directors' critiquing their actors' performances. And on yet another level, the scene recalls the very 'rules' of the Dogma 95 movement itself and its penchant for the rituals of self-criticism, critique and confessions.

This self-awareness extends to the explicitly documentary dimensions of the film itself, where von Trier – off-camera – asks the characters after-the-fact questions about the motivations for, and consequences of, spassing. In several exchanges reminiscent of discussions regarding who originally came up with the Dogma 95 concept and Vow of Chastity, the interviewer asks one of the spassers whose idea this all was, to which she replies 'Axel says it was his idea. I think it was Stoffer's.' Jeppe himself says 'It was my idea, but it was Stoffer who wanted to do something about it.'

The plot of *The Idiots* involves people who pretend to be something they are not for audiences in order to elicit emotional responses, a process which makes it very difficult to know how to read the intensely emotional, even melodramatic, scenes in the film. For if *The Idiots* continually reminds us of the very process by which we ourselves are being manipulated, what are we to make of the painfully intense close-ups of Karen, the woman drawn into the world of spassing? This really becomes a problem of audience identification: to which characters – if any – are we expected to extend our sympathy? Are we to view the spassers – who clearly are framed in such a way as to indicate a righteous piercing of hypocritical bourgeois attitudes towards the mentally disabled – as characters with whom we are supposed to identify on some level? Are they speaking and enacting a 'truth' that, however harsh, is sincerely expressed? It would be difficult to accept this, given that the spassers are shown to be indulgent, selfish and cruel, and given to excess. As Murray Smith asks: 'Where, then, does *The Idiots* – and the Dogma manifesto – leave us in terms of the Romantic appeal to the simple and the authentic? Is it annihilated by irony – or does some shred of it remain?' (Smith 2003: 119).

If there is any romantic appeal in *The Idiots* – if there is any uncorrupted sincerity – it comes closest to being embodied in the character of Karen who, we learn by the end of the film, has recently lost her child and who has left her family, presumably out of grief or shock. She, more than anyone else in the film, questions the spassers, and Stoffer in particular, about the moral and ethical dimensions of their game. Stoffer's indignant defences of spassing as a way to expose the hypocrisy of bourgeois prejudices regarding the mentally handicapped (and perhaps, by extension, any marginalised group) are repeatedly undercut by Karen's quiet questioning. In many ways, she serves as a surrogate for the audience, standing in for the viewer who wants to ask, 'why?' One of the more poignant moments comes when the group is in the woods and Karen directly confronts Stoffer: 'But there are people who are really ill. It's sad for the people who are not able like us. How can . . . how can you justify acting the idiot?' His response – 'you can't' – can be read as a profound, philosophic response that suggests it's as silly to ask about acting the idiot as it would be to ask why Dadaist art doesn't make sense. Or, it can be read as the response of an anarcho-nihilist, the sort of person who, like Tyler Durden in *Fight Club*, addresses the blankness of his generation:

> I see in fight club the strongest and smartest men who have ever lived – an entire generation pumping gas and waiting tables; slaves with white collars. Advertisements have us chasing cars and clothes, working jobs

we hate so we can buy shit we don't need. We're the middle children of history, with no purpose or place. We have no great war, no great depression. The great war is a spiritual war. Our great depression is our lives. (*Fight Club*)

The Idiots raises the same questions that *Fight Club* does: to what extent are the protagonists of the films symptoms of a broken-down culture, more to be pitied – or feared – than admired? Or, do the films ask us to identify, if not with the specifics then with the general programme of the spassers in *The Idiots* and Tyler in *Fight Club* which, like a fire, clear away the dead-wood conventions and habits of middle-class life? Does the anarchist sensibility that pervades both films point to a profound social unease ignored by 'official' culture, or are the actions of the characters little more than philosophic posturing dressed up as profound social critique?

Dancer in the Dark continues this and even blurs further the line between so-called authentic emotion and irony. In our post-modern age, can a musical about the death penalty by a Danish director who is, to say the least, ambivalent about the Hollywood tradition, be considered anything other than ironic? Can a film made in the year 2000 hark back to Hollywood's golden age of musicals in a way that doesn't involve camp, or parody, or irony? *Dancer in the Dark's* signal achievement might very well be that the audience is never sure. The director himself has disavowed any satirical impulse, telling Jan Humboldt that he didn't care for Dennis Potter's *Pennies From Heaven* because 'it was too much parody, something I wanted to avoid at all costs in *Dancer in the Dark*' (Lumholdt 2003: 163). Von Trier has also said that 'Maybe, it doesn't look like a conventional musical, but it's a musical to me. So it's not like I'm trying to change anything. This is what came out of it.' (ibid. p. 156)

Irony, like any other code, is always a product of context that involves many factors, including not only the director (or author, or singer, or actor, etc.), but the audience as well. For, if the film is either sincere or ironic (and it can be both simultaneously), it is only because of the expectations that we, as viewers, bring to the material. In this sense, the new punk sensibility is as much a way of seeing, of reading, as it is a way of making things. For an American audience schooled in the poetics of irony, as described by David Foster Wallace and others, *Dancer in the Dark* can't help but be read as 'ironic'. In the era of relentless deconstruction, remakes, television shows about television shows, *Nick at Night, Talk Soup*, the Internet, and other cultural formations that are at their core about the making of themselves, there is no way to avoid the question of irony when it comes to *Dancer in the Dark*.

What is so intrguing – and emblematic – about *Dancer in the Dark* is its refusal to acknowledge this. Nowhere in the film do any of the characters 'wink' at the camera to acknowledge that they are, in fact, part of an old-fashioned musical in an age when old-fashioned musicals are impossible. In navigating the terrain between sincerity and irony, new punk films find themselves in the position of encouraging audiences to identify with their central characters, even as the films make known that gestures of identification are always risky, especially for audiences conditioned to the relentless deconstructing of master narratives in everyday life. In 1944, Max Horkheimer and Theodor Adorno ended 'The Culture Industry' with the following observation: 'The triumph of advertising in the culture industry is that consumers feel compelled to buy and use its products even though they see through them' (Horkheimer and Adorno 1944: 167). The relaxing of critique in the face of the overriding entertainment apparatus of the culture industry, has, today, become the signatory gesture of new punk cinema.

PART II

SCREENING NEW PUNK CINEMA

5. DVD AND THE NEW CINEMA OF COMPLEXITY

Graeme Harper

Film, as we have known it for over a century, began its death in the later 1970s. Though it still exists, it is no longer what it was prior to this, and never will be again. Its death continues to be awkward and, religious connotations aside, if this death is to result in a resurrection we must, firstly, remove the veil of nostalgia that attaches itself to the picture palace and celluloid era and we must, secondly, embrace a new way of understanding and reading the moving image and its attendant sounds, styles and strategies, as well as its technical meta-text.

Unlike the background to the emergence of the punk movement, which occurred in the same period, the death of cinema was not produced by disaffection with establishment practices or, indeed, by a promotion of a philosophy of amateurism; paradoxically, cinema's death was brought about by an over-affection for the mainstream (in cinema's case represented largely by the professional operations of Hollywood). By 'cinema' I should differentiate here between that building we know as 'the Cinema' and the art-form we know as 'cinema' or 'film'. That building, the Cinema, has adapted to the prevailing post-1970s' conditions to incorporate a broader public entertainment ideal and a discourse of choice; the movie multiplex is the prime example of this. Likewise, because of the changes of the past thirty years, neither 'film' nor 'cinema' is now an entirely suitable term for the visual and aural medium we're discussing; for the moment, however, both, or either, words will have to do. Film's death has been technologically driven, founded on the emergence of home videotape recording and, soon after that, home computing, leading to, ultimately, film's redefinition at the end of the 1990s in the launch of Digital Versatile Disk or Digital Video Disk: in short: DVD.

Videotape, which had been in commercial use since the 1950s, became affordable as a home-recording and playback medium in the 1970s. Soon afterwards, by the early 1980s, in fact, income from home videotape sales outstripped income from Cinema releases in almost all world film markets and, it could be said, from that point onwards the life-span of the building we know as the Cinema was limited. It is, of course, no coincidence that, in this period, we begin to see the move towards building the movie multiplex – connected with what I will later refer to as the cinema of complexity – which sought to reintroduce variety into the market for mass film consumption, attempting to counter the stepped-up roll-out of videotape releases by supplanting the single-screen Cinema experience. It is important, however, to be wary of drawing a direct line between the increasing popularity of home film viewing on videotape and the emergence of the multiplex.

The movie mutliplex was as much a result of the multiple-choice philosophy of post-1950s' consumer culture as it was a direct product of the impact of domestic videotape on mass single screens. Indeed, the general movement in the West from the Fordist, or productionist, ethos of the earlier twentieth century to the consumerist ethos of the 1960s and onwards has been driven by increased leisure time brought about by a decrease in general working hours and by generally improved working conditions. Alongside this, there are labour-saving home appliances and a burgeoning service-industry sector that have been capable of absorbing some previously time-consuming domestic work. Income patterns have also changed, not least through an increased recognition of the equality of women in the work-place, if not always a direct change in their status and income. There has been considerable improvement in communications and transport, allowing for the increased global distribution of products and services. And late modern Western capitalism, as a political system, has continued to highlight its success, less challenged today since the crumbling of a number of alternative economies in the late 1980s. The arrival of movie multiplexes, which certainly made much of the factors of choice connected with home film viewing, was therefore also in keeping with the pattern of consumer desire-satisfaction-renewal-of-desire that is at the heart of late modern consumerism, and has connected well with the fundamental change in the pattern of film consumption that videotape introduced in the 1970s. But it was not just videotape that heralded the death of cinema. The home computer was, and is, at the heart of traditional cinema's demise.

Of course, it is provocative to suggest that either film or the Cinema is dead or dying. Talio Balio has written, albeit nearly a decade ago now, that '[C]ontrary to predictions, the new technologies did not kill the motion picture theatre; rather, they stimulated demand for more motion pictures, spread the risk of production financing, and enhanced the value of film libraries' (Balio 1996: 23). This is perfectly true, but only in part. The initial impact of the new film technologies of the later 1970s was to begin to unburden film producers from the incredible cost of producing cinema. While the tying-up of mainstream film production and distribution prevented the entire opening out of film-making to smaller, independent producers, the impact of post-1970s' technologies did at least offer the opportunity for the independents to produce more product and videotape, which, while not matching the quality of celluloid, increasingly provided an alternative distribution medium for the low-budget film-maker. In this way, the arrival of tape-based domestic film consumption moved film further away from the studio systems of classical Hollywood towards a post-classical ethos in which horizontal integration of production could at least entertain the notion of independence, if not always provide it. Paradoxically, it was not always provided because this was also the era of the high-budget block-buster which sold in part on the back of its high production values and, tellingly, on the back of its high production costs. This was not a phenomenon only of the film industry: book publishing throughout the 1980s saw large author advances met with even larger expectations and, as with these block-buster film releases, publishers attempted to saturate their outlets, too, in order to maintain profit margins. Thus, although videotape opened up the possibility of cheaper film production, incredibly strong commercial imperatives limited their exploitation, and the commercial need for market saturation limited viewer choice.

In addition, videotape allowed the powerful majors to tie the market into a staggered system of world film releases that maximised profits by alternating between release in the Cinema and videotape release, between PAL and NTSC release, and between one national release and another. In effect, regardless of the ownership of the product, videotape gave distributors several bites at the cherry and thus increased the possibilities for profit, even for the least popular films. It also raised the stakes, however, in relation to the movement between small-screen, domestic film viewing and the large-screen, mass cinema culture of the pre-1970s.

Media Literacy

Videotape film viewing, domestic and personal, helped to ground film as both home entertainment and as a televisual art-form which was not always directly televisual in an aesthetic sense but certainly televisual in the sense of the viewer's relationship to the medium. Already no longer an art-form only for mass response, because of the impact of television, by the end of the 1970s, film was increasingly a tradable home consumer product even for those audiences who could not regularly attend the Cinema. Although the Film Avid market – that is, the audience for film aged between fifteen and twenty-five years of age, who are the primary audience for the Cinema, making up about 40 per cent of world audiences – was able to access film in the home arena, so, too, were those sections of the film-going public who were outside the Avid market and previously disadvantaged by the public-ness of film distribution. These included children, of course, but, more significantly, early middle-aged parents, whose ability to leave the home was limited by family responsibilities. These early middle-aged film-viewers re-entered regular film consumption earlier than in the previous generation and, as they were more financially secure, formed the basis of the strong early take-up of video players and recorders. Not only that, with television forming part of the screening philosophy for film since mid-century, and videotape adding familiarly to this, the fact that film could be consumed in the home by both parents and post-1960s' children meant that a form of home-based education was set in motion which was to affect contemporary and future film style and content.

It is no coincidence that the heir to the 1950s' and 1960s' teen flicks of Elvis Presley, Annette Funicello, Cliff Richard and others were such films as *I Know What You Did Last Summer* (1997), *The Faculty* (1998), *Scary Movie* (2000) and even *Pulp Fiction*. In all of these films both theme and plot rely on the media savvy of characters and audience; these are just a few examples of the way in which media literacy has increasingly informed film-making itself. More recently, DVD has converged media literacy and audience expectation to create a level of filmic epistemology not known previously.

The emergence of the post-1960s' media-literate generation relates directly to the impact of videotape and to those attendant new punk film-consumption practices. It is paralleled by the growth in consumption of video games and an increasing variety of television programmes, some of which by the end of the 1960s had already taken on the form of being 'historical' and thus formed the basis of what can be called a 'master-to-acolyte' exchange. As television had enough of a history by the end of the 1960s to have produced a recognised canon, a selection of 'TV Classics', it was easy enough for parents to be Masters while children, absorbing this recent media history as Acolytes, were fed increasing amounts of new knowledge about the media and derived from the media. These parents were learning an entirely new history; their children, however, were born into a media-focused world. The post-1960s' generation found media literacy as ordinary as book literacy had been to the generation before them. Likewise, the idea of film as largely a medium delivered firstly in a cinema, and only then into a domestic arena, was at this point substantially diluted.

For the generation growing up in the 1970s and 1980s, film quite simply had two distribution platforms, The Cinema (multiplex and otherwise) and the television. Even this was a significant evolution from the situation understood by their parents. In the late 1990s, a third, mode-setting medium arrived. This was DVD, and it was DVD that brought to fruition the changes introduced, firstly by television then, more significantly, by domestic film-viewing on videotape – providing for either the demise of film or, seen another way, for its death and resurrection in a new form.

Home Computing

Personal computers started appearing on the market in the early 1970s. One of the first, the Altair 8800, sold mostly in kit form and had limited application. Incidentally, this was in 1975, one year before the seminal punk rock group, the Sex Pistols, released their first single 'Anarchy in the UK'. It arrived with the first personal computer, the Altair 8800, which sold mostly in kit form and had limited applications. In 1977, however, Apple Macintosh released its pre-built Apple II personal computer, and the future of home computing seemed, at the very least, partially secure. The Apple II had its own keyboard and add-on peripherals providing the possibilities of expansion and additional software applications. Significantly, it was also the first home computer with colour graphics. By 1984 the Apple II had made Apple the first computer company to reach annual sales of $US 1 billion. In anyone's terms, the Apple II was a phenomenal success.

A detailed history of microcomputing should perhaps not take up too much space here. And yet, it is true to say that the history of new punk cinema is fundamentally linked to the history of home computing, and cannot be devolved from it. Key computing moments map easily on to changing modes of film reading. In 1992, for instance, Apple released its Quicktime software, software allowing computers to play video clips. Other systems emerged alongside this to do likewise, effectively for the first time making the free-standing computer a site for film viewing. Even before this, however, technological changes were occurring that, directly or indirectly, built on the impact of videotape in relation to the way in which film was made, consumed and critically read. The Compact Disk, or CD, and Compact Disk Read Only Memory, the CD-ROM, were the most significant.

And yet, before moving on, pause for a moment and think about the changes domestic videotape had already brought about to film viewing, prior to the arrival of the CD-ROM in 1985. The formation of the idea, for example, that a film need not be viewed all at one time; rather, that it could be stopped while the viewer went about some other business, and then resumed at the point of departure. How about the idea of 'rewinding' or 'fast-forwarding' of film: no longer was a film a mono-directional entertainment. Perhaps, indeed, it was no longer even a teleological, or goal-directed, art-form. Did it really matter, that is, if you didn't get to the end? In fact, if the viewer wished they could fast-forward over the bits they found inadequate and repeat, over and over and over again, the bits they found most interesting or entertaining. How different is this to the single thrust of the mass film-viewing experiences of the pre-1970s' era?

Media Convergence

When, in 1985, the Dutch electronics film Philips launched the CD-ROM (a development from the audio CD) it did so on the back of the CD-ROM's storage capabilities, and the initial impact was on the storage of text. CD-ROM, with a storage capacity of 650 megabytes, could provide access to data and, indeed, databases, previously able to be held only on computer hard drives. And it was able to trade on the selling point established by CD, a technology introduced in the 1970s also by Philips: that is, it emphasised the clarity of the medium. As it was, however, Philips had continued strong competition from Asian manufacturers and, at first, adoption of the new CD-ROM technology was not as spectacular as might now be assumed, due largely to the high initial cost of CD-ROM drives. Writing in 1998, Brian Winston, notes that 'the CD-ROM itself could not support its own hype. In fact, it was oversold since its 0.64 gigabyte capacity gave it limited capacity for full motion video. Philips and Sony were promising a Digital Video/Versatile Disk (DVD) with six times the CD-ROM's for the late 1990s; but the damage to multimedia as a mass medium had been done' (Winston 1998: 238). But Winston is overly dismissive here; and, certainly, his emphasis on debunking what he calls 'the hype' surrounding CD-ROM clouds the issue. While CD-ROM didn't stretch right across the market from consumption of text, sound and still images to the leisurely consumption of full-length motion pictures, it did provide the initial sense in which media convergence could be possible.

The term 'media convergence' relates essentially to the idea that the personal computer and the television would, at some point, come together to form one media portal. In its various historical and contemporary forms, the telephone offered a third technology to this scenario. Free-standing gaming hardware, such as the highly successful Gameboy platform, provided a fourth. The concept goes deeper than this but that was its essential skeleton and, currently, it remains so – though a high degree of convergence has already occurred. Beyond this skeleton, the flesh of the idea revolves around the forms and access points to a variety of media. This can be traced today to technologies as distant as the first satellite television and as new as the mobile/cell videophone. As an emerging technology of the late 1980s, CD-ROM, was tactile, referencing the tactility of book and videotape culture, and interactive, referencing the discourse of the Internet. It was portable. And it was more durable and stable than videotape or, at the very least, gave the impression of being so. Thus, its limitations in terms of full motion video, regardless of the technical issues needing to be overcome, were not as significant as the impression it gave of moving towards convergence. In an arena in which 'the medium is the message' (McLuhan 1960: 1) CD-ROM's message was plain: visual and audio culture was not separate from that of the computer; in fact, it might well be intimately linked to it. Despite technical limitations, Compact Disk Read Only Memory heralded the merging of videotape film and interactivity, even if it couldn't entirely provide for it.

Digital Versatile Disk/Digital Video Disk (DVD)

DVD/DVD-ROM arrived on the world scene in 1997, and its origins can be traced back, appropriately, to work on double-density compact disks in the early 1990s, 1993 being the key development year. Debates surrounding DVD's release were driven by issues relating to technology and issues relating to ownership. Decisions about what would emerge as the world's universal DVD format dominated the period from 1994 to 1996. Throughout 1996 discussions around copyright dominated. The ability to control copyright had already become a key issue associated with the growth of the mass media. International copyright, which had historical relations to the British Statute of Anne of 1710 – in essence, empowering booksellers to hold to legal account rival booksellers – to French Revolutionary ideas of 1791 and 1793, and to the Berne Convention for the Protection of Literary and Artistic Works of the late nineteenth century, had not for some time had a challenge as big as that which occurred with the explosion of domestic videotaping, and nowhere near what was predicted at the launch of DVD. The system of regional encoding of DVD disks that ensued owed its origins to the intensity of industry concern.

Of course, DVD regional encoding was largely a failure. If increased media convergence meant anything, it meant the ability of one media technology to support another. The use of television advertising to sell film releases was one example. In DVD's case, the ability to buy disks over the Internet was the key. This reduced the opportunities for film distributors to control staggered national and regional disk releases, provided consumers additional opportunities to arrange 'hardware chipping' (the operation that allowed a single-region DVD player to be made multi-region), and alerted consumers to the growth of DVD across the world. In effect, the global nature of the Internet by the 1990s made DVD the first truly global domestic film platform, and the multi-language capabilities it provided ensured this quickly became the case even more readily. Suddenly, film was the most universal of home entertainments. Even at the birth of the Internet, such universality of communication that DVD provided could not have been imagined in any form. As DVD could be consumed either on a free-standing player, like videotape, or on a computer, just a raw view of the technology itself suggested universality.

Consequently, major global entertainment companies, such as Warner Bros, MGM/UA, Paramount, Viacom, Disney and Columbia, were involved in deciding on a universal technical format for DVD, in investigating design issues associated with the platform (not least the relationship between primary film and 'supplementary' sections of the disks), and in worrying over the vast copyright issues that prevail even today. It took until 1996 to get general industry agreement on the technical specifications relating to DVD and, even then, debate continued after the technology was released. For example, it was not until 1998 that a principal studio like Paramount announced it would release films on DVD at all. On a personal note, in 1998 I directed the UK's first 'DVD and Film' research conference. The DVD choices offered to British consumers by participating film distributors were at that time very limited indeed; hardware sales, though predicted to increase substantially, were negligible.

What was at stake? It would be instructive to consider the technology *per se*, as Brian Winston has done with earlier media technologies. What was at stake, in that sense, is perhaps best summed up by Jim Taylor when he says that 'DVD is the ideal convergence medium for a converging world. We are witnessing watershed transitions from analog TV to digital TV (DTV), from interlaced video to progressive video, from standard TV to widescreen TV, and from entertainment to interactive entertainment. In every case DVD works on both sides, bridging from the "old way" to the "new way"' (Taylor 2001: 2).

But even more was at stake than this.

THE CINEMA OF COMPLEXITY

Up until the arrival of domestic videotape in the late 1970s, cinema had been a reactive, rather than an interactive, medium. It was like many of the most traditional of theatrical forms in which the audience is passive, participatory only in absorbing and recalling the experience. Even more so, there were considerable technical and cultural limitations on consumer individualisation. The culture of film viewing was one in which the audience was discouraged from associating with the act of production and pressed to undertake one mode of consumption. The quiet, darkened Cinema literally restricted the audience from devolving their experience from the central presentation and, in a reverent fashion, asked for complete dedication to the primary performance. In addition, the sameness of this performance was one of the industry's unique selling points in that it was suggested that the text of a film screened in The Cinema would be the same no matter in which Cinema you might view it.

Domestic videotape issued considerable challenges to these practices. It introduced the idea of film viewing in an atmosphere of light and noise. Domestic film viewing *per se* was far less reverent and far less separate from the world beyond film than films viewed in The Cinema could ever be. It was also far more participatory. Videotape viewing placed control of the medium in the hands of the viewer; it introduced the notion of film viewed non-sequentially, film viewed on demand, and film viewed as part of everyday life, rather than separate from it. The movie multiplex, picking up on the discourse of choice and 'on-demand' consumption that videotape installed in the home market, struck back in the name of traditional mass viewing, but it soon became more of an 'entertainment complex' than was associated with a traditional Cinema and thus referenced the auxiliary nature of film consumption in which complexity, or a new cinema of 'related ideas, activities and things', was to flourish. CD-ROM capitalised on its storage capacity, not necessarily to provide full-length feature-film viewing, but to highlight the clarity and portability that media consumers had come to value. Significantly, CD-ROM made disk technology a technology of information and knowledge, with its emphasis on databases, encyclopedias, text, still image with interpretative text, moving image as sample and example, and both denotative and connotative graphic design.

When DVD arrived in 1997, consumers were not only familiar with demand-led, domestic, choice-based film viewing but also with disk-based interactivity. The final point of DVD-based convergence was to make mainstream cinema no longer simply a medium primarily of entertainment but to make it equally a medium associated with knowledge acquisition, regardless of its genre. This was the knowledge acquisition that CD-ROM had heralded. DVD was a perfect technology for a media-literate generation, and an ideal technology for late-modern consumerism: informed, on demand driven, infinitely renewable and thus able to maintain the cycle of desire-satisfaction-renewal-of-desire upon which late-modern consumerism relies.

The new cinema of complexity, which is the cinema of choice and knowledge, is also the cinema of death and resurrection. Whereas to watch a film more than once was, in the past, mostly the domain of cult-film fandom, or was merely repetitive, DVD introduced the idea that traditional mono-directional, or sequential, cinema was just one component of the moving-image experience, and that repeat watching was not only acceptable but was almost required. Rather than a film having one life it might, in fact, have many.

The cinema of complexity, the emerging new punk cinema, is today, similarly the cinema of supplementary-ness born out of the supplementary-ness of videotape and CD-ROM technology in which activities beyond the visual and aural content of the primary medium are highlighted in its consumption. Complexity, or the grouping together of similar ideas, activities and actions, makes the centre of DVD not the film itself but what has, until now, been considered auxiliary material in the practice of film viewing. Though the word 'supplementary' is used here to describe that material (this word having its origins in multi-media design discourse), the material is, in reality, no longer supplementary at all.

A DVD is produced with a primary narrative. That primary narrative is a mono-directional film text. Discounting occasional 'Director's Cuts' this primary narrative remains fixed. It is, for all time, the same product – good, bad or indifferent. In that sense, beyond its convenience, DVD had nothing more to sell than videotape had to sell for the twenty years preceding it. It's worth noting that DVD still remains relatively unstable compared with hard-drive storage or, in some ways, even with videotape. Its surface is highly sensitive. It relies on multi-layering in which production quality control must be very high to guarantee success. In some world markets – those relying on less managed production processes – imperfections in the disks are comparatively common and render a proportion of disks unwatchable. But all this is only a sidelight. DVD offers, as its consumer draw-card, something more than that we would consider to be in the domain of traditional film viewing.

'Supplementary-ness', or the provision of additional product seemingly for the same unit price, has a long marketing history. This is a history not driven only by the principle of 'value for money'. At least in part, supplementary-ness is about personalisation, or the buying of mass-produced product without buying the feeling of sameness. A product that can be personalised is a product that can encourage great consumer loyalty. Personalisation equates to ownership and ownership to consumer commitment. Consider, for instance, the car industry's use of 'optionality' in order to change what is mass production into what appears to be personalised consumption. Videotape, too, allowed for the personalisation of film viewing, incorporating choice, a wide variety of home-taping strategies, and a system of non-mercantile exchange through which film could be sent around a peer group, creating a fan base that did not necessarily work inside the corporate structure of mainstream film distribution.

While not immediately replicating the home recording strategies of videotape, DVD nevertheless echoed the aspects of non-mercantile exchange through its supplementary knowledge base. An increasingly media-literate audience could immediately exchange broadly fan-based information gleaned from DVD supplementary platforms. Supplementary-ness, therefore, picked up on the prevailing discourse of media literacy and, as it allowed for an increasingly complex relationship with the core film, referenced the previously auxiliary aspects of film consumption that had become, by the time of DVD's arrival, part of the audience's primary viewing experience.

Almost from the outset, supplementary platforms on DVD incorporated three identifiable content paths: that associated with production information (background information on the production processes of the film), that associated with the film's release (trailers, information about cast and crew and so forth) and that associated with language and subtitling which allowed the disk to be consumed in a variety of markets, and/or to reference multi-language or multi-market production histories. While consumers were aware of these things, it was not until the arrival of the cinema of complexity that they became part of the central discourse, and it was not until the arrival of DVD that these could be effectively incorporated into the core viewing experience.

Additional changes in film reading resulted. Whereas videotape could be paused to allow a break in the film, or to incorporate any number of other personal activities, DVD could be paused to increase the knowledge of the film viewer about the film itself. Pause the film, discover something more about the film from the disk, and continue. This was unique. In addition, as disk designers could consider the specific audiences likely to view the film, supplementary platforms could be designed to reference the interests of those audiences. Children's films on DVD, for example, quickly included game-based supplementary materials. Classic films, equally, incorporated detailed cast information. Horror films, seeking a wider market, might incorporate historical or contextual information that sought to ground the film in a wider tradition or to make a case for it as seminal within the canon. Many DVDs today include 'gag reels', picking up on the popularity of television 'bloopers' programmes. Others include archival material, casting sessions, trailers for future releases, scripts, storyboards and production notes and stills libraries. The inclusion of this material already has a short but notable history. Finally, supplementary-ness allowed for the otherwise largely singular viewing experience of the primary narrative to be made infinitely renewable.

While it is true that, beyond the smaller phenomenon of 'Director's Cuts', a film once made remains the same film no matter what, supplementary materials on DVD can be changed. One early marketing strategy connected with this was to release some films with limited supplementary materials, and then re-release these films as 'Special Editions' with the supplementary platform intact. Another strategy was to include cast and crew supplementaries in the first instance and then to update the film with additional production materials, interviews and commentaries in order to create a 'Box Set' or 'Collectors' Edition'. And there continue to be any number of other versions of all these strategies. Importantly, not all of this is only of interest to consumer analysts.

Supplementary-ness, referencing the discourse of the cinema of complexity, also references the requirements of late-modern consumerism because here is a product that can die and be resurrected as many times as its auxiliary materials can be renewed. As consumer culture depends on a cycle of desire-satisfaction-renewal-of-desire, so DVD is able to renew the desire for a single film text by widening the concept of what that text entails. To say that the supplementary material is, in fact, auxiliary to the film is to miss the fact that the viewer's reading of the film itself can be adjusted by changes in the disk's supplementaries – not only the selling power of the disk's traditional film text but the relationship between this film and the discourse of the cinema of complexity. For example, a film that provides more filmic knowledge via its supplementary platform than its competitor films might well be considered more desirable by a media-literate generation. But what if, given the historical impact of domestic videotape film viewing, the activities of 'pause', 'rewind' and 'fast-forward' can be enhanced by slower fast-forwarding, staggered rewinding and freeze-frame pausing? DVD provides this and enables close textual reading of film in a way not previously available. How this will affect film scholars' approaches to *mise-en-scène*, acting, film colour and style, screenwriting, in fact every element of cinema, is yet to be determined.

Post-Cinema?

From the outset, the discourse of DVD heralded the culmination of thirty years of change in styles of film production and film consumption. Its background as a technology relates to the emergence of the immediate new punk technologies of videotape and CD-ROM; but its technological origins are far less interesting than the impact it had, and is continuing to have today, on modes of film viewing. These modes extend, without doubt, to the scholarly study of film, and its attendant theories and methods, but they are also fundamentally associated with an increasingly media-literate world population. DVD has broadened the viewing experience to include, in one platform, activities once considered to be either 'core' or 'auxiliary', but certainly not melded in the same time and place. Film or cinema, as we once knew it, has died. But it has been resurrected as a twenty-first-century art-form. Whether it is appropriate to continue to refer to this art-form as 'film' or 'cinema' is up to the reader to decide. Certainly DVD has combined several technological and cultural changes to create something distinctive. If these are, strictly speaking, no longer 'movies' then perhaps they are 'digitals', the gathering together of multiple digital experiences into one image-based experience. Perhaps they are 'ROMs', because they involve many levels of reading and memory. Perhaps they are simply 'new movies' because, of course, it would be wrong to suggest that all that has gone before has disappeared and indeed, for now, the experience of public film screenings still remains similar to past experience, despite the great changes.

Whatever film or cinema might best now be called, DVDs' continued effects on the modes of production and reception of the moving image owe their origins to the technological and societal changes that began in the late 1970s. Simply put, the filmic past and the filmic future converge in this one technology.

6. DIGITAL TECHNOLOGIES AND THE POETICS OF PERFORMANCE

Bruno Lessard

Utopian and dystopian discourses have accompanied the rise of digital techniques of cinematic production and post-production. While some enthusiastic directors, film critics and spectators have found that digital technologies have already reshaped cinema, others, offering a more temperate, almost Luddite perspective, believe that digital technologies have not brought substantial changes and will not modify the cinematic experience as we know it. In other words, a century after the birth of cinema, digital technologies might show the limits of celluloid and traditional montage practices, but they will remain in a state of infancy that does not call for the revolution in cinematic practice foretold by many.

What I propose in this essay is to adopt a more balanced approach to the use of digital technologies in contemporary films, bearing in mind that Utopian and dystopian positions are complementary rather than mutually exclusive. Digital technologies have favoured a certain democratisation and transformation of cinema: new film-makers direct their first films at minimal cost, and more experienced directors perform technological 'tricks' that may not have been possible prior to the advent of digital media. Digital technologies, however, do not erase a century of film-making practices and cinematic heritage overnight. Issues of representation, mise-en-scène, montage and performance do not disappear with the advent of digital media; they come back to life in forms that are mediated in a new way. Dogma 95 and new punk films exemplify the manner in which contemporary cinema has used digital media creatively but without breaking with the cinematic past.

In this chapter I discuss the manner in which digital media have refashioned production and post-production techniques, and I illustrate my argument with the help of Mike Figgis's *Time Code* which I perceive, among other new punk films, to be the most sustained cinematic engagement with digital technologies. While movies such as *Toy Story* (1995) or *Final Fantasy: The Spirits Within* (2001) draw extensively on the computer, *Time Code* is a hybrid form of cinema in which digital technologies and live performances come together to experiment with film form and content in an unprecedented manner. One should see in Figgis's work an experimental form of film-making; as film demands new formal properties from technology, it also begs for new criteria of evaluation from critics and for new skills from spectators. *Time Code*'s revolution not only concerns the history of cinema but it also confronts institutional and personal modes of reception that paradoxically bring us back to the birth of cinema.

First, I give a general outline of the Dogma 95 movement's use of digital cameras, and then I explore the philosophical and cultural underpinnings of the concepts of realism and performance privileged in Dogma films. Moreover, I place Dogma 95 and new punk productions within a discontinuous history of cinema that several digital media theorists have proposed lately. This framework underlines the manner in which digital technologies reactivate the almost-forgotten cinematic tension between spectacle and narrative a tension at the heart of early cinema. I depart from the current state of digital criticism when I claim that what can unite spectacle, narrative, and 'digital realism' is the concept of performance: the performance that the digital technologies offer as spectacle and the actors' performances in the narrative. In addition, several new punk films, such as *Time Code*, *Run Lola Run*, and *Memento*, demand a certain cognitive 'performance' on the part of the spectator. This cognitive performance is the notion I adopt to replace the controversial concept of 'interactivity' so much discussed in the field of digital media.

Dogma Ethos, Realism and Digital Technologies

The identity of the Dogma 95 movement centres around the renewal of film practices and conventions in small nations that cannot compete with the Hollywood industry. The ethos of the movement, its manner of living and eventually of dying, posits originality and creativity as supreme achievements. The main target of the movement being a certain portion of Hollywood productions that emphasises spectacle and illusion to the detriment of more 'profound' psychological issues, the Dogma brethren desire Danish cinema to be a counter-movement that would accentuate the performance of the actors and the realism of the narrative. Dogma 95 incarnates a desire to do more with less, to rejuvenate an art-form gone awry. The manner in which this was to be realised concerns a certain politics of film-making that is proposed in the Dogma Manifesto co-signed by film-makers Lars von Trier and Thomas Vinterberg.

The Dogma 95 movement has been described as the most radical cinematic enterprise since the French New Wave. Dogma criticises, and departs from, film-makers such as Godard, Truffaut, and Resnais, however, for having developed a bourgeois culture, individualism and artistic drive it sought to denounce in the first place in the *'cinéma de papa'*. Dogma thus fights the *auteur* film, that is, individualistic cinematic practices that would not be representative of the 'real' world. Indeed, Berys Gaut has emphasised that 'The [Dogma] programme criticises the *auteur* theory for granting supreme power to the individual director, whose pursuit of an artistic vision threatens the presentation of truth' (Gaut 2003: 99).

The Dogma film-makers' desire to globalise film-making is one way in which they feel the representation of truth and reality is best served. In order to do so, 'Dogma 95 avoids the kind of nostalgic investment in the local that is a feature of dominant types of heritage film and thus emerges as an appealing non-nationalist response to globalisation' (Hjort 2003: 38). Dogma films are not about ethnic purity nor Nordic essence; they feature the manner in which a minor cinema resists assimilation by opposing the society of the spectacle Hollywood has contributed to developing with the help of digital technologies. This way of opposing relates to self-imposed rules that concern the concept of cinematic creativity.

In his novel, *Immortality*, Milan Kundera discusses the manner in which individuals can cultivate uniqueness and originality. The narrator mentions that there are only two ways to be creative: by subtraction and by addition (Kundera 1992: 100). I would argue that Dogma films use a peculiar strategy that combines both subtraction and addition: they have subtracted the spectacle, the apparent illusions, and the implausible narratives characteristic of popular Hollywood productions, and they have reinserted the concepts of impressive performances and challenging narratives into the picture, so to speak. In other words, the Dogma manifesto redefines the rules of the cinematic game 'to create the conditions that enable citizens from small nations to participate in the game of cinematic art' (Hjort 2003: 35).

The war on spectacle, special effects and the cinema of illusions in which Dogma films engaged in the 1990s tried to restore authenticity and realism in the film industry. This fight against the reliance upon computer-generated imaging and special effects is a search for existential truth and genuine feelings. Arguing that the film of illusions masks reality, the founding fathers of the Dogma movement criticised the manner in which mainstream movie plots were becoming more and more superficial, depriving audiences of authentic emotions. Gaut writes: 'Dogma films, in contrast, aim to show the audience how the world really is, and to evoke the emotions appropriately grounded on that understanding' (Gaut 2003: 90). This position, of course, calls to mind a certain discussion about cinematic realism.

Film theory has focused on the issue of realism and of illusion for several decades. André Bazin's distinction between the cinema that privileges reality and the one that believes in images and montage to provoke thoughts and feelings is famous. Bazin went so far as to claim that representing life without mediation and in its entirety is the 'myth of total cinema' that fuelled Muybridge's and Marey's venture in moving images. The 'apparatus theory' of Jean-Louis Baudry and Jean-Louis Comolli took issue with the Bazinian depiction of reality, showed the ideological workings of cinema, and argued that realism is, in fact, the illusion of immediacy which the apparatus performs through false identification and hidden subjection.

Therefore, the return to realism advocated by the Dogma manifesto would certainly make some pause. What are we to make of this plea for an aesthetics that wants to bring us back to realism? Indeed, how can cinema progress with a critical position that recalls Bazin's seminal essay on the ontology of the photographic image as one that records reality, that shows it untainted by human intervention? In fact, the post-recording facilities that digital technologies allow have led to a host of doubts regarding the supposed 'reality' of what is recorded, and this interrogation seems to question the very premise of representing 'reality' with digital tools. Moreover, it testifies to the importance of realism in the collective mind. Indeed, from photography to virtual reality, realism has been the most talked-about issue in the development of these visual representations. As far as realism and digitality are concerned, the use of digital cameras has moved a number of critics to claim that Dogma films contradict the very ideal of the manifesto. For example, Gaut has claimed that 'the technical means for doing so [the democratisation of cinema through new technology] involved the very technology that Dogma had initially sought to ban. In that respect, at least, Dogma has been a success despite itself.' (Gaut 2003: 100).

I disagree with Gaut's conclusion and argue that we need to distinguish between the end and the means to that end. It is true that Dogma films promote the use of hand-held digital video-(DV) cameras. The information those cameras record, however, is not meant to be manipulated extensively in the post-production process in order to create another cinema of the spectacle; in Dogma and new punk films the data are not used in special effects, in morphs or in digital composites. Directors shoot on DV to enhance the potential and creative aspects of film-making. Even though the cinema they offer may be seen as another disguised illusion, it is one that, at first glance, does not look like an illusion or at least does not want to be one.

In contemporary films there is a subtle but important distinction to make between the belief in the possibility of representing reality and the performance of this very same representation. Whereas philosophical and ideological motivations underlie the will to represent 'reality', the performance of this representation relies upon material means that cannot be omitted from any discussion of recent films. The role digital technologies play in the shaping and subverting of conventional story-telling and aesthetics must be discussed in the context of film practices that have come to substitute the representation of reality for the representation of performance. The 1990s occupy a central place in this account of film history.

The year 1995 marks a turning point in the development of the movie camera.[1] The release of Sony's mini-DV camera would lead the way to a counter-cinematic movement that would question a certain tradition of film-making procedures. This inexpensive format would allow new film-makers to shoot their first films without dealing with financing and elaborate casting, among various other imperatives. The same year, Lars von Trier and Thomas Vinterberg co-signed the Dogma 95 Manifesto. Three years later von Trier's *The Idiots* and Vinterberg's *The Celebration* were presented at Cannes, the latter winning Jury Prize. It was the first step in a long series of award-winning cinematic projects that would use DV cameras to shape a different cinematic aesthetics.

It is very interesting to observe the manner in which the digital recording of more realistic narratives has allowed new ways to capture performance. For instance, to record a particular scene in von Trier's *Dancer in the Dark*, a hundred cameras were used to capture Björk's performances. The cinematic rendition of those performances is the result of the manner in which digital cameras were easily transported, attached and manipulated. One can only imagine the logistical ordeal that would have been the result of an attempt to use a hundred analogue cameras to shoot the very same scene: the cost of film stock would have been exceptional and the manipulation of cameras a time-consuming enterprise. The Icelandic singer's song-and-dance numbers benefit from the emergence of digital cameras in a way that shows how the recording of performance depends upon technology to be more effective in terms of time and money.

Von Trier and Vinterberg, the two prominent Dogma directors, promoted the return to realism and the use of hand-held DV-cameras. The most famous Dogma films, von Trier's *The Idiots* and Vinterberg's *The Celebration*, were shot using a DV-camera, and several new punk films that have been made since follow the recording procedure proposed by the two directors. Interestingly, several new punk directors have found in the DV-camera the right tool to record their version of 'reality' without necessarily adopting a dogmatic or metaphysical concept of reality advocated by von Trier and Vinterberg. Indeed, the notion of performance seems to be at the core of their concept of 'reality', pointing to how any cinematic account of reality corresponds to an analysis of film as the performance of digital tools and of cinema as the site of performing agents.

Given that Dogma film-makers indulge in a rhetoric that promotes a return to 'reality', the ontological nature of human experience they propose is devoid of illusion and promises a renewed authenticity. The performance of the body in the context of DV-cameras would be linked to the originality and authenticity film-makers desire to convey in their productions. As Peter Schepelern has remarked, the hand-held camera has always denoted 'a character's intense sense of self (subjective camera) . . .' (Schepelern 2003: 66). This claim, however, should not blind us to the fact that an 'intense sense of self' is not immune to fantasies and illusions on the part of directors. We should bear in mind that the self that is represented via the use of a hand-held camera translates the immaterial will to be authentic, original, and free into the embodied performances of camera-persons and actors. In other words, the ideals the Dogma manifesto express would never have seen the light of day without the appropriate equipment to record certain movements and the bodies of those who perform the film-makers' cinematic visions. One could even argue that the writing of the manifesto relies more upon technological means than upon 'original' ideas that clearly relate to preceding cinematic movements of the 1940s and 1960s. Finally, Schepelern refers to the (analogue) camera of the *cinéma vérité*; in the case of several Dogma and new punk films, it is a hand-held DV-camera that is used. What are the consequences of the use of a DV-camera for issues of representation, spectacle and illusion?

Digital 'Realism' and New Punk Aesthetics

Discussing *Time Code*, Lev Manovich has rightly made the distinction between two very different digital aesthetics: 'special effects driven spectacle and documentary-style realism striving for "immediacy"' (Manovich 2002: 213). He has proposed to use the expression 'DV realism' to describe films that depart from digital special effects and computer-generated imaging. Manovich, however, comes to question the innovative nature of DV realism, for the 'DV realist school' would recall Italian neo-realism and *cinéma vérité*, the only difference lying in the instruments contemporary directors use to record 'reality'. While Manovich speaks of a documentary-style aesthetics, I suggest that new punk aesthetics is one that may recall that of the documentary but that does not strive to be similar to that of the documentary. Indeed, the 'reality' that the DV-camera records is not that of a documentary; new punk films emphasise a narrative in which improvised and rehearsed performances merge, and those films certainly do not believe in an all-encompassing concept of reality. Dogma and new punk directors know perfectly that what they present to us is not pure reality; what they offer is another illusion based upon an idea of reality.

The expression 'DV realism' does not help us conceptualise the manner in which digital technologies affect performance and the representation of reality in new punk films. In fact, Manovich's comments on *Time Code* do not seem to grasp the aim of Figgis's project: 'Although it [*Time Code*] adopts some of the visual conventions of computer culture, it does not yet deal with the underlying logic of a computer code' (Manovich 2002: 217). Actually, why is it that *Time Code* would have to 'deal with the underlying logic of a computer code'? The point is precisely not to confuse the tools and the performances they can offer, nor to subject the performances to the technology, even though they can function together at times. New punk aesthetics seems to stress that technology should serve the performance and not the other way around. Watching Figgis's *Leaving Las Vegas* (1995), *The Loss of Sexual Innocence* (1999) and *Time Code*, one doubts that the director will ever engage in the exploration of the computer code. He seems more interested in actors' performances and in the ways in which recent technologies challenge pre-conceived ideas about film-making, actors and spectators.

Certainly, the concept of the code is at the heart of many new punk films, most notably in Darren Aronofsky's *Pi*. Yet, assuming that the codes to which the film-makers refer do not possess a more significant meaning in the age of genetic decoding seems to be mistaken. Technological codes are crucial in the computer manipulation of data but, in terms of narrative, their meaning is still to be assessed. For example, Manovich ends his discussion of the language of new media with the claim that contemporary cinema is no longer just cinema, it is a code: 'in a computer age, cinema, along with other established cultural forms, indeed becomes a code. It is now used to communicate all types of data and experiences, and its language is encoded in the interfaces and defaults of software programs and in the hardware itself' (Manovich 2001: 333). In Manovich's formalist account of digital media, the different codes he perceives are to be found in digitised images, software and database structures, among others. The films he has in mind are ones in which animated sequences or characters are created on the computer. One can see such use of digital technologies in *Jurassic Park* (1993), *Terminator 2: Judgment Day* (1991), and in the more extensive use of digital tools in *Toy Story*. These films, however, do not take issue with the task of cultural decoding, as *Time Code*, *Memento* and *Pi* do. What if taking issue with the code involved precisely a cultural detour via embodied presence and performance?[2] I would suggest that memory and codes function in various repetitions of cinema and of video that call for a performative spectatorship. New punk films articulate and rehearse what it is to *decode* the various 'codes' and meanings contemporary culture displays.

Interestingly, Manovich opens the door to a political understanding of the code, but he does not develop it. He argues that one of the 'effects of computerization on cinema proper' is 'Filmmakers' reactions to the increasing reliance of cinema on computer techniques in postproduction' (Manovich 2001: 288). He illustrates the description of this effect with Figgis's *Time Code* when he mentions 'Films that focus on the new possibilities offered by inexpensive DV (digital video) cameras' (ibid. p. 288). Indeed, what of *Time Code*, a Hollywood film that challenges the Dogma attempt to confront Hollywood? Clearly, the creative agenda that undergirds *Time Code* is a case in point that deserves more critical attention. Moreover, is not Manovich's mention of *Time Code* as an exemplary film that explores the new paths opened up by digital technologies characteristic of an ideological position that implies that what the film has to offer is purely technological in nature? What if the use of digital cameras and new editing possibilities would contribute to a new definition of actor performance and to the role of the spectators in their reception of the film? In other words, what if the computer code were a cultural code in the first place?

Decoding and Performing Time Code

Time Code is an exemplary film to analyse because it is one of the most discussed and misunderstood new punk films and certainly the most controversial in terms of reception. For example, Rhys Graham has said of the film that 'innovation has not been employed to enhance the scope of cinematic potential but rather for innovation's sake and in praise of the technology alone' (Graham 2000). According to Graham's comments, what are we to make of the extraordinary effects the actors' performances have on the spectators and of the complex spatial and temporal narratives the split screen offers both human memory and cognition?

Shot in four continuous takes of ninety three minutes and using separate Sony DSR-1 digital cameras, the distributed version of the film is the one Figgis selected after fifteen improvisational performances.[3] The screen is divided into four quadrants that show four interrelated narratives that centre around a Los Angeles-based film-production company called Red Mullet. The ninety-three-minute journey offers shocking story-lines that deal with betrayal, rage, jealousy, lust and murder, among others.

While it is true that *Time Code* has visual precedents,[4] it nevertheless remains an example of experimental cinema: its 'success' cannot be assessed based on criteria that relate to other film forms or genres. Even though *Time Code* may recall Italian neo-realism and *cinéma vérité*, it creates a form and a genre characteristic of the digital era. Let us see how performance could be the key to a preliminary understanding of the film. Approaching *Time Code* involves dealing not so much with the issue of representation in the age of the digital revolution but with the question of performance in the realm of digital culture. One should bear in mind that Figgis's background is in the performing arts. Indeed, Figgis is a trained musician whose notion of art is always related to performance. The emphasis Figgis places upon performance and improvisation in *Time Code* must be at the forefront of any analysis of the film. In fact, Figgis's understanding of *Time Code* is closely related to the performance of a musical piece. For example, the series of fifteen improvisational performances around a given structure recall jazz music sessions. Moreover, at several points in the film the DV cameras come together to offer moments of almost musical synchronicity, and often one quadrant will enter into a contrapuntal dialogue with another, contradicting or complementing the meaning of a sequence. Finally, Figgis wrote the script of the film on music paper, conceiving the four narratives as a string quartet. Digital film, for Figgis, is cinematic 'music' and performance of that visual 'music'.

Moreover, in his director's commentary Figgis makes analogies to other areas of the performing arts that link his digital cinematic experience to performance. For example, he mentions how in European experimental theatre the space of the stage is often used to show a maximum of narratives and characters. Similarly, in *Time Code* Figgis uses the space of the screen and the four quadrants in a way that would revisit and remediate the space of a theatre stage, conceiving the visual space as a drama on four screens. Finally, Figgis mentions dance techniques when describing the choreographies the camera-operators had to perform in order to record the appropriate action on the right occasion.

As is the case in choreographies, the performing arts in general imply the presence of a physical body within a given space. In digital art the function of the body of the spectator has been discussed using a controversial concept: interactivity. 'Interactivity' points to the manner in which the body of the observer, spectator or interactor participates in the making of the work. Two of the most important aspects of digital media are their immersive and simulational qualities. No longer subordinated to the will of the artist, the person interacting creates both work and meaning with his or her body and mind.

This fairly incomplete overview of interactivity has been challenged lately by scholars who have proposed to use the term 'performance' instead of 'interaction'. Of course, as many scholars have remarked, all forms of art demand a certain interactive cognition to be appropriated. Discussing database 'narratives', Marsha Kinder mentions that contemporary films, such as *Pulp Fiction, Memento, Run Lola Run, Mulholland Drive* and *Time Code*, are works that demand a more 'active' participation but these works cannot be called 'interactive'. In fact, Kinder claims that 'interactivity' is an illusion because 'the rules established by the designers of the text partially limit the user's options' (Kinder 2003: 351). Kinder's words bring us back to the question of illusion in interactive environments. This critique leads her to propose 'performance' as a more effective tool with which to discuss contemporary digital productions: 'the user as a "performer" of the narrative – like an actor interpreting a role, or a musician playing a score, or a dancer performing traditional moves, contributing her own idiosyncratic inflection and absorbing the experience into her personal archive of memories' (ibid. p. 351).

Of course, performance can be as problematic as interaction. Indeed, how are we to compare the memorisation and performance of a piano concerto with the actions of someone who clicks on a mouse to explore a CD-ROM? In other words, performance, too, can function as an illusion. The performances in a film such as *Time Code*, if we are to attribute them to the spectator, would begin with the cognitive efforts he or she has to make to incorporate four different story-lines at the same time. Moreover, the actors' performances have to be understood as difficult improvisational sessions in which anything can go wrong. Kinder's suggestion that 'as narratives map the world and its habitants, they locate us within a textual landscape requiring a constant refiguring of our mental cartography with its supporting databases, search engines and representational conventions' (Kinder 2003: 353) would be more plausible in this context of improvisation and performance.

Without alluding to performance, Gene Youngblood has mentioned how the 'simultaneity-effect' of the split-screen narrative 'enlarges our concept of a cinematic event' (Youngblood 1989: 159). The overload of information the parallel event-streams create is the challenge contemporary spectators face in the case of *Time Code*. Their performance begins with the task of visual and cognitive incorporation of data. As Philip Rosen has suggested: 'If interactivity is the trump card of the digital utopia, then its claim to radical novelty depends on a claim for new modes of subjectivity' (Rosen 2001: 347). The spectator's new mode of cinematic subjectivity would bear witness to the various performances on screen (that of the actors and that of the technology itself) and then would assess its own performative assimilation of this cinematic material. The digital code would then take a cultural and embodied signification that is seldom envisaged.[5]

In movies, such as *Time Code* and Harmony Korine's *julien donkey-boy*, the body and the camera-eye are intertwined in a manner that suggests other possible modes of subjectivity and embodiment. For example, in Korine's film, at times the camera is attached to the body of the actor and seems to function as a body part endowed with vision. The spectator's point of view becomes that of the arm and moves around the actor. Several years ago, Youngblood mentioned that 'in interactive image synthesis, the spectator is the camera' (Youngblood 1989: 161). In Korine's film, the spectator takes on the role of camera via the illusion of embodied subjectivity.

Reminding us that the digital 'revolution' is one that can lend itself to formalistic accounts, Janet Harbord writes: 'Yet there is a familiar ring to the revolutionary appeal of new technologies and aesthetic strategies, which bypasses the social embedding of those forms' (Harbord 2002: 142). Indeed, if digital media's roots are to be found in early cinema's soil, as Manovich and other scholars believe, we should not forget to include discussions of performance. Indeed, in pre-cinematic forms of entertainment, the live presence of the physical body was crucial to the spectacle and to the narratives. Moreover, in magic-lantern shows and in early displays of the cinematic technology, what attracted spectators was physical and technological performance. The digital 'revolution' may thrive on the spectacle-narrative tension but, in the evaluation of the digital 'revolution', performance has to be considered in its digitally remediated forms.

Notes

1 I will refer the reader to the very useful timeline 'D Cinema' (2004) in *The Velvet Light Trap*.
2 For a cultural and psychological understanding of the code in terms of nostalgia, loss and repetition, see Murray (1999).
3 The US DVD edition of *Time Code* features improvisational sessions 1 and 15. The spectator can compare the first performance with the last.
4 Arguably the most famous cinematic precedent, Hitchcock's *Rope* (1948), tries to simulate the recording of a film in one continuous take. A more recent example of live split-screen recording is *D-Day*, a Danish multi-chanel television production that was screened at the turn of the millennium. For an analysis of *D-Day*, see Roberts (2003).
5 Exploring forking-path narratives, David Bordwell has also mentioned how recent cinematic productions challenge cognition and human memory in ways that combine our longing for narrative closure and craving for new cinematic experiences: 'It [a film] must therefore work particularly hard to shape the spectator's attention, memory, and inference-making at each moment. No wonder that filmmakers balance potentially confusing innovations like the multiple-draft structure with heightened appeal to those forms and formulas that viewers know well.' (Bordwell 2002: 103)

7. NAVIGATING CHAOS

Silvio Gaggi

> So let's start with the title. *The Fabulous Destiny of Amélie Poulain* was kind of hard to find. It was a story of chance and destiny, and chance and destiny were deeply intertwined in this project.
>
> (Jeanne-Pierre Jeunet [2001])

A fly lands on a street and is run over by a car, leaving a small red spot on the road. In a restaurant the wind causes a table-cloth to billow up, making two glasses dance as if by magic. A man returns to his office and erases a name from his address book. Another man's sperm penetrates the egg of his wife, the wife becomes pregnant, and a baby is born. As these events – including the conception, pregnancy (shown as a fast-motion set of jump-cuts of the woman's changing body) and childbirth – are shown visually, a voice-over narrator describes them with a cool, scientist-like detachment:

> On September 3, 1973 a blue fly capable of flapping 70 beats a minute landed on St. Vincent Street in Montmarte. At that moment, on a restaurant terrace nearby, the wind magically made two glasses dance unseen on a tablecloth. Meanwhile, in a 5th-floor flat on Avenue Trudaine, Paris 9, returning from his best friend's funeral, Eugène Colére erased him from his address book. At the same moment, a sperm with one X chromosome, belonging to Raphael Poulin, made a dash for an egg of his wife Amandine. Nine months later Amélie Poulain was born.

This description – containing details such as the exact date, the rate of the fly's flapping wings and specific street names – contributes to the rationalist effect, as if precision is important because there is some significance to the fact that these events (except for the gestation and birth) occurred simultaneously.

The juxtaposition of words and images adds to this truth effect. Words and images are often combined so that they complement and mutually reinforce one another: news photos with captions; photo IDs with names and birth dates; paintings of Biblical scenes accompanied by scriptural passages. In this introductory sequence of Jeanne-Pierre Jeunet's *Amélie* (*Le Fabuleux destin d'Amélie Poulain* [2001]) each event described and depicted carries with it some of the added truth effect that results from word/image complementarity. It is as if the film is trying to convince the audience of the importance of each event, and also, more importantly, suggesting something (what?) about the fact that they occurred simultaneously. And yet there is no hint about why these events are important or why they are cinematically juxtaposed. Apart from the fertilisation, gestation and childbirth, compressed into a few seconds at the end of the series, it is unclear what the connection among these events might be. The causal connection from fertilisation to childbirth (the birth of the film's protagonist) is obvious, but it is unclear how that series of events is related to the other events – the fly's death, the billowing of the glasses and the erasure of the friend's name.

This series of visual images and verbal statements takes place in less than a minute, the first minute of the film, just prior to the introductory credits. Juxtaposing shots creates the impression that the events represented are in some way connected; causal or symbolic connections are most common. One person speaks; a second answers. A fuse is lit; an explosion occurs. Workers are shot; cattle are slaughtered. A bone twirls in the air; an orbiting station spins in space. The introductory series of shots of *Amélie* – combined with the dispassionate, scientist-like voice-over description of them – thus suggests a connection among events described and pictured. Why else would they be juxtaposed? But it is also possible that the point is just the opposite: this series of images may suggest the arbitrariness of events in the world. The 'point' may be that things do happen by accident and that coincidences in time do not necessarily mean anything at all. Things are what they are; one creature is killed; another dies; a third is born. So what?

This set of images pointedly introduces one of the key questions of the film. Are we to regard these disparate events (and by extension the disparate events of life) as somehow connected, or are these coincidences (and thus the coincidences of life) essentially haphazard? Is some complex, unexplained causality at work? Or is the cinematic juxtaposition of these seemingly unrelated events suggestive of the fundamental randomness of the events of life itself?

Many recent films deal with this issue: the knotty ambivalence between viewing things as related and as not related, and hedging between these two perspectives. There may be an order, and things may be related but, if there is an order, it is difficult or impossible to discover, describe and explain. Such films suggest an ambivalent middle ground, difficult to conceptualise, between classical conceptions of causality and a vision of the world as disorderly, random and meaningless. These films describe a vision of connectedness/disconnectedness, order/disorder that is subtle, indirect and so complex that predictability is impossible.

This is an order (if it is an order) that can only be described as it manifests itself, retrospectively. Understanding often comes after the fact. That may seem to be a distressing recognition, given the fact that previous views of understanding assumed that with intelligence came the possibility of predicting an outcome prior to the manifestation of the outcome. But, in this world, which hedges between order and disorder, it's the best we can expect. This order in chaos can't be predicted in advance of its manifestation–at least not perfectly. It is the kind of order/disorder described by chaos theory and emergence theory.

David Lynch's *Mulholland Drive* (2001) is a complicated, nearly incomprehensible narrative which continually teases the viewer into believing that a coherent explanation or interpretation can be found to explain the seemingly inexplicable sequence of characters and events depicted. Did a particular scene really happen, or was it someone's dream or hallucination, or was it a resurfacing memory of an amnesiac character? Or are such questions irrelevant? Is one set of scenes a dream and another the 'reality', or vice-versa? If the same actor has different names in different scenes, are they supposed to be different characters or is the character using a pseudonym in one of the scenes? A naïve and seemingly inexperienced woman suddenly performs a love scene that is startlingly erotic. Do we revise our view of her supposed innocence, or simply decide that she is a remarkably good actor? Characters fragment and reconfigure themselves. The two major characters – two women clearly distinguished at the beginning by their contrasting colouring and by their contrasting personalities – become less distinguishable as the film progresses. Are they different characters or symbolic representations of different sides of the same personality? A seemingly new character, resembling one of the original ones, appears. Is the former brunette now made up to look more like the blonde? Or does this represent an entirely new character? And yet, despite the confusions, there remains a sense that there is a hidden truth to be discovered, that there is a way of explaining the connections between characters and events. The film does not permit the viewer to dismiss the events it relates as arbitrary – there are too many threads and echoes among the scenes and characters. But it is nearly impossible to come up with a plausible explanation of how it all relates. There seems to be a method to the madness but it is almost impossible to work out what that method might be.¹ Not quite order, but not quite disorder either.

Mike Figgis's *Time Code* consists of four ninety-three-minute takes – no cuts or dissolves – projected simultaneously on to a screen split four ways. All four takes represent sequences or threads of action taking place in different parts of Hollywood. Sometimes more than one of the threads converge at the same location so that different cameras present the same events simultaneously, though from different angles or ranges. The film becomes a Borgesian 'garden of forking paths',² a network of events that sometimes are linked – diachronically within the same thread or synchronically through cross-over characters or converged locations – and that sometimes diverge – the characters and events of different threads having only an indirect (though not non-existent) connection among them. The viewer, like someone navigating a hyper-text (or life itself which is, after all, a huge hyper-text itself, which we navigate through the various choices we make), makes choices regarding which particular thread to attend to at any particular time. The film becomes a microcosmic metaphor of the larger complexity of human existence, and asks questions about causality and chance, order and accident. When an actress, who has compromised herself (in all the standard ways) to get a part in a movie, has, despite of these compromises, been rejected for the part, she encounters, as if by accident, an entirely different director who hires her without even a screen test; one glance and he knows she is right for the part of his character. It is an apparent accident, and yet there are indirect connections between the two of them that make the accident less than complete.

Tom Tykwer's *Run Lola Run* broaches similar questions though the strategy is quite different. Rather than present the complexity of complex events, Tykwer presents three narratives representing alternative possible outcomes for the same dilemma. The protagonist, Lola, is called by her boyfriend, who has lost DM 100,000 which he was supposed to deliver as the take on some illicit operation. The film presents three variations of Lola's desperate twenty-minute 'run' through Berlin, including her attempts to come up with the DM 100,000 that will save his life. The film incorporates numerous filmic foregrounding effects: fast action, shifts to black and white, still photographs, and animations embedded within a basically live-action movie. Each version of Lola's run differs from the others, resulting in three different endings. As in *Time Code* we are given different views of the same time period though, in *Lola*, they are not different points of view of the same or related events but are different possibilities – very different consequences – resulting (as in chaos theory) from apparently small differences in early conditions. Also unlike *Time Code*, *Lola* reconfigures the three corresponding times of different possible universes into a single linear sequence which represents different versions of the same twenty minutes, whereas *Time Code* splits the screen so that we see simultaneously four aspects of the various intertwined events. Still, both films raise similar questions about causality and the complex relationships among events in the world.

There is a perpetual ambivalence between reading these works as post-modern paranoia, in which there is always the suspicion that things are not what they seem, that there is some hidden other truth which lies behind the surface of events, and as post-modern flatness, in which things are simply what they are, phenomenal surfaces, and there is, as Andy Warhol famously said of himself, nothing at all behind that surface. And so the 'solution' to making sense of what we see may be that of a detective or a scientist trying to discover the truth that explains events – or at least maintaining a faith that such an elusive truth exists. Or it may be coming to a realisation that, since there is nothing behind those surfaces, that things are what they are and nothing more, the best we can do is describe those surfaces, aestheticise them, and treat them with the careful attention of a fetishist of the banal. *Amélie*'s narrative intrusions can be interpreted as implying both these opposing possibilities.

There is also a third option: the middle ground that lies between or reconciles order and disorder, causality and randomness. Relatively new scientific theories, such as theory, emergence theory and fuzzy logic, all struggle to create models of systems that recognise the complexity and indeterminacy of life without, at the same time, creating a picture of the world which is disordered or random. Most significantly, they accept a degree of non-predictability without regarding human agency as impossible or action as futile; on the contrary, they attempt to empower human beings by creating a kind of reasoning that accepts the fact that decisions and actions must be based on judgements and qualitative calculations. The anticipated effects of actions are hoped-for outcomes, probabilities at best, and not certainties. In chaos theory the famous 'Butterfly Effect' or 'sensitive dependence on initial conditions' (Gleick 1987: 8) suggests that small inputs into complex systems can produce, over time, huge differences in outcomes. Emergence theory discusses how complex systems can emerge from extremely simple initial states: sets of 'cellular automatons', elementary 'agents' with the simplest of instructions, might, according to this theory, 'evolve' into the most elaborate and complex dynamic systems. Such complex systems could, in fact, result in galaxies, organic entities, intelligence and even self-consciousness; at the same time, the state of the system at any point cannot be predicted from information about its beginnings (e.g. Holland 1998: 125–42; Morowitz 2002: 179).[3] Fuzzy logic attempts to systematise the complex, multi-factored judgements that go into decisions, so that the kind of real-world determinations that people make all the time can be systematised and emulated in artificial computerised programs. Instead of regarding propositions as simply true or false, fuzzy logic enters factors that rank *degrees* of truth, quantifying them, for example, on a decimal scale ranging from zero to one. This kind of methodology allows information to be entered that – in its very lack of precision – more accurately corresponds to the kind of real world 'fuzziness' implied by statements such as 'She is tall' and 'The soup is hot' (Kaehler 1998; Sowell 2004).

Within this disorderly order or orderly disorder, intervention in the world is still possible, passivity and powerlessness are not inevitable outcomes. True, complete certainty is not a possibility; human life is not classical mechanics. Operating in the world always involves risk, always is a matter of making educated guesses and taking your chances. In *Amélie*, before Amélie comes to understand the kind of qualified control she can exert on the world, she hedges between a paranoiac belief in the power of her ego to control events and a feeling of helplessness to affect the circumstances of her own life. She is portrayed as an individual who suffers from a child-like feeling of omnipotence, of magical control, along with a retreat from close relationships – partly in fear of the destructive possibilities of her (imagined) power, partly as a result of her emotionless and repressive parents and her consequent isolation.

Amélie sees images in the clouds. This is a common experience, clouds providing a readily available Rorschach test of everyday life. The viewer sees these images, as if through Amélie's eyes, and the images – a bunny, a teddy bear – appear remarkably well formed. Of course, we are seeing through Amélie's eyes and not looking at 'real' clouds which, though they do invite diverse readings, seldom seem so well drafted. As she photographs these images, a road accident occurs. A man approaches her and accuses her of causing the accident with her camera. Thus begins her delusion of omnipotence and her fear of the potentially destructive power of her will. She stares at a television, believing that the disasters she sees represented there are her fault: a fire, train derailments, the crash of a jumbo jet. Later she takes revenge on the individual who tricked her by manipulating his television aerial, causing him great frustration while he is watching a soccer game. But days later her mother is killed by a tourist from Quebec who commits suicide by jumping from a tower of Notre-Dame cathedral and landing on her. Is the strange accident that resulted in her mother's death a fluke of events, or is it to be connected with the revenge Amélie has taken? Amélie grows up guilt-ridden, petrified and rendered impotent and incapable of action. Although she works and relates to people, as is necessary for her to survive, she is isolated, introverted, and more of an observer than a participant in life.

She begins again experimenting with her power after her 'accidental' discovery of an old box of toys and memorabilia. She is shocked when she hears on television the news of Princess Diana's death and drops the cap of a toiletry bottle. In the process of retrieving it, she discovers a loose tile at the bottom of the wall of her bathroom. Hidden behind the tile she finds a box containing various items – including a toy racing-car, a toy bicyclist, a whistle, a jack-knife – all placed there by a boy forty years earlier. She decides to perform an experiment. She will locate the owner, return the box to him secretly, and observe his response. If his life is positively altered by the return of this time-capsule from his childhood, she will attempt to engage the world of humans. It is as if she is making a compact with God or nature or the universe of possibility: a positive outcome to her experiment and she will risk engagement; a negative outcome and (it is presumed) she will remain as she is.

After considerable detective work, she identifies the individual and creates a situation in which he 'accidentally' discovers the box. He is intensely moved by the inexplicable retrieval of the long-lost box and, as a result, decides to re-establish relations with a daughter from whom he has been estranged. Amélie regards the experiment as a success. The sequence of events that led to this new, more engaged Amélie, recapitulates in form the introductory sequence of the film as well as the key questions suggested in that introductory sequence: the television that broadcast the news of Di's death; Amélie's dropping the cap of the bottle; its rolling toward the loose tile; the hidden box; Amélie's decision to use the box to perform an experiment with life. Eventually this all will lead to Amélie's fuller integration with life but was this all a series of accidents and meaningless coincidences? Or was Di's death somehow destined to be connected, via a long chain of causes and effects, with Amélie's 'cure'. Was that 'cure' a fortuitous result of random rolls of the dice or is there an order to the events? The unfolding of events was unpredictable; but does that mean that there is no order to it all?

Unfortunately, instead of using the results of her successful experiment to change her own life, Amélie, decides first to engage in a series of new, similar experiments in which she secretly intervenes in people's lives in an attempt to do good. Rather than apply her lesson about intervention and the possibility of change to her own circumstances, she avoids that more difficult decision by applying her knowledge to others in her neighbourhood, in the small café where she works, and to her own father. Most of the film is episodically structured, showing Amélie's various attempts constructively to intervene (mostly successfully) in the lives of various people. She creates rumours that result in an affair between two unlucky lovers, a co-worker and an *habitué* of the café. She booby-traps the apartment of a vegetable merchant who abuses his mentally handicapped employee. She intervenes in the life of her father, 'freeing' his garden gnome and arranging for photos of the inanimate statue to be sent to him from famous tourist locations around the world: in front of the Empire State Building, the Parthenon, Angkor Wat, Santa Sophia. She plays God, intervening in a causally chaotic universe. Of course, her role in creating the startling and inexplicable coincidences that affect the people she knows might be applied retroactively to her own situation: has some unseen force (God, Nature, the laws of causality and probability) been controlling the events of her life, just as she now controls the lives of others?

Raymond Dufayel, known as the 'Glass Man', is an elderly man who lives in an apartment across from Amélie's. He occupies the role of an archetypal 'wise old man' figure, and becomes her counsellor and confidant. He seems to understand her, her motivations and her difficulties, and, at times, he indirectly offers her sage counsel. At the same time, there is a kinship between them; they seem to be personally connected or in some way similar. At one point Amélie sends Dufayel a video-clip with unlikely incidents and odd characters: a horse jumping a fence and joining a bicycle race; an acrobat who performs with a dog; an African-American woman standing out of doors, passionately singing gospel and playing guitar while accompanied by a choir. Although the significance of this tape eludes the viewer, Dufayel responds to it as if it is a message with meaning.

Because of a congenital defect, Dufayel was born with brittle bones and has remained indoors for twenty years. Thus, Amélie's isolation is echoed in him although his has physical causes and hers emotional. Before they actually meet, and continuing after they do meet, the two spy on each other through their windows, he using binoculars, she a small telescope. In presenting their respective views of each other, Jeunet takes great liberties with visual probability, presenting much greater detail regarding their activities than would be likely to be actually visible; at times they even seem to hear the noises the other makes. These voyeuristic intrusions on each other's privacy suggest a form of cinema or cinematic surveillance. In representing their lens-mediated points of view the film invokes cinema itself.

This meta-cinematic aspect of the film manifests itself constantly in Amélie. At times toys or other objects come alive as if in response to events in the narrative. We know that such images aren't supposed to represent real events, nor can they always be explained by suggesting that they are events that occur in a character's imagination; rather, they are blatant cinematic tricks, the animated objects providing a means of commenting on the action, fulfilling, in a whimsical way, the role of a 'chorus' in a play. The voice-over narrator makes sudden intrusive announcements, again foregrounding the artificiality of cinema. At one point the narrator enters, stating that Amélie and Nino, whom Amélie falls in love with from a distance, grew up only 5 miles from each other; this narrative intrusion is accompanied by an aerial shot of Paris with their respective neighbourhoods identified with arrows and red letters; then there is a split screen of the two of them impossibly signalling each other with mirrors from their childhood homes. Of course this detail, along with the narrative intrusion, reminds the viewer of the same recurring question: is the fact that they grew up so close to each other and that they are now, as adults, in effect courting one another (though they have not yet actually met) significant? Is there a 'destiny' or at least some sort of trajectory of nature that is bound eventually to bring them together? Or are their crossings of paths simply some of the coincidences that inevitably occur in a world filled with people and events? Amélie at times turns to the camera and winks or gestures, breaking the illusion and suggesting that the audience is being let in on a joke or stratagem in which she is engaged. And, of course, there are constant inclusions of different kinds of representation in the film: torn photographs collected in a scrap-book, letters real and forged, televisions with video-players, and video-cameras. Frequently the camera shifts to fast-motion, there are jerky zooms and jump-cuts; the colour is intensely controlled and often unnaturally saturated. The result of all these manipulations is a cinematic playfulness; film as film is fore grounded; and the tone is shifted. Amélie might almost be regarded as a fluffy, 'feel-good' film but its playfulness, its refusal to take itself too seriously and its insistence on making obvious the artifice of the art tend to counteract the emotional manipulation that is characteristic of more common kinds of sentimental exploitation.

Dufayel has spent his isolated years segregated from the rest of the world, copying over and over Renoir's painting *Luncheon of the Boating Party*, always trying, but never quite able, to make a perfect replica. This exercise, on one hand, evokes a Zen-like repetitiousness, like a meditative attention to a single object or sound, an exercise that might seem pointless to minds accustomed to rationalising their actions on the basis of a belief in progress or purpose. But, on the other hand, it also reinforces, along with a lot of other images and situations in the film, a sense of death-in-life, and it questions the possibility of an individual who is dead – emotionally if not literally – being reborn. A past painting, already made, the work of another individual, can hardly be redone. Copying a great work is a legitimate exercise for a novice artist but, in itself, it cannot result in an authentic work by a different artist working in a different century.[4] Numerous other images in the film echo this theme. Photographs recur constantly in the film – photos from photo-albums, the postcards Amélie's father receives from his errant gnome, the torn photos of the film's various characters that appear with the final credits. Photos are always mixed messengers: traces of the past, indexical signs linked by a causal chain of light and chemical reaction to the individuals and events they represent. But, as representations, they are unable to recoup those past individuals or events. They tease us with their undeniable link to the past, and frustrate us because they remind us also that the past is irretrievable.

Most important are the torn ID photos collected by Nino and mounted in a scrap-book, which Amélie obtains and shows to Dufayel. One person in the collection keeps recurring. Why, they wonder, would someone keep taking his picture in a photo-machine and always discard those photos? Dufayel says he's afraid of growing old, and Amélie says, 'He's dead! . . . He's scared of being forgotten. He wants to remind people of his face. Like faxing his portrait from the afterlife.' Dufayel takes seriously this interpretation, comparing the photographed individual with the figures in his Renoir painting, who are dead, but who will not be forgotten. This interpretation turns out, in the end, to be completely wrong. The individual is, in fact, simply a technician maintaining the photo-machines and using his own face to check them. Amélie's and Dufayel's hermeneutic effort suggests major issues related to identity and mortality, and it evokes in the audience the issue of epistemological paranoia: there may be an explanation below the surface of events; explanations are usually just possible models for what is impossible to see directly. A profound explanation might be completely wrong, and the truth might end up being something much more banal. Is there depth or is there only a shallow surface?

Perhaps Amélie's most elaborate application of her insight into the undecidability of human explanations occurs during one of her interventions. One of her neighbours is a pathetic woman who perpetually laments a decades-old loss: her philandering husband who ran off with another woman and later was killed in a car accident. A letter arrives suddenly, forty years late, in which the husband laments his actions, declares his abiding love, hopes for forgiveness, and looks forward to his return. The revelation contained in the letter results in her transformation from a pathetic, port-drinking woman who will force her sad story on anyone willing to listen, to an individual who has been redeemed, who has found love and validation late in a life which, from her perspective, had been indelibly marked by failure. Of course, it was Amélie who created the forged letter. Earlier, we were shown her creation of the letter, partly in fast-motion and frequently making direct eye contact with the viewer, as if demonstrating for our benefit the methodical procedure in which she engaged to create the forgery. If history is a speculation about what we can't see, based on the relatively few details we can see, why not change the details in order to construct a history that better serves the purposes of the present? In this case the present that is better served is the happiness of an old woman. And who knows? It's possible that Amélie's restructuring is closer to the truth. Perhaps her husband did regret his decision and wished he could return to his wife. Since the outcome of his romance cannot be known, why assume that the outcome was a happy one?

Amélie discovers and falls in love with Nino, a young man who collects the torn and discarded pictures found below a photo-ID-machine in a railway station. These torn photos suggest fractured individuals dissatisfied with their lives as well as with the images that allude to those lives. Nino, like Amélie, is an individual very modestly placed in society. He has at least two jobs, one in a porno shop, the other dressed as a scary character in an amusement-park ride. His hobby of collecting the discarded ID photos allows Amélie to connect with him: they are both observers of, more than participants in, life's curiosities. Amélie, however, has done some practising in constructive intervention. Consciously intervening in the messy processes of the world can change outcomes. A slight alteration in conditions at a certain time can have large effects later on. A few casual remarks designed to get rumours started can result in two individuals, who barely noticed each other previously, falling in love.

The question is, is Amélie prepared to apply the strategies she has applied to others to her own life? She begins a series of stratagems that are designed to provoke a meeting with Nino and to hold off that meeting. She leaves a note on his moped that he should meet her the next evening at five o'clock. 'Bring five francs', it states, implying that this is what it will cost him to get his scrapbook back. The note is written on the back of one of the ID photos. When he arrives she directs him, via a contrived phone-call, on a quest that recapitulates her own quest to achieve order, control and, finally, intimacy, within a complex, indeterminate system. The quest on which she sends him requires that he navigate a kind of hypertext of links and nodes. Various clues ('Follow the blue arrows', for example) lead to other clues and, if the navigation is successful, these individuals who are in love will be brought together. Unfortunately Amélie lacks the courage to do her part to see the game through, and only leads him to the point where she can view him from a distance, through a telescope. She does return the scrap-book but, when he finds it, she is gone.

She and Dufayel work out the drama that is unfolding between her and Nino by identifying the two with figures in the Renoir painting. Dufayel says, 'Is she in love with him?' She says yes. He says, 'I think it's time she took a real risk.' 'She might', Amélie replies. 'She's devising a stratagem.' 'She's fond of stratagems', Dufayel says. 'Oui', she says. He says, 'In fact she's cowardly. That's why I can't capture her look' (as if speaking of a girl in the painting). Immediately afterwards, a movie on television seems to enact Amélie's situation, a science-fiction drama with dialogue redubbed in such a way as to refer to Amélie and Dufayel. 'Dufayel's attempts to meddle are intolerable. If Amélie chooses to live in a dream and remain an introverted young woman she has an absolute right to mess up her life!'

The game continues, involving messages and disguises. Nino leaves notes in the railway station, 'Where, when?' in response to her 'Do you want to meet me?' It's like navigating a hypertext but, in this hypertext, the 'nodes' are not pages but positions from which, ultimately, two human beings might find each other. She photographs herself wearing a Mexican hat and mask, disguised as the character Zorro from the American television show. Somehow the message of all this is that life is a confusing mess, and the odds are against us. It is disorganised, and there are lots of crazy, lonely people. It has a complicated structure, like a hypertext, without clear directions and markers, and we can easily become disoriented and lose sight of our goal. Still, against the odds, it *is* possible to succeed: people do find each other, love does happen. It's luck, it's accident, it's constructive intervention, but it happens.

In the end, and only with some constructive intervention on the part of Dufayel, Amélie and Nino meet and consummate their love. There is a recap of some of the film's characters. An aspiring, though chronically 'failed', author from the café walks in the street, stares at an attractive young woman, and seems not entirely unhappy. Amélie's first intervention – the man whose toy-box she found – strips a chicken and feeds pieces of it to a grandson, son of the daughter from whom he's been estranged. Dufayel works on his eternal Renoir. And Amélie's father leaves for the airport – presumably to strike out, to travel, willing for the first time in his life to take some risks, following the lead of his errant (though now returned) gnome.

The voice-over enters with a series of incidents that recapitulates in principle, though not in specifics, the kind of series that began the film and that has recurred throughout it:

> September 28, 1997. It is exactly 11 a.m. At the funfair, near the ghost train, the marshmallow twister's twisting, while in Villette Park, Félix Lerbier learns there are more links in his brain than atoms in the universe. At the Sacré Coeur the Cardinals are practicing their backhands. The temperature is 24 degrees Celsius. Humidity 70%. Atmospheric pressure 999 millibars.

These words, accompanied by appropriate visuals, are followed by quick cuts of Amélie and Nino, in speeded-up motion, riding on his moped through the streets of Paris. Sometimes Amélie looks directly at the camera, continuing the film's meta-cinematic tendencies. The final cast credits are given against torn and pasted pictures of each character, like the torn photos in Nino's scrapbook.

The film ends, conforming self-consciously to 'happily ever after' 'feel good' romance and romantic comedy conventions. And yet we do not feel cheated by this ending, as we might with a 'straight' romance. Partly, this is because *Amélie* is so blatantly conventional and has gone to such lengths to foreground itself as a stylised, whimsical representation. But also because the film presents its happy conclusion partly as the result of luck and partly as the result of a new kind of wisdom: a willingness to intervene constructively in complex multi-causal systems in which things are not so ordered that simple causes produce anticipated effects, but not so disordered that nothing can be done, a world in which chaos does not mean the absence of all order, in which outcomes emerge in ways that are not irrational but are not fully predictable either, and in which an intelligent use of fuzzy thinking often can produce desirable results.

NOTES

1 N. Katherine Hayles and Nicholas Gessler present a quite convincing interpretation of the film, and even include a chart diagramming the various 'narrative states' that alternate in the film in their essay 'The Slipstream of Mixed Reality' (Hayles 2004b).
2 Jorge Luis Borges's 'Garden of Forking Paths' has often been cited or alluded to as a story that anticipates a hypertextual structure. Stuart Moulthrop's hypertextual story *Victory Garden*, for example, has numerous allusions and references to the Borges story. See Gaggi (1997: 132–4).
3 These ideas were summarised by Hayles during her keynote address at the 20th Century Literature Conference (Hayles 2004a). Thanks to Dr Hayles for providing me with a copy of her lecture.
4 Post-modern 'appropriation', a standard artisitic strategy of the later twentieth century, does involve sometimes exact copying of previous works of popular, commercial or fine art. But, in such cases, the recontextualising of the work makes the 'new' work quite different from the old work. Such 'new' work nearly always involves a putting in quotation of the old work. Thus, the content becomes very different, despite the fact that the works may look exactly alike. Dufayel seems to be doing something quite different from post-modern appropriation; insofar as we can tell, he seems genuinely to be trying to recreate something essential about Renoir's original.

8. NON-LINEAR NARRATIVE

Bruce Isaacs

The Golden Age of Hollywood

Charting a revision of – or diversion from – a particular kind of cinema presumes that cinematic trends are coherent and that such trends can be identified through a series of texts, authors and what can loosely be defined as distributors. This is often less instructive than it initially appears, and can sometimes lead to broad and occasionally meaningless generalisations. Contemporary critical writing, however, distinguishes classical narrative cinema as the zenith of the Hollywood studio film of the 1930s, '40s and '50s, exemplified in the work of Frank Capra (*Mr Smith Goes to Washington* [1939], *It's a Wonderful Life* [1946]), Howard Hawks (*Scarface* [1932], *The Maltese Falcon* [1940]) and John Ford (*Stagecoach* [1939], *The Grapes of Wrath* [1940], *The Searchers* [1956]). Though directors such as Orson Welles and Alfred Hitchcock had produced films that constituted a departure from the classical model (Welles's *Citizen Kane* [1940]) and Hitchcock's *Rope* [1948] spring to mind as deliberate attempts at formal innovation), the studio film thrived on the founding principles of an often reworked and imminently recognisable formula. I use the phrase 'founding principles' to avoid the oversimplified (and yet perennial) notion that a single homogeneous film structure constituted an entire cinematic tradition, which is clearly not the case. This essay will not take the position that the studio film offered one product in a variety of disguises. It was rather a rich and complex body of texts (reflecting numerous aesthetic traditions) that informs a contemporary American cinema as much as it offers a vital point of departure.

David Bordwell's influential work on narrative highlights a number of features common to the studio film (Bordwell 1986: 17–34). Though there were anomalies (we will consider Welles shortly), the focus of the classical narrative was on realism, both aesthetically (photography, lighting, editing, etc.) and thematically (in the choice of plot-lines and characters). The dominant formula – introduction – development – denouement – constructed the staple narratives of Hollywood melodrama (*Gone With the Wind* [1939], *Casablanca* [1942]), the social/political treatise (*Mr Smith Goes to Washington*, *The Grapes of Wrath*), film *noir* (*The Maltese Falcon* [1941], *The Big Sleep* [1946]) and the biblical epic (*Samson and Delilah* [1949], *The Ten Commandments* [1956]). Though diverse in subject matter and produced in response to a variety of social and historical phenomena, these films exemplified the abiding narrative formula. Hollywood productions reflected the dominant ideology (resulting in a demographic mainstream, a concept that exists in current studio marketing strategies), particularly its conception of an American 'reality' that functioned self-evidently on relations of cause and effect in the pursuit of historical truth (the quest for narrative truth offered a cinematic substitute). Thus, a remarkable number of studio films depict protagonists who attempt to solve a mystery using a prescribed set of clues that amount to a comprehensive back-story, the plot (what was actually depicted) and probable future developments (the causal consequences). Narrative closure was presumed, in spite of increasingly convoluted story-lines (Raymond Chandler confessed to a less than comprehensive picture of the plot of *The Big Sleep* such that even he as author and, later, a script consultant on the Howard Hawks film, was not certain who was responsible for the death of the chauffeur), and rarely challenged.

A second feature to which Bordwell alludes – and on which Robert Ray significantly expands (Ray 1985: 32–55) – is an hermetically sealed frame of representation. Action depicted on film was required to cohere within the sacrosanct boundaries of the film narrative. Formal cinematic technique was predetermined by the story, of which narrative was merely a necessary and unobtrusive function. Simply put, cinematic narrative was an enclosed, insular world that functioned without intrusion of an extraneous agency, whether creative or administrative. While a Howard Hawks film drew audiences because it was a Howard Hawks film and a Selznick production stamped an authority of big budgets, glamorous stars and soaring melodrama (alerting audiences to a particular cinematic 'reality'), the narrative itself rarely functioned with an acknowledgement of the director's input or the studio's interference; Hitchcock appeared momentarily in each of his films, but few cinema-goers of the 1940s and '50s would have recognised him. The conventional narrative presented the story according to the dictates of a 'real world' that was presumed to inform the cinematic world holistically. Indeed, directors such as Frank Capra and John Ford, were esteemed in American popular culture because of a fidelity to the 'real'. Ford's long shots of Monument Valley in *The Searchers* are an elegy for that which makes the American frontier what it is in the collective (and reflective) imagination. Paradoxically, the hermetically sealed world of the Hollywood narrative assured the lasting influence of realism in American cinema. The greater part of contemporary American cinema seeks to erase the 'screen' that separates the image from the audience. In spite of (and perhaps even due to) alternative cinematic trends (beginning with the Hollywood New Wave of the 1970s), the dominant aesthetic of American cinema is founded on realism. A mass audience view films in a darkened room, insulated from an external reality, as audiences once did in the presentation of silent cinema or at the advent of sound, to sustain disbelief that it is viewing a world fundamentally divorced from its own, a world based upon a technological and textual construct. Classical Hollywood cinema, in forbidding the intrusion of the cinematic conceit, at least in part constructed the foundations of what André Bazin termed 'the myth of total cinema' (Bazin 1974: 17–22).

Locating the impetus for a new punk cinema, particularly in terms of narrative experimentation, requires us to return to Welles and Hitchcock, and to dabble somewhat in the notion of the '*auteur*'. *Auteur* theory, championed by the French film director, François Truffaut and his *Cahiers du Cinéma* colleagues, located the creative force of a film in the director, or more correctly, the director/writer; Truffaut was less accepting of material that was not directed by the script-writer. Among other things, *auteur* theory, apart from a philosophy of film, collected a group of young French film-makers into what was later (though remarkably quickly) termed 'The French New Wave' (Marie 2003: 13); whether this wave represented anything cohesive, aesthetically and thematically, is still debated. What is indisputable is that Truffaut and Jean-Luc Godard (two iconic figures of the French New Wave) made films partially as a response to a tradition of French cinema founded on classical narrative structures, high production values and a reified cinematic realism. Thus we have in Godard's *Breathless* a protagonist who addresses the camera, collapsing the boundary between filmic (narrative) reality and the medium that once merely reproduced a 'real world' in complete and unerring form. Indeed, *Breathless* represents a seminal moment in the dawning of cinematic self-awareness (if not the first) since the advent of talking pictures and the shift from theatricality to realism in Hollywood cinematic narrative.

The film-makers of the French New Wave identified themselves almost immediately within a tradition of *auteurs*, including Jean Renoir, Alfred Hitchcock and, significantly, Orson Welles. Welles epitomised the *auteur* in his experimentation with the classical Hollywood film and his incompatibility with the auspices of the studio system. *Citizen Kane* is a landmark in the transition from a classical to a post-classical narrative film and informs substantially the experimental narrative cinema of the French New Wave, the Hollywood New Wave, and the rise of the 'Hollywood Independent' in the late 1980s. If Welles had not conceived of a cinematic self-awareness as boldly as would Godard in 1960, he had certainly distanced his narrative from the hermetically sealed classical structure founded on closure, completion and cause–effect determinacy. Kane's story is subject to perpetual revision, a quasi-fictional account illuminating the ephemeral nature of identity and the discontinuities inherent in a narrative history. Formally, the film plays out as an expressionistic portrayal of a narrative conceit – the figure of Kane – visible intermittently through looming shadows, fractured accounts and knowing subversions of narrative truth. Kane is equally a construct of news reports, personal anecdotes and fragmented memories, and an overarching narrative trajectory that frames this collage. And in that lies Welles's lasting subversion of the classical Hollywood narrative: the 'truth' of Kane cannot be separated from the narrative structure employed by the *auteur* in the telling. Welles has himself conceded that the Rosebud 'solution' was more of a gimmick for audiences craving an answer to Kane's inherent mystery (Welles 1998: 53). For many contemporary critics, the film's resounding conclusion remains the reporter's final words: 'Charles Foster Kane was a man who got everything he wanted, and then lost it. Maybe Rosebud was something he couldn't get or something he lost, but it wouldn't have explained anything . . .'

The New Punk Aesthetic and the Input of the Hollywood Independent

Auteur theory is now somewhat unfashionable, extinguished in the wake of Roland Barthes's *Death of the Author* (Barthes 1977: 142–8) (among numerous other post-structuralist attacks) and theories locating the essence of a text in an organic relationship between forces of production and consumption. Common sense and practice also encourage the analysis of cinema as a co-operative enterprise, less subject to authorial intent than the novel which predated it. Before the contemporary film reaches the studio magnate, it has had the input, in some cases and to varying degrees, of hundreds of people. The input of studios at the level of content (whether formal or thematic) renders the finished product subject to further revision at the behest of a test audience or studio executive, an evil satirised in Robert Altman's *The Player* (1992). It is significant that David Fincher's final cut of *Fight Club*, a film I would place squarely in the new punk tradition, was altered at the instruction of Rupert Murdoch, Fox's CEO. Nonetheless, after a poor showing at the box-office, the film's producer was fired.

In part because of this textual heterogeneity, locating a new punk tradition beckons the recuperation of a watered-down *auteur* theory, or at least the collection of a number of film-makers who consider their product, if not antithetical to the studio fare, at least somewhat alternative. It is difficult to speak of a cinematic tradition in terms of the studio executives who green-light the project; it is equally limiting to identify a tradition in terms of a reductive sample of its perceived audience, a frequent abuse that occurs, for example, when the terms 'mainstream' and 'Hollywood' are conflated with a homogeneous cinematic aesthetic – Hollywood studio films do not all look the same. Quentin Tarantino, David Lynch, Spike Lee, David Fincher, Paul Thomas Anderson are names synonymous with a generation of American film-makers displaced from the figureheads of what Ray and numerous others refer to as the Hollywood New Wave of the 1970s (Ray 1985: 247–94). If Coppola, Scorsese and Altman engineered an alternative to the classical narrative film, Coppola's *The Conversation* (1974) offers one of the most innovative revisions of the closed narrative; Scorsese's protagonists dwelling on the fringe of respectable society offer an urban paranoia and psychological neurosis as the contemporary malaise; Altman's multiple, and ever-proliferating subjectivities in *Nashville* (1975) and *Short Cuts* (1993) prefigure Anderson's *Boogie Nights* (1997) and *Magnolia* (1999); Tarantino, Fincher, Lynch and others explore a revolutionary narrative self-awareness, an aesthetic phenomenon significantly removed from Godard's playful and ironic narrative 'visibility'. New punk narrative highjinks are less a reaction to an accepted and traditional narrative model (and less a pointed rebuke), than an acknowledgement of a developed and accepted textual reality. Simply put, narrative experimentation is no longer the privileged domain of the European art film but commonplace in American studio productions. One possible reason for the growth of an art-film aesthetic (of which narrative experimentation is a recognisable element) is the transformation of a once marginalised art-house commerce into a lucrative corporate marketing reality. *Pulp Fiction, Fight Club, American Beauty* (1999), *Eyes Wide Shut* (1999), *Boogie Nights* and *Being John Malkovich* (1999) are each the product of a major studio or subsidiary. Michael Moore's recent *Fahrenheit 911* (2004) exemplifies this convergence of an art-film aesthetic and corporate studio product: initially scheduled for distribution through *Miramax*, Disney (Miramax's parent company) refused the distribution owing to Moore's politically sensitive material.

If experimentation on classical narrative structures is commonplace in the new punk tradition, a measure of innovation lies in the degree to which a film can expand on acknowledged boundaries, and the degree to which this experimentation then impacts on that cinematic tradition. Does the fact that Tom Tykwer's narrative experiments in *Run Lola Run* were labelled 'post-Tarantino' (or that Richard Kelly's narrative inversion/reversion in *Donnie Darko* [2001] was labelled 'Lynchian') reflect this impact?

It is necessary, though not comprehensive, to talk about iconic film-makers in the formation of a new classical, post-punk, narrative cinema. While one ought to be suspicious of *auteur* theory in its mid-1950s' incarnation, especially contemporary cinema produced within the Hollywood studio system, it is pointless and facile to reject the possibility of a discernible 'vision' (for want of a better word), albeit a vision constructed within a highly complex and fluid dynamic. Lynch's *Blue Velvet* (1986), *Lost Highway* (1997) and *Mulholland Drive* (2001) seem to me quintessential Lynch as much as *Taxi Driver* (1976), *Raging Bull* (1980) and *Goodfellas* (1990) are quintessential Scorsese.

In this essay, I use the term new punk to refer to a strand of post-modern nihilism in American cinematic subject matter (Fincher's *Se7en* [1995] and *Fight Club* come to mind). It might also be useful as a category of cinema charting social alienation, abject loneliness, psychological fracturing (Mendes's *American Beauty*, Kelly's *Donnie Darko*). If punk was a reaction to a political, economic and social mentality, new punk might refer to a deflation of values and purpose, a resignation that the battles have been fought and lost. Yet these are only generalisations, especially when considering an entire cinematic tradition. *American Beauty* is equally cynical surburbanism and quaint nostalgia. *Fight Club*, chic nihilism that it is, wants also to trash destruction, to recuperate romantic attachments of men to men, men to women, the individual to its essential self. Contemporary cinema, particularly of the current generation of American film-makers, responds to a plethora of historical, social and economic phenomena. Locating an harmonious politics or aesthetics of this generation is fraught with difficulty.

Three Resounding Narrative 'Voices': The New Punk Frame

Quentin Tarantino

Tarantino's recent *Kill Bill* [2003–4] returns discussion of his work to the study of genre, particularly a genre hybrid sometimes referred to as meta-film – a tradition of films 'about' other films. The French writer Jean Baudrillard has written similarly about the Italian director Sergio Leone, an obvious precursor to Tarantino (Frayling 2003). Narrative innovation, once Tarantino*esque*, has been pushed to the background. To recall the degree of that initial innovation and its impact on a cinematic tradition,[1] however, I want to discuss a narrative device in *Pulp Fiction* that appears to have gone largely unnoticed.[2]

The film opens on Ringo and Honey-Bunny in the quintessential American diner scene with a twist. Deciding that restaurants are safer to hold up than petrol stations, Amanda Plummer (on crowd control) leaps on to a table and says: 'Any of you fucking pricks move and I'll execute every motherfucking last one of you'. The camera freezes and we move to credits. In the film's final set piece, we discover (from a different point of view) that Ringo's and Honey-Bunny's hold-up forms a frame to this unwieldy narrative. Linear narrative has been dispensed with: Vincent sits on a toilet though he was shot by Butch in an earlier scene. Now returned once again to the diner, we shift from Vincent and Jules for the moment it takes Ringo and Honey-Bunny to announce the hold-up. We watch again as Plummer leaps to the table for her (now) anticipated line: 'Any of you fucking pricks move and I'll execute every one of you motherfuckers!'

Tarantino fractures the one coherent and wholly conventional narrative device – the frame. The narrative frame recalls an entire cinematic tradition, encompassing Billy Wilder's *Double Indemnity* (1944) and *Sunset Boulevard* (1950), seminal American *noir* films made within the studio system and emblematic of its great achievement. The narrative frame extends to the realist novel of the nineteenth century, particularly Mary Shelley's *Frankenstein*, and is predicated on a conventional causality. Cause and effect *must* operate to return the beginning of the narrative to its natural end. In *Pulp Fiction* the frame is fractured by a character, Amanda Plummer, when 'revising' her earlier exclamation. 'Any of you fucking pricks move and I'll execute every motherfucking last one of you' becomes 'Any of you fucking pricks move and I'll execute every one of you motherfuckers'. Though not overtly a narrative self-awareness, it is still a narrative *reflexivity* that reflects the growing acceptance of non-realist narrative devices, and more specifically, the intrusion of alterior narrative frames into a master narrative. Plummer's revised line literalises what was only metaphorical in *Citizen Kane*: that story is ultimately and resoundingly the contrivance of its narrative framing, subject to revision, reversion or, in the case of David Lynch's best work, dissolution.

David Fincher

Fincher is responsible for two seminal new punk films, *Se7en* and *Fight Club*. While *Se7en* recalls the dystopic cityscapes of *Bladerunner* (1982) and the metaphysical themes at the core of a post-modern film tradition, it is less obviously (and deliberately) experimental in narrative structure. His 1999 film of Chuck Palahniuk's cult novel *Fight Club* is arguably one of the most interesting narrative experiments since Brian Singer's *The Usual Suspects* (1995). The film charts a presentation of a post-modern odyssey into destruction, oblivion and, ultimately, the recuperation of the self – in this it diverts from Palahniuk's novel which, in its conclusion, is unremittingly bleak: the protagonist ends up in a mental institution when his explosive charge malfunctions and history is relegated to a perpetual present (Palahniuk

1997: 206–8). The film's narrative appears to function conventionally, again with the use of the traditional framing device. In the opening scene, the nameless narrator and Tyler Durden share a conversation which digresses into a depiction of the events that culminate in that conversation. When the viewer returns to the scene, Tyler is unveiled as a destructive (and, paradoxically, regenerative) split personality, a degree of sensationalism that, in my opinion, weighs upon the film's magnificently rendered (and very fashionable) anti-sensationalism.

One of the film's motifs involves depicting a scene in reversion. The title sequence inverts the conventional cinematic gaze: we begin inside the narrator's mind and exit through a point between his eyes. Fincher's preponderance of experimental cinematic devices – jump-cuts, fades, a reduced colour ratio – convey the constructedness of the narrative. Tyler's splicing of porn images into family entertainment parallels Fincher's control of the film narrative, de-framed by Norton's fractured self. The Tyler persona intrudes initially into Norton's narration in fleeting still-shots, mirroring Tyler's splicing of frames of film into a master narrative; it is worth watching the first twenty minutes of the film very closely to observe this bold and yet remarkably subtle intrusion into the linear, cause-effect narrative.

Unlike Tarantino's frame that collapses without the impetus of a character, Fincher places the narrative in the control of the characters framed within it. In this sense, the narrative is written, and rewritten at the whim of the characters that are traditionally its components. An example of the reflexive narrative frame (Plummer's line in *Pulp Fiction*) expanding to the self-aware, ironic placement of characters as creative agents occurs when we return to the frame in the final scene of *Fight Club*. The shot materialises on Norton sitting on a stool with a gun in his mouth. The opening credit sequence – a shot reverting from a central point (Norton's psychosis) to the exterior reality – recurs with Norton's voice-over: 'I think this is about where we came in'. The two alternate versions are reproduced below.

The Opening
TYLER: Three minutes. This is it. Ground Zero. Would you like to say a few words to mark the occasion?
NARRATOR: I can't think of anything.

The Closing
TYLER: Three minutes. This is it. The beginning. Ground Zero. [The narrator's voice-over: *This is about where we came in.*] Would you like to say a few words to mark the occasion?
NARRATOR: I still can't think of anything.
TYLER: Hmm ... flashback humour.

A Tarantino-like alteration occurs with Tyler's insert 'The beginning', which does not appear in the original conversation. Tyler's acknowledgement of the narrator's 'flashback humour', however, reflects a radical narrative self-awareness. And beneath that is an ironic appreciation by the *auteur* of the essential constructedness and contrivance of the traditional narrative form. On one level, the 'flashback humour' is presented as functioning within the narrator's psychosis – that is, it makes sense because it is only to be expected of an irrational mind fumbling over an otherwise accepted sequential narrative. On another level, a narrative origin (cause) is unrecoverable because it is reflected upon by an internal presence. The narrator is also a narrative trickster insofar as he is able to alter a narrative sequence (conversation 1) required to perform its repetition (conversation 2). Tyler's and the narrator's simultaneous awareness of the narrative revision fractures what began as whole and must thereafter regress to a point of entropy. This is not to say that the narrative fractures into nonsense, merely a radically indeterminate *kind* of sense.

Linearity and causality, Fincher seems to declare, are merely select way*s* of telling a story subject to the intrusion of an indeterminate narrative voice that is aware of its presence within an hermetic structure. It is a textual conceit that ultimately has very little to do with an external 'reality'. Various narrative realities converge, each an indeterminate construct of the other, each compromised in its integrity by the existence and performance of the other.

Christopher Nolan

Memento, Nolan's much discussed entry in the new punk tradition, involves an imminently recognisable (if not clichéd) *noir* protagonist named Leonard Shelby, a man who suffers from the unique 'mental' inability to make new memories. Shelby was in the insurance industry and recalls Walter Neff, the protagonist of Billy Wilder's *Double Indemnity*. While the narrative of *Memento* is all but impenetrable on a first viewing, repeated viewings illuminate a simple plot: Leonard is searching for his wife's murderer but is disadvantaged by his condition. He relies on notes, Polaroid photographs, tattoos and other inscriptions of the truth in lieu of the truth itself which, even were he to discover it, he would soon forget.

Memento, narratively, is not as remarkable, and certainly not as radical, as *Fight Club*. Temenuga Trifonova suggests that contemporary cinema offers two instances of a triumph of the 'virtual' over the real: on the levels of cinematography and point of view (Trifonova 2002: 14). In examining alternatives to conventional narrative forms, this essay has investigated the fracturing of the objective point of view and the ascendance of its artificial, or virtual, equivalent. Thus, in *Fight Club* and *Pulp Fiction,* while the narratives appear ostensibly to tie up the loose ends, a comprehensive (and hermetically sealed) narrative frame is fractured by a number of intrusions from a 'virtual' presence: Honey-Bunny's and the Nameless Narrator's revision of an earlier 'quotation' are two such instances. The virtual is not merely artificial – or a simulation of an objective narrative viewpoint – but the destruction of perfect objectivity. The significant distinction in *Memento*'s case is that, while Leonard shares something of the new punk narrator's schizophrenia, the viewer is offered an objective and relatively seamless perspective from which to view the events: the more Leonard forgets, spiralling toward psychical dissolution, the more the audience learns and the nearer it moves towards narrative closure. Narrative truth, rather than an illusory and debilitating obsession, is maintained in spite of – and perhaps because of – Leonard's failing grasp on that truth.

Cinematically, Nolan's film embraces many aesthetic devices in the new punk *œuvre*: juxtaposition of colour and black and white, jump cuts, an aural track often dislocated from the image – a voice-over frequently accompanies a prior or succeeding shot. Also remarkable is Nolan's deliberate investigation of the possibilities of the cinematic narrative form, particularly its rejection of traditional realism. The cause–effect model championed by the studio system is literally inverted: the viewer is a witness to a phenomenal effect before its cause is illuminated – in this sense, it offers a form of narrative entropy, a disassembling of the master narrative to a point of indeterminacy. The only narrative progression is a subplot involving Leonard's investigation of the insurance claim of Sammy Jankis. Narrative progression is depicted in black and white, while regression, the dominant trajectory, is depicted in colour. The film opens on its narrative conclusion, the death of Edward Gammel (though this closure is ultimately only a temporary measure – Leonard is imprisoned within a narrative that returns eternally to the place at which it began).

Genuine indeterminacy is only maintained, however, if filtered through the point of view of Leonard. Leonard's plight is literally indeterminate, untethered from a narrative cause and affect. Conventional cause and effect relys on the functioning of memory and insist on narrative closure as the necessary culmination of a set of visible and retrievable designs. In *Memento*, Nolan offers a *noir* protagonist not only trapped within a convoluted plot, but simultaneously the progenitor of it.

Film *noir* represents one of the most significant movements in American cinema after World War II. Interestingly, the new punk *auteurs* have returned to its subject matter and accepted styles: consider The Coen Brothers (*Blood Simple* [1984]), David Lynch, Fincher's *Se7en and* Ridley Scott's *Bladerunner*. Traditional *noir* essentially maintained the strict tenets of the cause–effect narrative model, exemplified in Hawks's *The Big Sleep*. *Memento* offers a contemporary revision of the narrative form, as well as a comment on the *noir* tradition. Pearce's bleached blond hair is deliberately anachronistic in this cinematic context. To this extent, *Memento* offers itself as a reflection (or simulation) of a traditional *noir* narrative, aware of its constraints within that realm, and the possibilities to wrestle itself free.

New punk as a Cinematic Aesthetic

To return to the point at which we began, establishing a tradition of cinema founded on aesthetic (or other) common grounds is increasingly difficult to do. Broad categories that once encompassed cinema as an art-form can simply no longer be maintained. Art films and studio productions converge in the Hollywood mainstream, at least in the American market. Mel Gibson's *The Passion of the Christ* [2004] is an independently funded production ranking quite highly in box-office sales. Conversely, Fincher's embattled *Fight Club* (charted as a Fox $40,000,000+ block-buster), fared miserably at the box-office but has had a remarkable life among the cult circuit, art-house crowds and academic theorists. Apparently there is a number of fight clubs operating in America, accepting disenfranchised young men into their folds.

Despite the disturbing (and occasionally enervating, as in the case of the Miramax-distributed big-budget *Kill Bill)* convergence of the studio and independent film, Jim Hillier maintains that the independent *aesthetic* has survived. 'But are *Boys Don't Cry* [1999], *Time Code* and *Being John Malkovich* [1999] "independent"? By all rights, they should be and are – in spirit' (Hillier 2001: 16). It is this spirit that forms the basis of any inquiry into cinematic traditions and the movements that innovate on them. Broadly speaking, the few examples offered in this essay appear to confirm, if not a dominant mainstream acceptance of alternative narrative practices, at least a healthy curiosity. Charlie Kaufman's recent screenplay, *Eternal Sunshine of the Spotless Mind* seamlessly blends a very traditional romantic narrative (boy meets girl, boy loses girl, and through some ingenious application, re-acquires her) and many of the characteristics of a new punk narrative. Joel Barish has the unique ability to construct his own memories, to intrude into his own narrative unconscious and thereby alter an external narrative reality. Kaufman's *Adaptation* offers a textual self-awareness in which twin brothers furnish an ending to a script Charlie Kaufman has been commissioned to write but is unable to complete. Charlie Kaufman represents a noble screen 'artist', his brother, Donald, a hack thriller screenwriter who is impressed with Charlie's serial-killer idea: 'take a guy who cuts up his victims into little pieces and calls himself the Deconstructionist'. When the two brothers write the ending together, the film, aware of Donald's 'intrusion', lampoons into a hybrid genre piece, pitching absurd comedy, poignant tragedy and the action thriller into a thirty minute final act.

Narrative self-awareness is merely one element of a broader ironic relationship that exists between the cinematic text and a contemporary audience for which film is, in many cases, not only the dominant art-form and means of entertainment, but the only one. The implications of this shift in aesthetic sensibilities are difficult to evaluate and, indeed, conceptualise. If new punk cinema (and the broader but now generally accepted corollary, post-modernism) reflects an increasing uncertainty in narrative truth, ideological right and existential purpose, the new punk *auteurs*, rather than shying away from the disturbing implications, seem to have embraced the aesthetic possibilities. This is nowhere more evident than in contemporary cinema. Aesthetic innovation, insofar as it is able to establish a 'wave', requires a sensibility and mind-set willing to receive it. Contemporary audiences (whether in mainstream or niche markets) are aware of cinematic traditions less as incarnations of an inherent and external 'real' than as a cinematic mythology. The hermetically sealed frame of representation, in contemporary cinema, has been inverted: accessing this cinema requires a profound and complex knowledge of cinematic traditions, to varying degrees of esotericism.[3] To what extent does an aesthetic appreciation of Tarantino's *Kill Bill* rely on a prior knowledge of Leone's *Once Upon a Time in the West* [1968]? To what extent is contemporary cinema merely a cinematic performance of prior texts and passed traditions?

One characteristic of the films of the new punk generation is the hyper-revisionism of its content, aesthetically and thematically. The cinematic image is a commentary on film, and by extension, a running commentary on itself. The film-savvy culture of the new punk milieu permits and embraces a radical new kind of mainstream-artistic appreciation that has its roots in art cinema and high culture – narrative experimentation, self-awareness, and the artistic frame as simulation[4] – marketed by major studio subsidiaries for mass audiences. The implication of this hyper-revisionism is the loss of an essential and literal realism that was once so pervasive in the Hollywood studio film. Tarantino, Fincher, Nolan and others reflect obsessively on a cinematic past, a cinematic mythology that informs the narrative frame of their films. Their protagonists are not only able to stand outside of the mimetic construct, they are able to locate themselves within a prior cinematic tradition.

New punk cinema has revised what in 1960 was coolly subversive, reinventing the innovative spirit of the French and American New Waves as the cinematic norm rather than a novel and unprecedented alternative. In relocating itself in relation to the 'spirit' of cinematic experimentation, it has shattered the pristine relationship between the interior and exterior of the cinematic frame by challenging the classical narrative structure (and its reliance on realism), subject to a traditional performance of cause and effect and the hermetically sealed narrative. Contemporary new punk cinema offers only an interior, a pervasive meta-cinema that has drawn the exterior 'real' into itself at its point of inception.

In a film culture in which studios turn out independent sleeper hits, *auteurs* inevitably suffer from the lack of the tools and purpose to offer material subversive of the cinematic norm. The subversive is perhaps itself a commodity aesthetic. Nevertheless, occasionally a striking moment appears on film, declaring its subject and cinematic performance as subversive of the norm, independent in spirit, and a return to a (nostalgic) punk/grunge aesthetic. One such moment begins *Fight Club* when we are offered the first melodic bars of a Hitchcockian major theme (or perhaps a Lynchian simulation of Hitchcock) only to be abruptly cut off by a staccato beat that leads into a techno track. For me, it is Fincher's reflective moment in which he says, 'fuck that shit off', only to acknowledge at the film's conclusion that genuine originality is merely transitory.

Notes

1. Recall, for example, Mr Orange's 'anecdote' in *Reservoir Dogs* (1991), told to maintain his cover with such veracity that he enters the anecdote's narrative, which intrudes on the film's master narrative. He addresses the camera, speaking in front of characters with whom he shares the screen, but who inhabit separate narrative frames.
2. For an excellent survey of 1990s' cinema experimenting with circular and other narrative models, see Villella (2000).
3. See Collins for an excellent reading of inter-textuality and cinematic literacy in Robert Zemeckis's *Back to the Future III* (1990): 'The fact that the hero's [Marty McFly] choices are all cinematic quotations reflects not just the increasing sophistication of the cinematic literacy *Back to the Future*'s audiences (and the profoundly inter-textual nature of that literacy), but also the entertainment value that the ironic manipulation of stored information now provides' (Collins 2002: 281).
4. See Baudrillard (1981: 3–18). Baudrillard's analysis of the text as simulation has gained a surprising currency in contemporary cinema. The Wachowski Brothers' *The Matrix* offers a number of sly references (a discussion of Baudrillard in the original screenplay was later omitted from the film). Peter Weir's *The Truman Show* (1998) explores similar territory (it functions as a rejection of the central features of Baudrillard's 'media reality'), although it does not explicitly reference Baudrillard.

9. MAKING IT REAL

Steven Rubio

> I wonder what we'll play for you tonight
> Something heavy or something light
> Something to set your soul alight
> I wonder how we'll answer when you say
> 'We don't like you – go away,
> Come back when you've learnt to play'
>
> I wonder what we'll do when things go wrong
> When we're half-way through
> our favourite song
> We look up and the audience has gone
> Will we feel a little bit obscure
> Think 'we're not needed here,
> We must be new wave –
> they'll like us next year'
> The Wonders don't care
> we don't give a damn
>   ('One Chord Wonders', The Adverts)

The Adverts were one of the earliest British punk bands of the mid-1970s that emerged in the wake of the Sex Pistols. The band was formed in late 1976 by two art students, TV Smith and Gaye Advert; early in 1977, several months before the appearance of *Never Mind the Bollocks, Here's the Sex Pistols*, the Adverts had released their first single, 'One Chord Wonders'. In August 1977, Ian Birch wrote up the band for *Melody Maker*, wherein he described a recent concert:

'[T]o put it mildly their set was a shambles. But, in a way, that is what has always appealed to me about the band. It never ceases to amaze me how they can stumble through one number, let alone a whole set. Every song constantly teeters on the verge of collapse as it careers along' (Birch 1977: n.p.).

While 'One Chord Wonders' in fact has more than one chord, the monomaniacal sound of the record convinces the listener otherwise. The band wasn't particularly concerned with technical skills on their instruments (they had apparently only recently learned how to play them, and the second version of the song, recorded for the album *Crossing the Red Sea With the Adverts*, is already a bit more adept in a technical sense), but songwriter Smith was always attentive to the importance of excellence in lyrics. In retrospect, even the title 'One Chord Wonders' suggests a logical-to-the-extreme extension of the infamous punk battle-cry, 'here's three chords, now go out and form a band'.

The band in 'One Chord Wonders' takes the stage, only to find the audience is unappreciative of the Adverts' technical skills ('Come back when you've learnt to play'). Unconcerned, the band plays on, only to find the audience has left. All of this takes barely more than half of the song's brief running time. The second half features the repetitive chorus, the lead singer working his way through variations of 'we don't give a damn' while the rest of the band chants ominously, 'THE WONDERS DON'T CARE!' and the drums pound simply and mercilessly.

Early punk bands such as the Adverts created their art, not only in response to their surrounding cultural milieu, but also in the context of a pop-music world that had increasingly embraced technical virtuosity as a cornerstone of excellence. The raw early Beatles of Hamburg and 'Twist and Shout' had given way to the lovely sheen of *Abbey Road*, which had influenced a generation of prog-rockers. Whatever the merits of 'progressive' rock, the genre was becoming increasingly stale by the time punk arrived, and part of the appeal of punk lay in the lack of instrumental virtuosity, which represented a slap in the face to those who would replace 'authentic' emotion with sterile professionalism. The Ramones showed that three chords were enough; the Adverts playfully suggested that three were too many.

As could perhaps be expected, an honest attempt to create a new art out of personal experience soon enough became the basis for an unspoken (even at times, overt) manifesto on the proper way to make music. There was a 'right' and 'wrong' way to be punk, which made it rather difficult for newly emergent punks to be personally expressive. Meanwhile, the audience was largely gone, the bands became 'a little bit obscure', and New Wave (capital N, capital W) was what people liked the next year. Punks and punk art remain to this day, but always and even intentionally on the margins; one wonders if nowadays people, punks and non-punks alike, can recall a brief moment in the mid-1970s when it seemed possible that punk would take over the world.

The mid-1970s was a crucial period in the development of the American film industry, as well. A batch of inspired film-makers had emerged during the previous decade, beginning around the time of *Bonnie and Clyde* in 1967. Coppola, Scorsese, Altman and the rest have been hailed so often at this point that a backlash is surely on the way, but the fact remains that something special was happening to Hollywood film between 1967 and 1975. Some of the films of that era shared with the subsequent punk-rock movement a disdain for technical virtuosity . . . at the very least, the tiny budget of *Easy Rider* (1969) demonstrated what could be done on a shoestring at least as effectively as did the first Ramones' album. Other films had grander aspirations and larger budgets. All of them assumed the possibility of personal artistic expression within the Hollywood system, and the system was mostly happy to oblige until one of those new directors, Steven Spielberg, delivered *Jaws* in 1975. *Jaws* was a box-office smash of titanic proportions, obliterating previous records, and when *Star Wars* blew *Jaws* out of the box-office water in 1977 (the great punk year), a trend had been established that continues to dominate the thinking of mainstream Hollywood studios to this day: the 'block-buster' mentality that spends extra attention, not on movies that offer the personal artistic expression of a director, but on movies that have the best chance not only of making a profit, but of ringing in the dollars on an enormous scale.

Pauline Kael, the best writer on the great American films of 1968–75, identified the post-*Jaws* problem so effectively in 'Why Are Movies So Bad? Or, the Numbers'. Her argument still largely holds true, many years after she wrote the piece in 1980. In particular, she noted the importance now placed on extraneous items (sales to television, promotional tie-ins, and the like) which increase the amount of money made by the studios. The studios no longer make movies primarily to attract and please movie-goers; they make movies in such a way as to get as much as possible from the pre-arranged and anticipated deals. Every picture (allowing for a few exceptions) is cast and planned in terms of those deals (Kael 1994: 820).

Kael argued that the ability to guarantee a profit in advance leads to movies which are unobjectionable before they are anything else, the primary concern of the producer being to avoid upsetting the *status quo* that will ensure profits. This works against the production of quirky individualist fare. Furthermore, the desire of the studios to protect themselves in advance leads to a preference for BIG: big stars, big directors, big productions.

If a big star and a big director show interest in a project, the executives will go along for a $14,000,000 or $15,000,000 budget (a lot of money in 1980) even if, by the nature of the material, the picture should be small. And so what might have been a charming light entertainment that millions of people all over the world would enjoy is inflated, rewritten to enlarge the star's part, and over-scaled (ibid. p. 824). The result is impersonal film-making (although I suppose it could be argued that George Lucas was creating his version of personal film-making when he came up with *Star Wars*).

In all of this, in the emergence of punk rock, in the American films of the golden era, and in the critiques of what has arisen in the wake of those artistic periods, I am making an assumption: that the personal expression of an individual or a group of individuals is a primary concern of great art and great artists. The situations may change. Punk rock was a cultural–musical response to the music of the past and the social conditions of the present, presented as a fuck-you to the mainstream, while a movie such as *The Godfather Part II* (1974) exists entirely within its cultural and artistic mainstream. But, in each case, the artists offer a personal vision (or a collective presentation of the group's 'personal' vision), and this personal vision is contrasted with what is seen by the artists as faceless pseudo-art, hiding a lack of vision behind technical excellence.

One primary difference between 1970s' punk and '70s' Hollywood film-making lies in the fetishised nature of 'authenticity' among more dogmatic punks. When he made *Mean Streets* (1973), Martin Scorsese may have been trying to give a sense of what 'real' life was like for him growing up, but he always used 'extra-real' methods to represent the real, piling on the nostalgic music and artsy camera movements. Punk, it sometimes seemed, was less interested in representing the 'real' than it was in simply BEING 'real'. This being the case, musical ineptitude was preferred to actual talent, since the inept musician was real in his or her awfulness. In was no surprise, then, that Sid Vicious became an icon of punk. Musically untalented, Sid was none-theless a perfect punk, or rather, Sid was a perfect punk precisely because he was untalented. That he couldn't play his bass or sing on key was proof that he was authentic; you would never mistake him for Sting. (His stupid death was further proof Sid was real, if further proof was necessary.)

In recent years, various film-makers have come along who, overtly or less obviously, have been influenced, not only by their predecessors in film, but by punk culture. Many of these film-makers operate within what can loosely be described as 'indie' film. Independent film was one area not anticipated by Kael when she wrote her anti-studio screed in 1980. While her analysis of the studios remains applicable today, what she missed was that a group of film-makers would come along who shared her sense of the irrelevance of the studios to personal artistic expression, and that an audience and a distribution system would emerge for these independent works. It is to these movies that we now turn.

> Culture is what we make it, Yes it is
> Now is the time, now is the time, now is the time
> To invent, invent, invent, invent, invent, invent . . .
> (Sleater-Kinney 2000)

In 1995, film-makers Lars von Trier and Thomas Vinterberg attached a 'Vow of Chastity' to the Dogma 95 Manifesto, Dogma 95 being 'a collective of film directors founded in Copenhagen in spring 1995' with 'the expressed goal of countering "certain tendencies" in the cinema today' (Kelly 2000b: 227–8). In the manifesto, it was claimed that 'a technological storm is raging' in film that will make it possible for anyone to make a movie. This 'ultimate democratisation of the cinema' is not necessarily a good thing 'because the individual film will be decadent by definition' (ibid. p. 228). (At this point, it is worth noting that it is rarely clear whether or not the Dogmatists are being ironic or straightforward.) The Manifesto decried the tendency in film to value technological capabilities over the authentic representation of life, claiming that advances in technology lead to films with 'illusions via which emotions can be communicated'.

The Vow of Chastity details various aspects of the film-making process that must be followed if a movie is to receive the approval of the Dogmatists. Among these restrictions on the process, the film-makers are required to shoot only on location, to use no sound that does not arise organically from the scene, to use hand-held cameras, to shoot only in colour without any optical filtering, and to avoid 'superficial action' (here they get specific: 'Murders, weapons, etc. must not occur') (ibid. p. 228). The point of all this chastity? The goal of the film-maker 'is to force the truth out of my characters and settings. I swear to do so by all the means available and at the cost of any good taste and any aesthetic considerations.' A Dogma film is interested only in 'truth', and as the manifesto argues, technological 'trickery' leads to films filled with superficial illusion and precious-little truth.

To the extent that we are to take the Manifesto and Vow of Chastity seriously, we can see some similarities between Dogma 95 and the punks of the 1970s. There is a desire to distance oneself from the bland, technologically adept mainstream productions of the time, which results in the attempt at a relatively primitive art which rejects technology in the name of deeper 'truth'. There is a celebration of outsider status. And there is an aggressive pride in confrontational possibilities. Nonetheless, there are equally important areas where Dogma and punk exist on opposing sides.

Punk's 'here's three chords' mentality celebrates the democratic possibilities in art. Many punks were first influenced by the Ramones, whose simple but brilliant work suggested 'hey, ho, you can do this, too!' You learned your three chords, you formed a band, you made music. Dogma recognises this tendency, but fears it . . . if everyone can make a movie, everyone will, and the resultant chaos will be good for no one (apparently, the Dogmatists assume most people will transform inexpensive, easy-to-use technology into yet more superficial crap). Again, with the caveat that the Dogmatists are winking at us, the Manifesto calls for an increased presence of the avant-garde, explaining that 'It is no accident that the phrase "avant-garde" has military connotations. Discipline is the answer . . . we must put our films into uniform.' Punk celebrates the You Can Do This spirit of chaos, Dogma runs frightened into the arms of discipline.

In this, Dogma is more like second-wave punk, after the first burst of delicious energy. It took a few years for punk to fossilise into 'punk', and took some time before the newness of the approach became just another set of rules to follow. Dogma begins with the set of rules, as if its proponents saw that someone said 'here's three chords, form a band' and decided such a statement proved the importance of setting standards.

Despite all of this, films with the Dogma imprimatur are as varied as the people who make them. Directors who make Dogma films often talk about the liberating aspects of the process, and this is understandable: to make movies outside the mainstream must surely be invigorating for creative talents. Some Dogma films, such as *julien donkey-boy*, are almost unwatchable; some, like *Italian for Beginners* (2000) are indistinguishable from mainstream movies (it is possible that the relatively conventional love story of *Italian for Beginners* is ironic, but the movie works only when it is clearly NOT ironic); some, such as *Camera* (2000), (the tale of a digital video camera, 'told' from the point of view of the camera, a nice twist of Dogma), are conceptually interesting but otherwise inconsequential. In every Dogma film, we must ask the question, is 'truth' being told here? And, as you might expect, the answer depends on the film.

But one thing becomes clear after watching a lot of these movies, and it's a problem that is often apparent when an artist strives for 'authenticity' in this way. To make a film that explicitly follows the Vows of Chastity is to announce to yourself and your audience that This Film Is Different. How is it different? It rejects the accepted mainstream definitions of proper film production, associating the mainstream with superficial illusion. How do we in the audience know the film is different? It works hard to remind us that it is not like all the other superficial films. How does this serve 'truth'? Not much at all, because the insistence on dogmatically low-fi technology draws attention to the style, reminds us we are watching a movie, not in a Brechtian sense of breaking the wall between film and audience, but in a showy, look-at-me sense. The Vows require that 'The director must not be credited' and demand that directors proclaim 'I am no longer an artist. I swear to refrain from creating a "work", as I regard the instant as more important than the whole.'

But nothing draws more attention to the director than an imposed style that bashes the audience with its studied anti-tech stance.

A recent film which illustrates the problem underlying the 'I am not an artist' approach is Gus Van Sant's *Elephant*. This movie – a fictional version of the Columbine shootings with the tagline 'An ordinary high school day. Except that it's not'– purports to be a depiction of 'ordinary', as if the absence of what the Vows of Chastity call 'superficial action' will get us to the core of 'truth' at the bottom of Columbine. But for a movie that wants to depict the ordinary, it's pretty busy.

Some of the best, most 'truthful' movies come when the film-makers refuse to pass judgement on their characters. *Sid and Nancy* is about junkies but doesn't pass judgement on junkies. Gus Van Sant has noted on more than one occasion that he was emphatic about not allowing the usual easy and trite explanations for the actions of the killer teenagers in *Elephant*. For this reason, it would have been far more appropriate for the director to adopt an 'artistic vision' that disappeared into the non-committal philosophy Van Sant claims to be proposing in this film, rather than drawing attention to the style as if Van Sant were channelling ostentatious directors such as Orson Welles. You are always aware of Van Sant's presence in *Elephant*, which seems to be the wrong approach for a film intent on a matter-of-fact presentation. The endless scenes of people walking, the shaky camera work, the unstudied acting, all of this is clearly intended to make *Elephant* look more 'real' than other films, but it has the opposite effect.

And despite Van Sant's claims that his movie was non-judgemental, he includes a scene that could have carried the Joe Lieberman Seal of Approval. Teenage boys play violent video-games, watch Hitler on television, read about guns on the Internet and kiss in the shower, then go off and blow innocent people away. Did Van Sant miss ANY hot points in the 'why do kids do this stuff' debate? Video-games? Check. Television? Check. The Internet? Check. Homosexuality? Check. (The last point was in some ways the most disturbing . . . if a straight director had pulled such a stunt, he or she would have been torn to shreds.) The style of the movie as a whole, and the representation of cultural artefacts in the particular scene in question, works against the supposed non-judgemental/hands-off approach that Van Sant is claiming for his movie.

Elephant demonstrates a fundamental problem with Dogma-style approaches to the 'real', to 'truth', to 'authenticity' in films. There are good reasons to be sceptical of films which promote their technological excellence while ignoring anything recognisably human on the screen. And, as Kael argued back in 1980, a movie-making system that strives for risk-free profits is unlikely to foster much of creative value. But it is not clear that the proper response to the current state of films is to concoct manifestos, ironic or not;

nor does it guarantee 'truth' to ask the artist to disappear. It's healthy for an artist to look beyond 'good taste', but it is simply an abdication of responsibility for an artist to pretend as if 'aesthetic considerations' are just something that gets in the way of 'truth'.

In contrast to these films, Michael Winterbottom's *In This World* (2002) doesn't shy away from aesthetic considerations, and is the better for it, as it walks a line between documentary, drama and docu-drama. Netflix describes *In This World* as a 'gripping documentary film', and there is a lot of voice-over narration that seems to be describing a specific journey taken by two specific people, Afghan refugees who travel from Pakistan to London. The credits for the film, though, include a cast of characters. The Internet Movie Database lists the two leads, Jamal Udin Torabi and Enayatullah, as playing 'himself', although the actual credits in the film have them playing 'Jamal' and 'Enayat'. (If Enayat is playing himself, he is also paying homage to William Holden in *Sunset Boulevard*.) The detailed production notes on the DVD explain that Jamal and Enayat had never acted before, and that director Michael Winterbottom (whose previous film, *24 Hour Party People* [2002], was a fictionalised look at mid-70s' English punk) let the two mostly improvise their dialogue, allowing them to experience the events of the film in a more immediate fashion than they could have if they'd had to memorise lines (and often, the two 'actors' were going through the events in the film themselves for the first time . . . their 'dialogue' consisted of the things they said to 'real' people in 'real' situations).

As best as one can work out, *In This World* is a fictional representation of a typical journey for refugees to England. The style of the film, shot with a small, inconspicuous digital video camera, adds to the documentary feel, and many scenes are, in effect, real in that Winterbottom placed his actors in a real situation and had them improvise their way, albeit with a narrative imposed on the scenes by the director.

Winterbottom may have some Big Things to say about refugees – in particular the complex laws which rule the offering of asylum in Britain – but he never gets around to those Big Things because the often harrowing journey of the two men is so captivating, it overwhelms the movie. In the end, *In This World* plays almost like an old-time serial: Jamal and Enayat get into one hair-raising situation after another, and the audience roots for them to escape to the next place on their journey. Despite all of the stylistic attempts (mostly successful) to give the film a documentary feel, what works is very basic story-telling: two men go on a journey, which consists of getting to a place, escaping the place, getting to another place. And the film ends up an interesting blend of fact, fiction and style, one which gets at some level of 'truth' about its subject.

In recent years, several films that play around with time in interesting if ostentatious ways, have been released. *Memento* is perhaps the most notorious in this regard. It is an ingenious story of a man with short-term memory loss who writes reminders everywhere (including his own body) to help him recall things he needs to know. The narrative is told backwards, in a way (scenes appear in reverse order of their occurrence, but each individual scene happens in the proper sequence), and this structure, along with the mystery tale at the core of the plot, make *Memento* seem important and revolutionary, because we haven't seen anything like this before. Director Christopher Nolan doesn't hide his stylistic moves; on the contrary, those moves ARE his film. Without them, you're left with a minor genre piece. We're a long way from the Vows of Chastity: Nolan completely reworks 'reality'. You can't say that Nolan is pursuing a more 'authentic' representation of the real, although perhaps he's doing his best to draw the audience into the reality of his memory-hampered protagonist. Mostly what Nolan is doing is showing off. Showing off has a fine and honoured tradition in film; without it, there would have been no Orson Welles. But Nolan doesn't appear to be having a very good time in *Memento*. He's so intent on his parlour trick that he forgets to enjoy himself, and the most the audience can hope for in terms of enjoyment is to exercise their brains, trying to work out what is going on.

A useful contrast is Tom Tykwer's *Run Lola Run*. Like Nolan, Tykwer impresses with his virtuosity, but we also sense joyfulness from the filmmaker. *Run Lola Run* plays with narrative, and plays with time, and plays with genre . . . the operative word is 'plays'. Tykwer seems to be having as much fun as Godard making *Breathless*, and his willingness to throw the kitchen sink into his film if it will help is delightful. *Run Lola Run* is an apt description of the film, which is about speed and running as much as it is about time and filmic conventions. Tykwer does a masterful job of integrating the soundtrack into the action (music on the sound-track being a Dogma anathema, of course) so that, among other things, *Run Lola Run* makes a perfect video for techno music. Even something as seemingly trivial as Lola's hair colour becomes earth-shaking here . . . the shocking red is as delightfully transgressive as the Beatles' mop tops were in the 1960s, or spiked hair for punks in later years.

There is little 'reality' in Tykwer's film. He doesn't seem to be concerned with capital-T Truth. One could easily dismiss *Run Lola Run* as a trivial romp driven by the music and the running and the red hair and the animation and the way the director co-opts the narrative structure of video-games in order to allow his heroine to re-enact events until she gets them right. But there is a truth of sorts in the kind of reckless enjoyment a movie like *Run Lola Run* offers. Strict Dogma films want the director to disappear (even though the act of disappearing often calls attention to the director). A movie like *Memento* trumpets the stylish moves of the director, but it feels like preening. But *Run*

Lola Run walks all over Dogma and tramples on solipsism. It's as showy as *Memento*, but it seems crafted for the audience's enjoyment, not 'look what I did', but rather 'look at what we can do, isn't this fun?' *Run Lola Run* demands a response, inspires the viewer to run out and dye their hair red. That inspirational factor is something it shares with punk.

> There were times, I'm sure you knew
> When there was fuck fuck fuck all else to do
> But through it all, when there was doubt
> I shot it up or kicked it out
> I faced the war and the world
> And did it myyyyyyyyy way
> (Sex Pistols, 'My Way')

The punk moment was more than music. If the global cultural impact wasn't quite what many might have hoped for, nonetheless the music itself inspired others beyond the people who went out with their three chords and formed a band. In its thrashing of the bland music of its day, in its insistence on the importance of every person's voice, in the way it encouraged people to say 'no' with such fury that the negative became an affirmation . . . in all of these ways and many more, punk influenced the world, and influenced artists far beyond the field of music. The Dogma 95 movement two decades later echoed many of the concerns of the punks, and offered a similarly low-fi attack on the vapid nature of much technologically advanced art, but the very existence of a Manifesto, whether or not the intentions were ironic, was antithetical to punk. The emergence of a full-blown 'independent' film circuit was more reminiscent of New Wave than of punk, but today, as in the period between 1968 and 1975, there are options for film-makers who want to make personal artistic statements while remaining at least partially connected to the mainstream, and the presence of even a compromised indie-film movement is a nice, and even punkish, step forward for creative film-makers.

Oddly, though, it was a relatively conventional film that best connected to the spirit of punk. Alex Cox's first feature as a director, *Repo Man* (1984), was an Los Angeles punk movie for about half its running time, and a very post-modern experience in any event. It barely prepared audiences for his next film, however, which also dealt with punks but which told its story in a more straightforward fashion. *Sid and Nancy* (1986) took one of the most famous, iconic punks of all time, the titular Sid Vicious, and made a movie that was punk to its core but was also, and essentially, a romance.

Sid Vicious may be a punk icon but, to a large extent, that only reflects a cartoonish vision of punk. The more intelligent (and scary) Johnny Rotten is still around, haranguing all who will listen and half of those who won't, but

Sid Lives because he's dead. As we suggested earlier, Sid personified that part of punk which was purposely stupid, in the process diminishing the impact of more dangerous punk philosophies. Meanwhile, Nancy Spungen was by most accounts an unlikable figure; as Jon Savage, chronicler of British punk has noted, 'It's hard at this point in time to find anyone with a good word to say for Nancy' (Savage 1998). Alex Cox takes these two disreputable punks, and makes a punk statement by the simple act of treating them like human beings, and by recognising their love for each other. The film is a *mélange* of 'real' and fantasy . . . Johnny Rotten probably thinks the movie is a lie. And the punk history, which takes up roughly the first half of the film, gets it only partly right. But once Sid and Nancy move to America, the romance kicks into overdrive, and, in an odd and even charming way, with that romance, the movie becomes legitimately punk. It thrashes expectations . . . Sid isn't a Hero, he's a junkie who pukes on people (in one scene, literally), and who would have thought to tell the story of punk by depicting the love of two people for each other? Perhaps no one, and that's the punk thing about it. *Sid and Nancy* rewards the punk spirit precisely because it denies your expectations. In the process, Alex Cox achieves what someone like Gus Van Sant in *Elephant* only dreamed about: he presents an honest picture of his characters, but doesn't judge them. Perhaps that's too easy on Cox: he does judge them, to the extent that he wants us to believe in their love.

And then, because Cox is tied to the historical record, Sid kills Nancy. And then Sid kills himself. That's a reality Cox can't escape.

PART III

CASE STUDIES

10. DOGMA BROTHERS: LARS VON TRIER AND THOMAS VINTERBERG

Shohini Chaudhuri

When Thomas Vinterberg's *The Celebration*, the first film to be made under the aegis of the Danish film movement Dogma 95, premièred at the 1998 Cannes Film Festival, audiences were astounded that what looked like a home movie had 'somehow wandered onto the screen' (Kelly 2000a). This was due not only to its story of incest and a dysfunctional family but also to its assaultive style, characterised by unsteady camera-work and shock-cuts – a result of following the ten film-making rules in the Dogma 95 Manifesto, designed to counter ' "certain tendencies" in the cinema today' (Kelly 2000b: 226).

Known as the 'Vow of Chastity', the Dogma rules stipulate location-shooting (no imported sets or props are allowed), direct sound (produced at the time of filming and not dubbed over the images afterwards), hand-held camera (always following the actors, rather than forcing actors to move to where the camera is standing), colour film stock and available lighting (rather than special film lighting) and Academy 35 mm format. They also forbid optical work and filters, superficial action (that is, murders and weapons 'must not occur'), genre movies, 'temporal and geographical alienation' (films must be set 'here and now'), and state that 'the director must not be credited' (Kelly 2000b: 227–8).

The Manifesto was signed by Lars von Trier and Thomas Vinterberg, the vanguard of the Dogma 95 collective which, at the time of its launch in 1995 at an event marking the centenary of cinema at the Odeon Cinema, Paris, also included two other Danish directors, Søren Kragh-Jacobsen and Kristian

Levring. Each member of this original collective, known as the Dogma 'Brotherhood', has released a Dogma film – so, in addition to *The Celebration*, the 'first wave' of Dogma films includes *The Idiots* (1998), *Mifune* (1999) and *The King Is Alive* (2000), all funded by Danish state television. In compliance with the rules, the directors' names do not appear on the films' credits. There has since been a 'second wave' of Dogma films from Denmark, including *Italian For Beginners* (2000), *Open Hearts* (2002), *Kira's Reason* (2001), *Truly Human* (2001) and *Old, New, Borrowed and Blue* (2003). The Dogma concept has also travelled internationally, inspiring a number of non-Danish Dogma films, such as the US indie *julien donkey-boy*, *Lovers* (1999) and *Fuckland* (2000), as well as works in other media (including dance).

Dogma has, rather unfairly, been dismissed as a mere publicity stunt, an 'apolitical' rehash of past film movements and has, somewhat prematurely, been pronounced 'dead' by sceptical critics who target the film-makers for not consistently following their own rules, thus reinforcing the belief that Dogma is simply a gimmick. Less sceptical interpretations of the movement have alluded to its creative use of arbitrarily chosen limitations – and the notion that limitations enhance creativity is one which film-makers invoke themselves. Mette Hjort, on the other hand, has presented the more compelling case that the rules of Dogma 95 are neither arbitrary nor apolitical: they represent a small nation's response to 'the inequities of globalising processes' (Hjort 2003a: 31). They are carefully framed in opposition to Hollywood's rules, so as 'to mount a genuine challenge to the ever-narrowing conception of what constitutes viable or legitimate filmmaking' – which is increasingly characterised by astronomical budgets, violent action and expensive special effects as a direct outcome of Hollywood's global market dominance. By doing this, the rules level the playing field on which cinemas of small nations such as Denmark compete with Hollywood (Hjort 2003a: 39). Von Trier has himself observed that Dogma rules liberate film-makers in small nations:

> If that is the only thing that comes out of these Rules, then I think that's fantastic – that people in countries like Estonia or wherever can suddenly make films . . . Because they look at Dogma and think, 'If that's a film, then we can make films too.' Instead of just thinking, 'Oh, if it doesn't look like *Star Wars*, then we can't make a film'. (Kelly 2000b: 145–6)

In this essay, however, I shall argue that the significance and impact of Dogma 95 goes much further than questions of 'national' cinema. As a film-making agenda, it is indeed pioneering and empowering for minor cinemas and the cinemas of small nations but this, in my view, makes it a prime example of the broader, transnational phenomenon of 'new punk cinema' – although the movement is also steeped in Scandinavian influences. Viewed in terms of a punk aesthetic, the apparent contradictions between Dogma's rule-making and rule-breaking begin to make sense, especially in the work of the movement's two main founders, von Trier and Vinterberg. Punk logic is what best encapsulates *their* ethos, if not the movement as a whole. This essay therefore presents case studies of their work following a general discussion of Dogma's punk idiom.

DOGMA AND ITS INFLUENCES

'My supreme goal', the Vow of Chastity declares, 'is to force the truth out of my characters and settings' (Kelly 2000b: 228). Dogma 95 advances a commitment to 'realism', supporting this with its emphasis on location-shooting, contemporary settings and hand-held cameras. This readily recalls the conventions of the Italian neo-realist movement of the 1940s' and 1950s' French New Wave film-making as well as 1960s' and 1970s' documentary film traditions such as America's Direct Cinema. Moreover, the practice of making the camera follow the actors rather than vice versa was famously pioneered by American Independent fiction film-maker, John Cassavetes, whose 16 mm Arriflex cameras facilitated an unprecedented intimacy with his actors in films such as *Faces* (1968). As a contemporary movement, however, Dogma 95 significantly transforms these influences which date from many decades ago. One of the most important factors in this transformation is the evolution of film technology; another is the punk movement itself.

Although the Dogma 95 Manifesto does not specify that films must be made on digital video, the movement is a product of the digital wave: 'Today a technological storm is raging, the result of which will be the ultimate democratization of the cinema', the Manifesto states. 'For the first time, anyone can make movies' (Kelly 2000b: 226). The rule regarding the Academy 35 mm format was originally intended as a deterrent to shooting on video which, the founding members believed, was more susceptible to manipulation than film: 'By using new technology anyone at any time can wash the last grains of truth away in the deadly embrace of sensation' (Kelly 2000b: 227). This rule, however, – like many of the other rules – has been freely interpreted so that film-makers can utilise the cheaper video format for shooting as long as they transfer to Academy 35 mm for exhibition. For economic reasons, both *The Celebration* and *The Idiots* were shot on digital video and in both cases the technology enabled the camera-operators not only to mingle fluidly with the actors – without camera mounts, tracks or cables getting in the way – but also to achieve an even greater intimacy than Cassavetes did with his 16 mm Arriflex cameras. Although Vinterberg maintains that 'it was not the idea to make cheap films' (Kelly 2000b: 123), one of Dogma 95's most valuable feats has been its legitimisation of low-budget digital-video film-making. This was underlined when Martin Scorsese and his jury awarded *The Celebration* the Special Jury prize at Cannes; it then went on to achieve critical and commercial success internationally, winning over audiences to a non-mainstream aesthetic.

Mike Figgis, whose *Time Code* and *Hotel* (2001) are partly inspired by Dogma 95, has been described as someone who 'foresees a new era of cinema – precipitated by advances in digital technology – that will be like the punk era in music. That is, stripped down, rule-breaking and totally revitalizing.' ('*Time Code* Production Notes' 2000: 1) I propose that the analogy between punk and Dogma 95 is even stronger than the one which Figgis makes between punk and the digital wave. Despite claims that Dogma was created for established film-makers seeking 'relief' from the apparatus of mainstream film-making (Stevenson 2002: 180), the Manifesto, with its rules simplifying film production, has widely been received as a Do-It-Yourself guide for aspiring film-makers. It removes the need for expensive equipment and makes the means of cinematic production available to all. This amateur, DIY sensibility is totally of a piece with the punk movement, which encouraged the belief that anyone could make punk music. Punk bands such as the Sex Pistols were accused of not being able to play – but their attitude to that was 'So what?' (Spencer 1995: 490).

The British punk movement was 'a positive reaction to the complex equipment, technological sophistication and jaded alienation which . . . formed a barrier between fans and stars' (Coon 1995: 491). Dogma's low-finance home-video aesthetic similarly positively erodes the barriers between film studios and the outside world, and makes people think, 'If that's a film, then we can make films too' (Kelly 2000b: 146). Set in this sort of context, the significance of von Trier's statement resonates far beyond issues of small nationhood. Aesthetically, as well as economically, the echoes of the punk movement are unmissable. Dogma is minimalistic, as punk was with its three-minute songs, basic chords and cheap equipment. It creates its own rules in order to liberate itself from mainstream cinema's rules, just as punk bands did to liberate themselves from the rules of the mainstream record industry. Dogma film-makers vow to follow the Manifesto 'at the cost of any good taste and any aesthetic considerations' (Kelly 2000b: 228), while punk bands celebrated a look and music style which was 'beyond considerations of taste' and indeed valorised bad taste (Coon 1995: 491).

Anarchy, aggression, arrogance and rebellion are the hallmarks of both movements. Both seek to confront – in some cases, to shock – audiences with jarring, hard-hitting, edgy work. Socially transgressive themes form the common denominator of many Dogma works. With their focus on close-knit social groups living in close quarters and dysfunctional families, the Danish Dogma films also show the legacy of Scandinavian theatre – namely the psychological family dramas staged in confined, intimate settings known as *Kammerspiele* (literally, 'chamber plays'), a genre which was adapted into film by Carl Dreyer and Ingmar Bergman, among others. Vinterberg acknowledges Bergman's *Fanny and Alexander* (1982) as a key influence on *The Celebration*, while von Trier's work self-consciously emulates the Danish art-cinema precedent set by Dreyer. While the close-up is a familiar device used in the *Kammerspielfilm* to lend emotional intimacy with characters, however, Dogma's home-camcorder-style punk anti-aesthetic installs an amateurish desperation in the scrutiny of intimate lives that is far from Bergman's or Dreyer's stately family dramas.

Despite eschewing aesthetics, Dogma 95 has become an identifiable aesthetic in its own right. Although some films, such as *Mifune* and *Italian For Beginners*, deploy a much calmer camera style, the rules requiring hand-held camera and available lighting and the prohibition of optical work and filters have resulted overall in a 'trademark' Dogma style centring around 'an instability and obscurity of the image' (Hjort 2003a: 32). This can be interpreted in terms of realist aesthetics – as an attempt to generate the impression of authenticity and present the audience with the 'truth' in the form of an apparently untampered record of events. Dogma films frequently make use of long takes with whip-pans instead of cutting away for shot / reverse-shot. This creates the illusion that the film we see is in a raw state, before being transformed and manipulated in the editing. Instead of point-of-view shots, Dogma films tend to use over-the-shoulder shots – another attempt to appear more amateurish, less constructed. This raw immediacy is in keeping with a punk aesthetic. But, rather than serving the Manifesto's realist claims, it actually highlights confusion as well as the limits to capturing 'the truth'. It also offers alternative ways of making meaning to Hollywood's 'realism', which depends on fixed codes of editing, lighting and *mise-en-scène*. Dogma 95 thereby further asserts its status as a new punk cinema that counters Hollywood's rules and exposes the hegemonic practices in its system of representation.

The Manifesto's final commandment of not crediting directors is, von Trier declares, 'like a punch in the face of all directors' (Hjort and Bondebjerg 2001: 221). It underlines Dogma's challenge to film history and the film establishment. Against the *auteur* concept, Dogma proposes a collectivist model of film-making: 'we must put our films into uniform, because the individual film will be decadent by definition' (Kelly 2000b: 226). Despite this, the Danish Dogma films have not at all been uniform and each one is visibly the work of its director, who has been able to work creatively within the rules, interpreting them as they wish and thereby always producing differing results. Genre, too, has proved unavoidable. The Manifesto's repugnance towards it can be understood in terms of the fact that genre is seen as conventional and shackled to the past, whereas Dogma's founding members want to be associated with the contemporaneous, the immediate, and the avant-garde.

The novelist Angela Carter once described punk as a 'predominantly masculine' style (Carter 1995: 512). Punk can be understood as a form of provocative self-fashioning and, of course, women can do it as well as men – as the 'second wave' of Dogma films has testified with women directors such as Lone Scherfig, Susanne Bier and Natasha Arthy taking up the Dogma baton. Notwithstanding the brief membership of documentary film-maker Anne Wivel, however, it is not by chance that the original Dogma collective was known as 'the Brotherhood' – it had a distinctively masculinist bent to its provocations. We can see this most clearly in the treatment of gender and sexuality in von Trier's work. With his increasing obsession with female debasement, martyrdom and rape, von Trier poses an extreme challenge to post-feminist sensibilities.

A Spit in the Eye of Tradition: Vinterberg's *The Celebration*

> The point is to get angry and do something different. The point is to reflect the movie business as it is – not just to give it another colour. But in some people's minds, Dogma just means 'hand-held films', you know? (Vinterberg, interviewed in Kelly 2000: 112)

Born in 1969, Vinterberg is the youngest member of the Dogma Brotherhood. After graduating from the National Film School, Denmark, his first film, *The Boy Who Walked Backwards* (1994), was a magic realist short. His first feature, the road movie, *The Biggest Heroes* (1996), was successful in Denmark but it was his second feature, *The Celebration*, which propelled him to international fame. Ironically, Vinterberg has become an international *auteur* as a result of Dogma 95, an ostensibly anti-*auteurist* movement.

The Celebration centres on the sixtieth-birthday celebrations of Helge Klingenfeldt at his country mansion. Invited to give a toast to honour his father, Helge's oldest son, Christian, reveals that Helge sexually abused him and his twin sister, Linda, when they were children; and that Linda's recent suicide resulted from this trauma. The family gathering repeatedly ignores Christian's revelations and tries to eject him from the party. It is only convinced when Linda's suicide note comes to light and confirms his story; the tyrannical patriarch is then ousted from his own party.

The Celebration's bourgeois family setting is nothing like Vinterberg's own upbringing – he grew up in a commune – but, as an atmosphere where behaviour is supposed to be controlled and rule-bound, it highlights transgression of rules. In one scene, Christian is banished from the house and tied up to a tree in the woods. As an ironic counterpoint, Vinterberg then cuts to a

Danish hymn sung by Christian's grandmother at the banqueting table. He calls this 'a spit in the eye of Danish tradition' – a phrase which sums up the spirit of the film (Kelly 2000: 120). *The Celebration*'s style complements its content, reflecting obvious aspects of the punk idiom: anger, explosive energy and anti-authoritarianism. Made to look like a home video of the kind that is shot at family gatherings, it perfectly embodies the undisguised home-made quality which is an essential component of Dogma's punk aesthetic. Of course, the film was not actually home-made but created by professional film-makers and released by the production company Nimbus Film. Its constructed amateurishness is emphasised by the cameraman appearing in the shot several times in the film, including in the rear-view mirror in the first scene when Michael orders his wife Mette and his children out of the car to make room for his brother Christian, whom they encounter on the way to the party; the cameraman takes their place in the car along with Christian.

In *The Celebration*, the cameraman represents the point of view of an extra guest at the party. When Michael later removes Christian from the dining hall and pushes him down the stairs, the camera, too, seems to topple backwards, reinforcing the impression that the cameraman is like a prying guest who is recording the proceedings and himself surprised by the developments. Unlike the omniscient camera of classical Hollywood narration, this cameraman's knowledge is seemingly as restricted as the audience's, unable to predict where the next centre of interest will be in any given scene. The use of palm-sized Sony PC-7 digital cameras enables actors to forget the camera's presence and react directly to each other yet, due to the confusion of the camera in the midst, the effect in Dogma films is not so much 'fly on the wall' film-making – as in the stated aims of Direct Cinema – but the creation of a 'camera personality' (Oxholm and Nielsen 2000). The camera becomes a participant who either physically intervenes in the action with 'a temperament and emotional life of its own' (Oxholm and Nielsen 2000) or becomes infected by the surrounding hysteria and frenzy. For example, when Mette arrives at the house after being forced to walk there, she greets Michael angrily and accidentally knocks the camera. Later, a screaming match between them ends with Mette hurling herself backwards on to the bed in frustration. As she falls out of the shot, the camera does a blurry pan around the room, before abruptly cutting away, mimicking her spent intensity.

As Vinterberg states, the Dogma rules 'call for brutality at the level of editing' (Hjort and Bondebjerg 2001: 281). This is particularly evident in the sound cuts, as when Christian's sister, Helene, quietly decorous at the banqueting table even while Michael initiates a racist Danish song to taunt her black boyfriend, Gbatokai, explodes in the bathroom – screaming, she thrashes around, hits the wall, and then is sick. The abrupt sound cut emphasises the contrast between these scenes – the contrast between rule-bound and rule-breaking behaviour. It has a direct analogue in punk music where songs stop abruptly rather than 'fading out'. In mainstream filmmaking based on Hollywood rules, sound is often carried over shots to create the illusion of smooth continuity and conceal the cut. In Dogma, by contrast, the cinematic minimalism imposed by the rules – here, the rule about direct sound – throws the cinematic apparatus into relief, revealing rather than concealing its ideological workings.

Vinterberg explains that when 'you have nothing to tell the story with other than the actors . . . you don't have music, for instance, to provide a crescendo, . . . you have to make [the actors] faint, or puke, or fight – something, to express what it is that you want to get out' (Kelly 2000: 114). The imposition of limits heightens the expressivity of the material resources at the film-makers' disposal, allowing them to explore the imminent fractal intensities within each of those resources: 'If the Dogma rules specify that no sound effects are to be used, then you're left with only your volume knob to work with and suddenly that volume control allows you to evoke a wide range of different moods', Vinterberg states (Hjort and Bondebjerg 2001: 276). *The Celebration*'s use of light illustrates this aspect just as well as its use of sound. As its cinematographer, Anthony Dod Mantle, recognises, the exigencies of working under available light and video-to-film transfer bring to the Dogma films an abstract 'aesthetic dimension' that has its own signifying potential (Combs and Durgnat 2000: 30). In fact, Dod Mantle deliberately enhanced this abstract aesthetic in several of the Dogma films he photographed by pushing the exposure to obtain even more 'video noise'. As darkness descends in the story time in *The Celebration*, the video pixels become increasingly visible on screen in such a way as to suggest that the image itself is decomposing. This sequence begins with Christian being cast out of the house to brood alone in the twilight. It comprises the chain-dance sequence (where all the guests, including the cameraman, romp through the house), Helene's public reading of the suicide note, the after-dinner dance, and Christian's collapse and hallucinations – all interior scenes shot under low-light conditions, sometimes just by candlelight. These scenes reflect the film's increasingly dark mood and the family's psychological breakdown. They end with Michael reacting to the truth of Christian's revelations of child abuse by physically beating up Helge in the darkness outside the house, thereby perpetuating the cycle of family violence.

The label of 'magical psychological realism', given to Vinterberg's earlier work, does more justice to *The Celebration* than the Manifesto's narrowly realist claims (Hjort and Bondbjerg 2001: 27). In scenes involving the discovery of the suicide note, the film cross-cuts between three locations to suggest connections that go beyond realism – Linda's old room where Helene reads the note to herself, Michael and Mette's room, and Christian's room, where Linda's ghostly presence is suggested by shots of his friend Pia submerged in the bath (Linda killed herself by drowning). The film works within the formal parameters of Dogma rules to evoke the presence of death-in-life, with slow-motion shots of the billowing curtain in Linda's bathroom and static overhead shots emphasising that we are now outside the viewpoint of the constantly mobile guest/cameraman whose flurried, nervous personality defines the rest of the film.

In addition to the Dogma certificate which opens each Dogma film and attests that the Manifesto's rules and intentions have been followed, Vinterberg invented the 'Confessions', in which film-makers reveal any deviations from the rules. For example, Dod Mantle confessed to violating the hand-held rule in one scene in *The Celebration* where he taped the camera to the microphone boom. Vinterberg states that he instituted the Confessions 'to emphasise how rigid I was; to make clear that we really observed the Rules' (Kelly 2000: 118). The Confessions encapsulate the paradox between rule-making and rule-breaking at the core of Dogma 95's punk ethic (although, like the Manifesto with its Ten Commandments, they also evoke religious imagery). A confession highlights the fact of trangression, and that to follow these rules is always to break another, more hegemonic set of rules.

Von Trier: The Punk *Provocateur*

The other co-founder of Dogma 95, von Trier, is the major force behind the movement. Born with the name Lars Trier, he has, at least since his time at the Danish National Film School (1979–82), adopted the aristocratic 'von' as a middle name – a gesture which, in a country like Denmark that prides itself on egalitarianism, was guaranteed to draw attention (Hjort 2003b: 139). With his leather jacket and 'studied sneer', von Trier became known during the 1980s as 'the punk provocateur of the Danish art underground' (Stevenson 2002: 59). Although he has since forgone this classic punk look, punk provocation remains central to his methods and has earned him the reputation of a charlatan and a cynical manipulator. Despite this, his stature as a director has grown and he is considered to be one of Europe's most original contemporary directors, initially rising to international cult fame for his début feature, *Element of Crime* (1984) and, more recently, winning the Palme d'Or at Cannes for his post-Dogma work, *Dancer in the Dark*.

Von Trier's early works – *Element of Crime*, *Epidemic* (1988) and *Europa* (1991) – were all meticulously realised projects, relying extensively on storyboarding, elaborate *mise-en-scène*, lenses, lights, gels and camera-dollies. Dogma 95 can be seen in terms of his own artistic trajectory, enabling him – and other established film-makers – to throw off the yoke of learned behaviour. Von Trier obsessively pursues this kind of rule-breaking in all his work since the

Manifesto as well as in his pre-Dogma works, *The Kingdom* (1994) and *Breaking the Waves*. *Kingdom* was the first project undertaken by von Trier's company, Zentropa, which he formed with producer Peter Aalbaek Jensen in 1992 in order to give himself complete artistic control over his films, although Zentropa has now evolved into a diverse, collectivist endeavour, especially with von Trier's 'Open Film Town' project which aims to make the business of film-making more transparent and accessible to amateurs (Hjort and Bondebjerg 2001: 227). A supernatural hospital soap television series inspired by, on the one hand, David Lynch's *Twin Peaks* and, on the other, the pseudo-documentary camera style of American television police drama, *Homicide* (1993–1999), *Kingdom* marks a turning-point in von Trier's career and a formative moment for Dogma. Shot on a fast schedule on location at Copenhagen's biggest hospital, the Rigshospitalet ('hospital of the Danish Kingdom'), it disregards continuity rules such as eye-line match and axis of action, using available light with shaky hand-held camera-work in most scenes.

In his typically provocative way, von Trier declared that he made *Kingdom* and his Dogma film *The Idiots* with his 'left hand', stating he 'circumnavigated that cultured right hand' (Hjort and Bondebjerg 2001: 219). *Kingdom* is full of technical flaws; von Trier instructed his cinematographer, Eric Kress, not to worry about 'bad' framing, excessively high contrast, or actors going into dark areas. The Arriflex camera used in *Kingdom* had hairs stuck in the gate – Kress recalls that 'Lars just loved it' and got very angry when a new camera with a hair-free gate was used for the sequel *Kingdom 2* (1997) (Thomsen 1998: 26). In this respect, von Trier has many affinities with American film-maker, Harmony Korine, who describes his own approach as 'mistakeist' (Kelly 2000b: 199). *Kingdom* made von Trier a household name in Denmark and became his first popular breakthrough work. It showed 'that seemingly sloppy and faulty filming and editing did not bother the public as long as the plot and the characters were interesting' (Schepelern 2003: 60). This has extremely liberating implications for film-makers. Since the silent era, von Trier explains, film has been governed by rules, such as the axis of action, which are designed to 'smooth things out', and 'people have been trained, are still being trained, to watch films like that' (Kelly 2000b: 146). He argues that there has to be 'a new film language' that is 'more abstract':

> I think that within the brain of the spectator, there is a will to find the 'story-line', if you want to call it that, or the logic between the things that are happening . . . I'm sure that this will is what we're working with, so we should dare much more.' (Kelly 2000b: 146)

Dogma 95 provides von Trier with a means of testing this out: film-makers impose their own rules to liberate themselves from established film-making rules. His film *The Idiots* even takes the form of a social experiment which mirrors Dogma's formal experiment. In it, a group of young able-bodied people form a commune and pretend to have learning disabilities, challenging each other to 'spass', as they call it, in public. They attempt to liberate themselves from society's norms, to provoke others and themselves by acting under self-imposed constraints, thereby exploring their own limits and society's limits. By the same token, we see von Trier, the able film-maker, 'spassing' with film form. 'Mistakes', such as blurred focus, jump-cuts, and apparently careless and unbalanced use of light, colour and composition (with the microphone boom occasionally appearing in shot), abound in order to jar and provoke spectators; the rules, in any case, forbid 'mistakes' of light and colour to be 'rectified' in post-production. Von Trier also made extensive use of improvisation, encouraging his actors to depart further from the script in each consecutive take, appearing to relinquish his own control of the work. Despite this, earlier takes, which were closer to the script, ended up in the film. In the final scene, the group's sceptical outsider, Karen, shows the strength of her conversion by returning to her family, who have not seen her for two weeks since her baby son's death, and spassing in front of them. Louise Hassing, who plays the commune member Susanne who accompanies Karen, states that as 'the essence of what the film was about . . . it was very, very important that every detail [in this scene] was just right' and, significantly, von Trier did not allow any improvisation here (Oxholm and Nielsen 2000).

Von Trier himself shot 85 per cent of the final cut of *The Idiots* despite having three other camera operators working on the film (Thomsen 2000: 22). He reasserts the control which he has relinquished as non-credited director by actually holding the camera – a Sony VX-1000 Digital Handycam, notably a much larger camera than that used in *The Celebration*. Von Trier has since continued to operate DV cameras, shooting all of *Dancer in the Dark* and *Dogville* himself. He is also present in *The Idiots* talking to the cast off-camera in pseudo-documentary 'interview scenes'. Although they are marked as taking place after the events of the dramatic narrative, the status of these scenes is unclear other than as a direct and provocative reference to the Manifesto's tenth rule. They follow the rules – von Trier does not appear in shot – yet break them at the same time, by asserting his claim to be acknowledged as the work's driving force.

The Idiots clearly pushes the limits of what is considered acceptable for public cinema release. Hjort writes, 'if the idea of able-bodied individuals voluntarily mimicking the involuntary behaviours of the disabled is intentionally distasteful and provocative in and of itself, it becomes even more so as a result of von Trier's decision to emphasise nudity and, more importantly, sexuality' (Hjort 2003b: 149). At a crucial turning-point in the film – that is, just before the commune starts to disintegrate – the members decide to throw a party which, at the leader Stoffer's behest, turns into a 'gang bang' – a scene which features real sex, including a penetration shot for which porn actors were hired. This ignited censorship scandals when the film was released abroad, including in the United States – although, surprisingly, the British Board of Film Classification released the film uncut, due, they claimed, to the brevity of the scene, its justification in the narrative and the film's sensitive handling of disability overall (Hjort 2003b: 153). Ironically, in view of the Manifesto, *The Idiots* clearly met the BBFC's aesthetic criteria, despite its conscious bad taste.

Von Trier's work deliberately stirs moral reactions, making it difficult to take a distance from it – but that, of course, is the point. Dogma 95 is by no means his first manifesto. For *Element of Crime*, he declared that film-makers must try to return to the time when their love for film was young, comparing it to a man with his mistress rather than his wife:

> We want to see mistresses of the screen vibrant with life: unreasonable, stupid, stubborn, ecstatic, repulsive, wonderful, but *not* tamed and made sexless by a moralizing grumpy filmmaker, a stinking puritan, cultivating the moronic virtues of the nice facade. In short, we want to see heterosexual films, for, about, and by men. (Hjort and Bondebjerg 2001: 216–17)

Sexual imagery is also implicit in the Dogma 95 Manifesto where, in the context of the Brotherhood, the 'Vow of Chastity' appears as a test of male celibacy, arguably another type of misogynistic posturing. Given this, it is interesting that all von Trier's films since *Breaking the Waves* have been women's films and melodramas – that is, feminine genres, notwithstanding Dogma's interdiction against genres. Despite their female protagonists (which his films never had before) it appears to be male psychology that they explore.

Breaking the Waves forms the start of von Trier's Golden-Hearted Trilogy, which includes *The Idiots* and *Dancer in the Dark*. The trilogy is inspired by a children's story about a girl who gives away her possessions to needy passers-by until she has nothing left; still, she believes, everything will be all right. In *Breaking the Waves*, where the Golden-Hearted heroine Bess sacrifices her life by submitting herself to a sexually sadistic sailor to save her paralysed husband, who has persuaded her to take other lovers and report back to him in order to aid his recovery, the Marquis de Sade's novel *Justine* is clearly another influence. Feminist critic, Ida Nilsson, has attacked von Trier's images of women as 'throwbacks' to the 'idealised depictions of docile, self-sacrificing women' of 1930s' Fascist propaganda (Stevenson 2002: 130). Harsh criticism has also come from Icelandic singer, Björk, who calls him an 'emotional pornographer' (Paphides 2000: 21). During her traumatic experience working with him as his lead actress in *Dancer in the Dark*, Björk decided that in *Breaking the Waves* von Trier is not 'with' Bess, as she had previously thought – 'he's the guy in the hospital bed who sits there because he can't partake in real life . . . and gets someone else to do it for him' (Paphides 2000: 21–2). Von Trier, she claims, 'needs a female to give his work soul and he envies them and hates them for it, so he has to destroy them during the filming' (Sweet 2004: 13). (Prior to *Kingdom*, von Trier's work was indeed widely regarded as 'soulless', although it was technically accomplished.) This attack is similar to that made against Alfred Hitchcock, who was famous for persecuting his actresses. In her book on Hitchcock, Tania Modleski describes this in psycho-analytic terms of denial and displacement: 'the male finds it necessary to repress certain "feminine" aspects of himself, and to project these . . . onto the woman, who does the suffering for both of them' (Modleski 1988: 13).

Von Trier's emotional manipulation is of a piece with his films' assaultive sensibility – one critic described *Dancer in the Dark* as having 'the force of an emotional bulldozer' (Matthews 2000: 42). Yet his tear-jerking strategy in the Golden-Hearted Trilogy is extremely ambiguous. On the one hand, its crudity seems to point to a kind of Brechtian distancing – raising the audience to a level of self-awareness about the manipulative excesses of any melodrama or women's film by making the voyeurism and sadism explicit – while, on the other, its adoption of the feminine mode appears ruthlessly opportunistic, not at all encouraging audiences to reflect critically. With however, *Dogville*, the first of von Trier's new USA-Trilogy, the arguments in favour of von Trier's critical engagement gain strength.

In order, he claims, 'to avoid repetition', Vinterberg has swung in a totally different direction since his Dogma work, *The Celebration* (Kelly 2000b: 114). In a subsequent film *It's All About Love* (2003), he deploys big budgets, studios, sets and tripods, determined to do precisely the opposite of Dogma requirements: 'I spat in Dogma's face', he declares (cited in Hjort 2003a: 35). Von Trier, on the other hand, despite also provocatively breaking Dogma rules in his post-Dogma works *Dancer in the Dark* (a musical) and *Dogville*, which were both the most expensive Scandinavian films of their time, has continued to be informed by the rules in crucial ways. *Dogville* is set in a Rocky Mountains town during America's Depression era. Von Trier, who has never visited the United States, allegedly due to his phobia of flying, shot the entire film on a sound stage in Trollhätten, Sweden (where *Dancer*, set in 1960s' America, was also shot). Using hardly any sets, with buildings and roads chalked in outline on the black-laquered floor and a minimum number of props such as a bench, a shop front, a desk and a bed, *Dogville* epitomises von Trier's search for an abstract, stripped-down film language. In important ways, it also harks back to Dreyer who, for his film *Ordet* (1955), asked his crew to fill the set with the items normally found in a rural kitchen, then systematically eliminated the props until only a few basic objects remained (Bordwell 1973: 11).

Dogville's cinematic minimalism does not extend to lighting and sound effects, which it uses extensively, nor to its cast, which features stars such as Nicole Kidman (who worked for a 'symbolic' fee). Kidman's Grace is a fugitive, on the run from gangsters, who offers her services to the townspeople in return for shelter. Their compassion degenerates into exploitation when they learn of the handsome reward they could gain by turning her in; and the men start extracting their own 'payment' by raping her; the absent walls in the stage setting underscore the rest of the town's complicity during these scenes, as we see everyone nonchalantly going about their own business. *Dogville* is a Brechtian reworking of *Breaking the Waves*, with Grace's sexual slavery and degradation made explicit – one of its few props being a neck collar by which Grace is chained to a weight after she tries to escape. That this is post-feminist provocation is also evident in the position of the camera – operated, of course, by von Trier himself, which emphasises that the dominant narrative point of view in his work is male, even when appearing to be female. In one of the rape scenes, which takes place in the applecart in which Grace tries to escape, a bird's-eye-view dissolve through the covering enables the audience to take the position of the rapist.

What also makes *Dogville* different is that, in a final chapter, Grace takes revenge, Old Testament-style, for the town's lack of charity towards her, assuming powers given to her by her gangster father, played by James Caan, a pun on his appearance in *The Godfather* (1972). When the destruction is over, Grace hears the barking of Moses, the town's guard-dog, which has miraculously survived. In the final, overhead shot, we witness Moses's chalk outline take flesh: a real dog barking at the camera. This gesture towards von Trier's own snarling provocation with the end credits which, with David Bowie's 'Young Americans' on the sound-track, display photographs of America's downtrodden from the Depression era to the present. This fleshes out the social injustices which von Trier has hitherto diagrammatically shown us. Although such injustices could take place anywhere, the photographs and music anchor the story to America. *Dogville* has therefore been interpreted as 'anti-American' – evidently, this time, part of von Trier's desire for provocation, with the disquisition on arrogance between Grace and her father anticipating charges of *his* arrogance for criticising a nation he has never visited. In *Breaking the Waves*, Bess sacrifices herself for her voyeuristic husband; in *The Idiots* Karen risks everything she has to prove to the commune members that their endeavours were worthwhile, while in *Dancer* Björk's Selma does the same to save her son; but in *Dogville* the townpeople are not even worthy of the heroine's sacrifice. America is known as the world's most Christian nation and the land where anyone can pursue their dreams regardless of who they are. Yet, von Trier seems to be saying, in terms of charitable welfare to the needy and underprivileged, it has not deserved God's mercy or his Grace.

Conclusion

This essay has argued that Dogma 95's audacious and unabashedly amateurish, DIY style and sensibility make it an instance of new punk cinema *par excellence*. It has explained the movement's paradox of sabotaging mainstream film-making rules and creating its own rules in terms of a punk ethic. The movement sets itself up as a resistance to authority – as a challenge to the cinematic establishment. There are also many ways in which it reinforces reigning ideologies and hegemonic assumptions, however, as seen in relation to gender and sexuality in von Trier's work – although, even here, the provocative mode of address facilitates a critical edge. Much more than a valorisation of low-budget and/or digital-video film-making, Dogma 95 creates a forum for debate in which the main point is to get angry – and to react.

11. MIKE FIGGIS: *TIME CODE* AND THE SCREEN

Constantine Verevis

In an essay entitled 'Towards an Archaeology of the Computer Screen', Lev Manovich describes four developmental stages in the screen's history: the classical screen of painting and photography, the dynamic screen of cinema, the real-time screen of television, and the interactive screen of the computer (Manovich 1998: 27–34). While this genealogy contributes to a broad understanding of screen technologies and visual cultures, recent new punk cinemas, and the mainstream *and* experimental film traditions upon which they draw, complicate Manovich's proposal. More specifically, Manovich claims that the arrival of the television and computer screen displaces the single 'window' that completely dominates the cinematic screen (ibid. pp. 28–9). Such a suggestion is complicated not only by the many *and different* historical examples of feature films that employ multiple windows – *Napoleon* (1927), *Pillow Talk* (1959), *Woodstock* (1970), *Wicked, Wicked* (1973), *Dressed to Kill* (1980), *Buffalo 66* (1997), *Requiem for a Dream, Kill Bill, Vol. 1* (2003) – but also a tradition of experimental film, most notably Andy Warhol's *The Chelsea Girls* (1966). Warhol's epic, dual-projection film was a spectacularly successful attempt to break down the 'art of duality' – the visual (experimental) and narrative (mainstream) modes of film-making – that polarised the New American Cinema of the early to mid-1960s (Warhol 1983: 139). More recently, the Warhol legacy – the ongoing exchange between the industrial and the artisan – can be found in the likes of the parallel plotting of films such as *Short Cuts* (1993) and *Magnolia* (1999), the surveillance television of *Big Brother*, and the real-time web phenomenon of

JenniCAM. More specifically, Mike Figgis's *Time Code* borrows from *The Chelsea Girls* its radicalised sense of time, its determined formality and its employment of multiple windows. Shot in real time (with no edits) on four digital video-cameras, *Time Code* has been touted as *the* film for a new generation of screen users, a work that allows – especially in its DVD edition – for an unprecedented amount of viewer control. This chapter considers the case of *Time Code* and its historical, structural and technological, near (and distant) relatives: audio-visions like *The Chelsea Girls*, *Magnolia*, and *JenniCAM*. It takes issue not only with the question of interactivity – the audience's selection and construction of narrative in *Time Code* – but also with how this film's experiment in digital video technology might contribute to an understanding of the archaeology of the screen.

Towards the end of *Time Code* a young, ambitious, eastern European filmmaker, Ana Pauls, supported by her rapper boyfriend Joey Z and sleazy agent, pitches an idea for a movie – a grid of four stories that would unfold simultaneously in real time – to a group of producers at Red Mullet Productions. Ana's voluble dissertation proceeds as follows:

> My film has the necessity – the urge – to go beyond the paradigm of collage. Montage has created a fake reality. Technology has arrived. Digital video has arrived and is demanding new expressions, new sensations. [. . .] My film will be an unmade film. Not just mobile. A film with not one single cut, but one continuous moment. A film with not one single cut. No editing. Real Time. [. . .] Imagine four cameras. Imagine four cameras displayed in a scene. Imagine a Situationistic type of play. A Guy Debord's type of play. The city as a jungle. Each of these four cameras [. . .] will follow a character and the characters are going to meet with each other creating the plot of the story, creating the plot of the film.

The film pitch – even more than the four earthquakes that interrupt, yet co-ordinate, the narrative developments of *Time Code* – is at the 'epicentre' of the film. Although ridiculed by Red Mullet producer Alex Green, who describes Ana's idea as 'the most pretentious crap [he's] ever heard', the pitch bears an obviously close resemblance to Figgis's film, standing *mise-en-abyme* for the grid-like structure and continuous shots that organise *Time Code* as a whole. More particularly, Ana's film pitch not only reflects *Time Code*'s distinguishing characteristics – the *long take* and the *multiple window* – but identifies the film's overarching theme of *realism*.

In a recent overview of the ways that cinema and new media interact, Manovich considers the manner in which the theme of realism accompanies 'the evolution of new media technologies during their four-decade-long history and the ongoing shift of cinema towards [it] being computer-based' (Manovich 2002: 210). Manovich begins by outlining two opposing tendencies in the aesthetics of digital cinema: on one hand, the big budget digital special effects of the Hollywood block-buster; and on the other, the modest reality film-making of digital video practitioners. In the latter instance, Manovich adopts the phrase *DV realism* to describe the 'use [of] multiple, often hand-held, inexpensive digital cameras to create films characterised by [the authenticity and immediacy of] a documentary style' and a capacity to *represent the real* (ibid. p. 212). Manovich puts forward, as examples of DV realism, American features such as *Time Code* and *The Blair Witch Project* and European films of the Dogma 95 group, *The Celebration* and *Mifune*. According to Manovich, the precursor to contemporary DV realism is the *direct cinema* movement of the late 1950s and 1960s:

> Like today's DV realists, . . . 'direct cinema' proponents avoided tight staging and scripting, preferring to let events unfold naturally. Both then and now, the filmmakers used new film-making technology to rebel against the existing camera conventions that were perceived as being too artificial. Both then and now, the key word of this revolution was the same: 'immediacy'. (ibid. p. 212)

Manovich's lineage for DV realism can be extended beyond the cinematic to embrace the mid-1960s' arrival of the (analogue) portable video-tape camera and the moment of 'direct video', or *street-tapes* (more on this below). Additionally, the *immediacy* that Manovich refers to – particularly in the case of *Time Code* – can also be related to André Bazin's strictures on cinematic realism and the long take.

In one understanding of the work of André Bazin, the long take contributes to a realist account of the cinema, one in which the exclusion of editing and the duration of the shot treats 'reality as intrinsic to the filmic process' (O'Pray 1989: 210). Appealing to the films of Erich von Stroheim, F. W. Murnau, and Robert Flaherty, Bazin rejected the 'tricks of montage' (typified by the work of D. W. Griffith and S. M. Eisenstein) to invest in the 'reality of dramatic space' (Bazin 1967: 27). Having challenged the 'aesthetic unity' of the silent film and divided it into two tendencies – the constructivist and the *realist* – Bazin looked to the development of editing, or *découpage*, in the sound film. Bazin stated that it was 'understandable . . . that the sound image, far less flexible than the visual image, would carry montage in the direction of realism, increasingly eliminating both plastic expressionism and the symbolic relation between images' (ibid. p. 27). Moving on from this, Bazin considered the dramatic effects of the 'shot in depth' or deep-focus photography advanced through the films of William Wyler and Orson Welles (and also the 'direct cinema' of the Italian neo-realists). Bazin argued that the techniques of deep focus and the long take conjoined the reality of dramatic space (the unified space and time of the single shot) and *découpage* (the dramatic editing of the sound film) to maintain the intrinsic realism of the photographic image (Elsaesser and Buckland 2003: 198). In his favoured examples of the sequence shot – in films such as *Citizen Kane* (1941) and *The Magnificent Ambersons* (1942) – Bazin found not merely a 'capital gain in the field of direction' but 'a dialectical step forward in the history of film language' (Bazin 1967: 35). Bazin's preference for the techniques of deep focus and the long take seems to be expressed in Ana Pauls's speech in *Time Code*, especially in her insistence upon 'the necessity . . . to go beyond the paradigm of collage'. As stated above, the long take is a key characteristic of *Time Code* (something returned to later) but it also informs a key precursor to Figgis's film: namely, Andy Warhol's *The Chelsea Girls* (and Warhol's early structural and dramatic films more generally).

The Chelsea Girls (1966) is an approximately three-and-a-quarter-hour-long epic made up of twelve thirty-three-minute unedited and unrelated reels projected in pairs. Each one of the segments features various Warhol Superstars – Nico, Ondine, Brigid Polk, Gerard Malanga, International Velvet, Ingrid Superstar, and others – playing themselves in episodes (ostensibly) unfolding in different rooms of the Chelsea Hotel. In the putting-together of *The Chelsea Girls*, Warhol drew upon his then recent experimentation with multimedia in such events as Jonas Mekas's 'expanded cinema' programme and Warhol's own *Exploding Plastic Inevitable* (1966), a New York 'happening' featuring live music and performance, multi-screen film projection and elaborate light shows. At the same time, *The Chelsea Girls* brought together two earlier aesthetic traditions – those of minimalism and camp – that had informed Warhol's previous film-making. As Callie Angell points out, it is possible to follow the development of Warhol's minimalist technique from the early experimentations with the multiple-camera set-ups and internal editing of *Sleep*, *Kiss* and *Haircut* (all 1963–4) through to the stationary camera and single-shot reels of *Blow Job*, *Eat*, *Empire* and *Henry Geldzahler* (all 1964) (Angell 1994: 125–6). Alongside these early 'structural' films, Warhol invested in a camp sensibility, sharing with film-makers, such as Jack Smith and the Kuchar Brothers, a fascination with Hollywood and its star system. Warhol's parodic output of the period included such films as *Tarzan and Jane Regained . . . Sort of* (1963), the unfinished *Batman* and *Dracula* films (1964) and Warhol's tribute to television producer Lester Persky, *Soap Opera* (1964). Warhol's *magnum opus*, *The Chelsea Girls*, adopted not only the long take, fixed camera aesthetic of the structural films, but followed the work of film cultists (such as Smith and the Kuchars) to narrow the gap between the underground and the mainstream, replicating in its 'widescreen' format and histrionic modes the methods of the Hollywood block-buster.

The use of the long take in Warhol's films – especially early structural films, such as *Blow Job, Eat, Empire* and *Henry Geldzahler* – might, as Michael O'Pray suggests, 'lead us to identify Warhol as a realist' (O'Pray 1989: 172). O'Pray argues that, in one version of Bazin's realist account of cinema, 'Warhol is a perfect example of a cinematic project which holds the object at a distance in its wholeness and integrity *qua* object, which treats of reality as intrinsic to the filmic process and where montage-like construction seems to have no hold' (ibid. p. 172). In this way, Warhol's cinema can be seen as a direct response to the 'fragmenting violence' of Stan Brakhage or Kenneth Anger (ibid. p. 174), but any easy alignment of Warhol with Bazin is complicated by Warhol's 'dramatic' collaborations with 'scriptwriters' Ronald Tavel and Chuck Wein, that lead to the staging of *The Chelsea Girls*. These early sound features – which included *Screen Test #1, Screen Test #2, Suicide, Vinyl, The Life of Juanita Castro, Horse, Kitchen, Space* and *Beauty #2* (all 1965) – typically consisted of two, single-shot, thirty-three-minute-reels and launched Warhol Superstars in a series of self-creating performances (Angell 1994: 132). In *The Chelsea Girls*, Warhol takes up the two, single-shot, 33-minute reel format of these films but complicates it by structuring the new film around a split screen, projecting the reels in pairs and in a phased relationship that separates the beginning of each reel by about five minutes. As Stephen Koch points out, the two sides of the split, wide-screen format not only exist in an 'unequal [and] contested struggle for attention', but the disjunction of the image is further compounded by the 'compositional style' – the sudden pans and abrupt zooms – of each panel (Koch 1971: 85). Koch argues that the net outcome of the 'restless, irresolvable pacing of [Warhol's] imprisoned camera' and 'the crack-brained conversations of each episode' are a frustration of one's impulse to focus upon an episode and then move, as one might with the earlier, silent structural films, *with time*:

> The result of this . . . drama of disjunction [is] to relentlessly set the operation of cognition against the arbitrary. As one becomes aware of this experience, one becomes equally aware that despite the implied mechanistic rigidity of the subdivided compositional field, despite any effort to concentrate on the simultaneous mini-dramas before our eyes, almost every movement of awareness is actually being determined at the outer edges of perception . . . *The Chelsea Girls* is not so much a narrative as a spectacle, but it is a spectacle in a state of perpetual disintegration. (ibid. p. 85)

Koch's comments on *The Chelsea Girls* point to the kind of tension that can be engendered by the coupling of the long take and the multiple window: the frustration of a meditative experience in the face – and in anticipation – of a televisual-type of fragmentation. *Time Code* is a film that might, at first, seem to adopt a similar pattern but a closer inspection suggests a different set of relations.

At one level, the formal composition (and total running time) of *The Chelsea Girls* and *Time Code* is similar: Warhol's film is made up of twelve thirty-three-minute sequence shots shown in pairs (396 minutes); Figgis's film comprises four x 93-minute sequence shots shown all at once (372 minutes). Additionally, just as *The Chelsea Girls* begins (according to established convention) on the right half of the screen space, *Time Code* also unfolds progressively, starting in the top right-hand quadrant and moving (after about two minutes) anticlockwise to top left then bottom left, and finally bottom right. But at another level – especially in the orchestration of 'narrative units' – the difference between the two films is considerable. Although the multiple reels of *The Chelsea Girls* are often arranged according to an established convention,[1] the fact is that they can be assembled in any combination and in any order. By contrast, the unfolding of the four shots that make up *Time Code* (at least in its theatrical edition) is fixed and unchanging.[2] Indeed (as indicated below) where the episodes of *The Chelsea Girls* depict what appear to be random and unrelated goings-on, the events in *Time Code* overlap and are carefully arranged and choreographed in accordance with a set of maps and charts.[3] More than this, the random encounter of Warhol's film is further assisted by the fact that each reel has a sound-track, the levels and switching (left, right or some combination) of which are left to the proclivity of the film-projectionist. The sound mixing for *Time Code* is, by contrast, attenuated to communication of salient bits of narrative information, with Figgis himself identifying music as the single most important element binding all four images together. Generally speaking, where *The Chelsea Girls* remains (despite of its 1960s' commercial success) a film that is resolutely experimental in its presentation, *Time Code* is one that adapts its new modes to the exigencies of the narrative feature film.[4]

The composition (formal narrative) of *Time Code* can be further understood by relating it to Christian Metz's study of syntagmatic relationships. Specifically, in his *Grande Syntagmatique* of cinema, Metz lays down a model for describing eight types of autonomous segments (Metz 1974: 119–33). The first of these types – derived from an operative distinction between those segments made up of more than one minimum segment (that is, more than one shot) and those made up of only one minimum segment – is the sequence-shot, a whole scene in a single shot (Heath 1981: 111). *Time Code* is evidently made up of this type of autonomous segment: that is, it consists of four (in number) ninety-three-minute sequence-shots. But things are complicated by the arrangement – the simultaneous presentation or *montage* – of these shot-sequences. Their placement in a grid (and their chronological relation) in fact suggests that (at least) two other types of segment identified by Metz are applicable here. More specifically, where *The Chelsea Girls* assumes no temporal relation between its various segments (something assured by the arbitrary coupling of shot-sequences), *Time Code* follows the operative distinction between achronological and chronological syntagms. That is, by turning upon a distinction between (chronological) syntagms that assume temporal simultaneity and those that assume temporal sequentiality, *Time Code* suggests itself as a variant of Metz's alternating syntagm. In this type of narrative unit, the film 'presents in alternation two or more series of events, each series offering a temporal sequence but the series together offering a simultaneity' (ibid. p. 113). Things get complicated here because this type of alternating syntagm is evidently meant for the successive presentation of simultaneous events (most obviously the case of cross-cutting pioneered by a film such as *Rescued by Rover* [1905]), but the split screen of *Time Code* (and also Bazin's account of deep-focus cinematography) enables the simultaneous presentation of simultaneous events (Bordwell 1985: 77).

This relationship is not immediately evident in a film such as *Time Code* because it initially unfolds (like *The Chelsea Girls*) as a series of (apparently) unrelated temporal episodes. As stated previously, the action begins in the top right-hand window (#1). This quadrant is occupied by a woman, Emma Green, wife of Red Mullet film producer Alex Green (the latter tends to occupy the lower – mostly bottom right – window/s). In this opening, Emma tells another woman, her therapist (it seems), about a dream: of a wound, a tiny cut, which bleeds and won't stop . . . After a couple of minutes, the top left-hand window (#2) opens up to show Lauren Hathaway descending a set of sweeping stairs of a large house. She strides purposefully to a car belonging to her lover, Rose, and deflates the front left-hand tyre . . . After about a minute, the bottom left window (#3) opens to reveal a bank of surveillance video-monitors. The camera then pulls back to show a security guard, who proceeds to move around an office building . . . Finally, after about four minutes of viewing time, the bottom right-hand window (#4) comes to life, picking up the movements of a man, Quentin, crossing a busy street to enter an office building. He approaches the reception desk of Red Mullet productions and – at this point – two windows (#3 and #4) converge upon the same space and action. This coincidence of windows is the first of a number of audio-visual cues – including the earthquake that shakes all four windows at the nine-minute mark, and the mobile-phone conversation between windows #2 and #3 at the twelve-minute mark – that enable the viewer to process the four sequence-shots as temporally simultaneous episodes.

The realisation that the four windows of *Time Code* present a series of simultaneous and overlapping dramatic actions helps define it as a sprawling soap opera, one of sexual jealousy and infidelity. The same – generically speaking – could be said of *The Chelsea Girls*, a film sometimes described as a ruinous remake of *Grand Hotel* (1932), or – to take an example nearer to Warhol's proclaimed taste – its direct remake, *The V.I.P.s* (1963). In the later 1960s and 1970s, Warhol's interest in both overwrought performances *and* in street-life realism seems to have been taken up by early practitioners of videotape as a way to demonstrate the limitations (formal and ideological) of conventional broadcast television. These direct-video groups embraced the shaky fluidity and real-time monitoring of the portapak. They conceded the difference in quality between their productions and those of the networks, and strove (like the *vérité* film-makers before and the DV realists after) to invent a new style that sought to impress through its ability to get to the 'real' issues of everyday life. More than this, direct video aimed not only to challenge the conventions of television and its genres – the soap opera, the domestic comedy – but to expand (as Warhol had) the limits of the television screen. Dierdre Boyle, for instance, remembers the example of Video Free America's *The Continuing Story of Carel and Ferd* (1972), a 'Warholesque' installation, advertised as an 'underground video documentary soap opera – a closed-circuit, multiple-image, videotape novel about pornography, sexual identities, the institution of marriage, and the effect of living too close to an electronic medium' (Boyle 1990: 54). While Boyle goes on to note that these multichannel video installations (of the expanded cinema-type) quickly became the province of the museum and the gallery, she notes, too, that practitioners of 'direct' community video quickly found a new outlet in the emerging public channels of cable television (ibid. p. 55). Boyle indicates the ongoing exchange between guerrilla and establishment television by way of the example of forty hours of *vérité* video entitled *The Police Tapes* (1976). Structured around nightly patrols with police officers of the 44th Precinct in the South Bronx, *The Police Tapes* was produced for public television but later edited down to an hour-long version for the ABC network. Further, *The Police Tapes* became something of a template for the ABC television series, *Hill Street Blues* (1981–87), and a precursor to the 'reality TV' of *Cops* (1989–) and (one might add) Kevin Rubio's internet fan-film, *Troops* (ibid. pp. 58–9).

While the explosive 'Pope Ondine Story' and sadistic 'The Queen of China (Hanoi Hannah)' reels of *The Chelsea Girls* link Warhol's film to *Time Code* as soap opera, another approach would suggest reality television and Webcams as their common ground. Manovich takes exactly this approach to *Time Code*, stating that its four-camera grid and real-time coverage of events are typical of the video-surveillance set-up that informs reality television (Manovich 2002: 216–17). A similar lineage can be drawn through *The Chelsea Girls*, where Warhol's early (minimalist) interest in the most private and often banal of actions (sleeping, eating, copulating) finds its way into reels such as

'Nico Crying' and 'Eric Says All'. Mark Sinker takes up this idea to locate the appeal of *The Chelsea Girls*s not only in its soap-opera-like domesticity – its yearning to be 'a species of safe family life' – but in 'a zone of alternative glamour [that] grounded its authenticity in tedium, where celebrity intersect[ed] with the radically mundane' (Sinker 1999: 28). This, together with *The Chelsea Girls*' interest in an intimate staging (or performance) of the self, and investment in exhibitionism-voyeurism, leads Singer to draw a connection through to *JenniCAM*, one of the first instances of the Webcam phenomenon. Dating back to 1997, *JenniCAM* came about when Pennsylvania student Jennifer Kaye Ringley placed a webcam on top of her Mac monitor and set it to capture 'action' in whichever part of her apartment it faced. A picture was posted on Jenni's website and was updated every three minutes. As Singer notes, occasionally Jennifer would (like Warhol's subjects) act up for the camera but mostly it recorded the mysterious beauty and/as boredom of Jennifer sleeping, Jennifer absorbed in computer work, or (often) Jennifer not there at all (ibid. p. 28). The more sensational aspect, and commercial application, of *JenniCAM* extend into such sites as *VoyeurDorm*, an eight-camera feed coming out of 'a Florida house equipped with 48 webcams where seven diversely attractive "students" live out their lives on screen 24 hours a day' (Stables 2000: 10).

The multiple-camera, surveillance set-up of *VoyeurDorm* not only leads to the reality television of the *Big Brother* households, but eventually loops back to *Time Code*, and its allegiance with the conventions of computer culture and *telecommunications*' technologies. Manovich draws out this type of connection, describing *Big Brother* as an unscripted registration of the interaction of the programme's participants and their environment *but* (because it is not presented as a continuous twenty-four-hours per day recording) never simply 'a window into life as it happens' (Manovich 2002: 214). Indeed, Manovich argues that a reality television programme such as *Big Brother*, 'follows well-established conventions of film and television fictions: a [goal-oriented] narrative that unfolds within a specified period of time and results in a well-defined conclusion [eviction of all but one of the house guests]'. In a similar way, *Time Code* seems to embrace the telecommunications technologies of reality television, forgoing any tight scripting, adopting the typical multiple-camera set-up of surveillance video, and recording its episodes in real time, 'rather than the artificially compressed time of traditional film narrative' (ibid. p. 214). But, as Manovich notes, 'the narrative that unfolds during [the film's] time period is highly artificial':

> *Time Code* is not exactly bare-bones telecommunication. It is not just a real-time recording of whatever happens to be in front of the cameras . . . We may think of [*Time Code*] as an edited surveillance video: the parts

where nothing happens have been taken out; the parts with action in them have been preserved . . . It is more accurate to think of *Time Code* as a conventional film that adopts visual and spatial strategies of video surveillance . . . while following the traditional dramatic conventions of narrative construction. (ibid. pp. 214–15)

While soap opera and reality television suggest likely kinships between *The Chelsea Girls* and *Time Code*, the conventional dramatic action of the latter suggests a further (and different) connection: namely, the multiple, overlapping format of a film such as Paul Thomas Anderson's *Magnolia* (1999). Like *Time Code*, *Magnolia* is a narrative that purportedly derives its integrity (and inspiration) from a musical composition: Anderson claims that it is patterned on The Beatles' song, 'A Day in the Life'. In addition to this, *Magnolia* brings together no fewer that twelve principal characters in a (melodramatic) narrative of surrogate families that unfolds across a running time (189 minutes) not dissimilar to that of *The Chelsea Girls*. *Magnolia* is, in turn, a film that is often seen as a homage to the masterful orchestration of characters and intertwined narrative strands found in the films of Robert Altman, most famously the sprawling ensemble of his classic *Nashville* (1975). Near the time of its release, *Nashville* was described as 'a brilliant modification [of] the multi-star, mounting doom, intersecting-plot format' of 1970s' disaster movies such as *Airport* (1970), *The Towering Inferno* (1974) and *Earthquake* (1974) (Hoberman 1985: 35). At one level, the 'disaster' of *Nashville* (set during a George Wallace-type pre-Presidential campaign and in the wake of Vietnam and Watergate) is America itself. But at another level, Altman lifts from the contemporaneous cycle of disaster movies the narrative device of a natural cataclysm (an earthquake), a plot mechanism he returns to in the finale of his rambling collection of Raymond Carver stories, *Short Cuts* (1993). *Magnolia*, too, takes up the (near) biblical dimension of cataclysm, uniting its San Fernando Valley residents not only (as in the case of *Nashville*) through music (specifically, their simultaneous singing of Aimee Mann's 'Wise Up') but via the film's inexplicable and torrential downpour of frogs. *Time Code* is linked, then, to this cycle, not only by its multiple and intersecting plots and the microphone techniques pioneered by Altman (Brooks 2000: 37), but (as previously noted) by its staging of four minor earthquakes.

Perhaps the most significant – in terms of its signalling and co-ordination of narrative events – is *Time Code*'s fourth and final earthquake. It arrives about twenty minutes before the end of the film, just as *enfant terrible* director Ana Pauls and boyfriend Joey Z are about to pitch their concept to the producers at Red Mullet. This is also the moment of *Time Code* in which the exchange and convergence between windows – much assisted by the amplification of salient audio information – is at its greatest. Following the tremor (itself a type of underscoring), Joey Z's music draws attention to the bottom left window and, within about a minute of screen time, the fourth camera (bottom right) has also converged upon the Red Mullet conference room. For the next ten minutes the sound-track is dominated by diaegetic sound from the bottom windows (#3 and #4). And – as Ana and Joey Z sing, rap and huckster their way through their routine – these bottom windows go through a series of reframings that typically settle – in conventional shot/reverse-shot pattern – on Ana performing on the left-hand side (#3) and Alex (or another producer) looking on from the right (#4). This culminates (as previously stated) in Alex's blunt assessment of Ana's monologue ('pretentious crap'), and then a momentary shift of sound focus to the upper windows. Joey Z's music quickly takes over again, underscoring the scenes of confrontation and seduction (in the upper windows) before a non-diaegetic pulse takes over and leads to the film's final minutes in which the spurned lover, Lauren, enters Red Mullet and turns a gun upon Alex. At this point, *Time Code* seems to owe something to the ending of the Paul Morrissey-directed *Andy Warhol's Heat* (1972), a reworking of *Sunset Boulevard* (which, coincidentally, is the location of the Red Mullet offices). The larger point, though, is that Ana's insistence that we embrace new media to 'go beyond the paradigm of collage' is mediated by an assemblage of images – an ordering of the flow of images – that leads to the 'intelligibility' of *Time Code* but limits the potentiality of its 'free play', its experimentation (Heath 1978: 36).

In a recent response to Manovich's account of digital imaging and visual culture, Janet Harbord argues that 'there is no separate object that can be designated "digital" film, but that digitalisation exists within and across the activities of production, distribution and consumption' (Harbord 2002: 138). More particularly, and as this chapter argues, an account of a recent DV-realism film such as *Time Code* requires that it be 'understood through the historical and cultural paradigms that pre-exist it, and that to an extent determine its shape' (ibid. p. 140). This chapter has sought to demonstrate the affinity *Time Code* shares with the earlier mainstream and avant-garde practices of audio-visions like *JenniCAM*, *Big Brother*, *Magnolia* and especially *The Chelsea Girls*. But, as Jonathan Rosenbaum has noted, any attempt to connect *Time Code* to a history of visual culture – something which Ana Paul's pitch requires that we do – might serve only to emphasise that which is shallow about the film: namely, '[its] dressing up of old content with new technology' (Rosenbaum 2000). It might be the case that the opportunity – the potential – of digital video in the example of *Time Code* is ultimately limited by a further pitch: a commercial imperative that *Time Code* be sold as a revolution in film-making, as 'a story that could only be told in four dimensions'. This said, the (new) aesthetic possibilities and ways of digitally 'recording reality' – history and memory, continuity and flux – might better be sensed (intuited) in something like *Russian Ark* (2002). Nonetheless, *Time Code*'s experiment – four cameras, one take, no edits, real time – belongs to the ongoing exchange between terms of duality: art and industry, mainstream and avant-garde, old and new.

Notes

1. For the conventional pairing of reels for the projection of *The Chelsea Girls*, see the illustration in *The Andy Warhol Museum* (1994: 136).
2. The Columbia/Tristar (region 1) DVD edition of *Time Code* does not allow for any manipulation of the image track, but features an interactive audio mix that enables the viewer to focus upon the audio in any one of the four windows.
3. See '*Time Code*: Digital Storytelling in 4/4 Time' (2000).
4. Closer to *The Chelsea Girls* (than *Time Code*) in this respect is *D-Day*, the Dogma 95 Danish television production. *D-Day* consisted of four seventy-minute digital-video recordings shot simultaneously in Copenhagen in real time and broadcast from 11.30 p.m. on New Year's Eve, 1999 to 12.40 a.m. on New Year's Day, 2000. The tapes went to air unedited on four different Danish television channels and in a split view of all four tapes on further channels. For an extended discussion, see Roberts (2003).

12. WHAT WAS THE NEO-UNDERGROUND AND WHAT WASN'T: A FIRST RECONSIDERATION OF HARMONY KORINE

Benjamin Halligan

A consolidation of the predominant characteristics of recent Hollywood filmmaking occurred in the success of two late-1990s' box-office hits: *Titanic* (1997), the zenith of the film-as-experience strain of 'High Concept' North American cinema, and *American Beauty* (1999), acclaimed for the originality of its approach to its material. The films came across as experiences for the taking, labelled as such for the multiplexes, 'must-see' 'water cooler' talking points. In this respect, the latter was 'art as entertainment', the former, 'entertainment as entertainment', a difference of degree between the two but the denominator is common and they both trailed Academy Awards in their wake.

Walter Benjamin once observed a phenomenon that seems, from this close distance at least, especially applicable to the 'art as entertainment' sensibility. The application is necessary because *American Beauty* seems to exemplify, and perhaps anticipates, a contemporary trend in North American filmmaking:

> ... we are confronted with the fact ... that the bourgeois apparatus of production and publication is capable of assimilating, indeed of propagating, an astonishing amount of revolutionary themes without

ever seriously putting into question its own continued existence or that of the class which owns it. In any case this remains true so long as it is supplied by hacks, albeit revolutionary hacks ... I further maintain that an appreciable part of so-called left-wing literature had no other social function than that of continually extracting new effects or sensations from this situation for the public's entertainment. (Benjamin 1973: 94–5)

The assimilating nature of *American Beauty* occurs in the successful translation of the style and preoccupations of an 'underground' into box-office material. The originality of *American Beauty* was nothing so much as a repackaging of aspects of 1990s' 'independent' American film-making (of the commercial fringe), as exemplified in, say, the films of David Lynch and Abel Ferrara. In this case, the bourgeois apparatus of production was the burgeoning Disney-to-be, DreamWorks SKG. The assimilation was in the nature of the 'Bodysnatchers': the film became an acceptable version of the same thing.

In terms of the matter of degree (art as entertainment and entertainment as entertainment), the 'art' sensibility manifested itself in *American Beauty* through incidentals and inessentials, elevated to the level of the all important. This is true of both individual moments – the bag blowing in the wind, for example, itself extracted from Antonioni's *Il Deserto Rosso* (*Red Desert*) (1964) – and underlies the nature of the narrative as a whole (the generically dysfunctional family unit within the milieu of 1950s-like American suburbia, *à la* Lynch). The experiential aspects of the narrative, that function to immerse the viewer in the pervasive superficiality of the generic suburb, give way to a sense of a critical distance from the film – a distance filled with irony, reflexive pastiche, 'knowingness'. This creates an environment in which the expected can itself expect to be usurped, and the audience warned not to feel alienated should this occur. Thus the film offers a sense of 'difference' within the familiar. This critical distance, in relation to art as entertainment, recalls Brecht's reading of film in the 1930s: the smoke-screen of 'art' obscures that which, in this case, posits a very tight spectrum of entirely passive expressions of 'rebellion'.

The nature of the assimilation, which received its final blessing in the success of the film, indicates the weaknesses and uncertainties of Hollywood film-making in the 1990s (an inability to understand or control audiences, or the 'digital revolution'). This translated, seemingly, into a knee-jerk plundering of left-of-field film-making in order to appeal to the more wayward audiences that the Hollywood industry felt were endangered. Such a move is a shoring up of market futures. This sense of endangerment had coloured Hollywood strategies since the near breakdown of the 1992 GATT trade talks with the European Union and the shift, in the late 1990s, to the majority of box-office returns for Hollywood films being reaped from outside North

America. To be crude about the perceived marketing strategy: since the non-Americans were noted sometimes to prefer art-as-entertainment over entertainment-as-entertainment – desired the 'difference' – then that element must also be addressed, repackaged and assimilated, and so find its position within the products of Hollywood. It becomes a matter of articulating a foreign language with a familiar 'filmic language', of placing the foreign language within a 'vernacular' system so that the foreignness becomes ultimately little more than a nuance, a quirk.

When even 'difference' becomes a commodity, then a certain equilibrium has been achieved. As in the Czech film industry under Soviet reorganisation in the early 1970s, all dissidence is annihilated: those responsible for it are either silenced or exiled, and the films and their nature either banned, appropriated or regurgitated. The North American film of the late 1990s fell into two camps: the monumental block-buster, of which *Titanic* was the most visible, the heart of a nexus of global products, or the film of 'difference' that then seemed to have been called into existence in order to mop up all audiences who did not buy tickets for the doomed ocean liner. All films caught in between are pushed towards one of the two poles, so that there can be no 'in between', merely binary oppositionism: a film was the same (entertainment-as-entertainment) or not the same (art-as-entertainment), and not to be the same was to come to be still the same; not being the same had been co-opted. And this co-opting occurs in the way in which those 'not the same' are products that aspire to must-have status: bought up by subsidiaries of major studios, forcefully pushed at festivals. So it was noted at the time that the success of *Titanic* heralded bad news for all smaller films – those that were formally 'in between'. This constitutes the eradication of 'real' difference through the *imposition* of a vernacular system; a reorganisation by stealth (artistically, the Czechs had it relatively easy). In Miramax's famed post-production re-edits and rewrites, this imposition can be seen in action.

The wider impulse for (and, alas, a desire for) assimilation can also be seen in the general trends of film-making of the formerly 'underground' or semi-underground American *auteurs* in the 1990s. At worst, they recast themselves as 'hacks, albeit revolutionary hacks' (particularly in the light of the challenging and newly re-emergent Russian, European and New Asian film scenes of the 1990s). But this shift to the mainstream by the Coens, Soderbergh, Jarmusch, Van Sant, Larry Clark, Lynch and others was tempered by one 'slight return': Harmony Korine, in his films *Gummo* and *julien donkey-boy*, went defiantly in the other direction. *Gummo* met with widespread criticism and condemnation upon its release; many felt Korine exploited the dispossessed that he filmed – offering a questionably voyeuristic experience masquerading as an exposé. This sentiment was shared by the right and the left; David Walsh termed it 'a libel against mankind' (Walsh 1997b).

In this context of a looming, bloated Hollywood omniculture, 'low concept' would be an applicable term for Korine. *Gummo* itself inverts the norm of the nexus of global products: rather than the television spin-off from the film, it comes across as a film spin-off from television (specifically, *The Jerry Springer Show* [1991-current]; indeed, one of the principal characters of *Gummo* was taken from the paint-sniffing segment of a drug prevention episode of *The Sally Jessy Raphael Show* [1985–2002]). The film has a self-contained still-born marketing campaign: a promise of pandering to the racist stereotype of the white-trash freak show, a Heavy Metal sound-track, outrage upon outrage piled up. Barely have the words New Line and Time-Warner first appeared on the screen than a torrent of juvenile obscenities fades in on the sound-track. On the face of it, the film seems tailor-made for the bored browser in the video shop: a spectacle that will offend; packaged outrage as entertainment.

This difference from the shift to the mainstream, in *Gummo*, can be understood in terms of the apparent aspirations. While the semi-underground *auteurs* of the 1990s looked to models of (troubled liberal) film-making, such as neo-*noir* and the 'issue' film, Korine looked to one of the idiosyncratic *auteurs* of the New German Cinema: Werner Herzog. Korine claimed to have fallen under the influence of Herzog as a Californian teenager of the 1980s and that Herzog, whose work represented an absolute foreignness to him – specifically in *Auch Zwerge Haben Klein Angefangen* (*Even Dwarfs Started Small* [1970]), a kind of cinematic 'abduction by UFO' experience, wrecked any evolving sense of what a film should or should not be. Herzog's influence informed *Gummo*, and Herzog himself was present in *julien donkey-boy*. There was no Scorsese, Coppola or Penn lineage for Korine. Rather, he looked to the monumental statements of Herzog and the New German Cinema: unwieldy metaphors, ambiguous relevance, insane propositions. Korine's model was the lack of a model particular to Herzog's unique vision and methodology. Herzog's 1970s' work had been characterised by allegories that refused to reveal the *actualité* of which they spoke: the vague sense of humanity against nature, or God, as parables of civilisation and capitalism (*Fitzcarraldo* [1982]), of revolution as a pointless and doomed activity (*Even Dwarfs Started Small*), of characters newly adrift in an alien landscape (the Bruno S films: *Jeder Für Sich Und Gott Gegen Alle* [*Every Man for Himself and God Against All*] [1974] and *Stroszek* [1977]). For the *auteur*s of the New German Cinema, because any human truth or 'meaning' fell short of historical fact, meaning itself was to be resisted in the art that invariably reflected recent West German history. It is Herzog's 'unstuck' metaphor – the grand gesture as a grand gesture, insanity as the only proof of life – that informs Korine's methodology. Herzog returned the compliment too, in a suitably idiosyncratic manner. In discussing *Gummo* with Korine, he commented:

> What I like about *Gummo* are the details that one might not notice at first. There's the scene where the kid in the bathtub drops his chocolate bar into the dirty water and just behind him there's a piece of fried bacon stuck to the wall with Scotch tape. This is the entertainment of the future. (Herzog 1997)

To which Korine replied, revelling in his difference (now authenticated by the master of difference): 'It's the greatest entertainment. Seriously, all I want to see is pieces of fried bacon taped on walls, because most films just don't do that.' (Herzog 1997) The authentification of 'difference' for *julien donkey-boy* came via a Dogma 95 certificate: Korine as a member of the brotherhood of Danish film punks. And for *Above the Below* (2003), from the discomfort of the onlookers at a man in a perspex box, suspended above them, starving.

Structurally and aesthetically, Korine's films exist beyond any familiar 'art-house' or underground category. They talk in a foreign language in these respects. In terms of the expected political critique, Korine invites and then rejects a liberal agenda with his no-hope sketches of the wretched underbelly of American life. On one level he articulates the neo-realist's question in terms of the type of imagery he presents – 'Why and how has this come to pass?' But the crux of his vision lionises the marginal along with the disregarded icons of late twentieth-century culture, reinventing them into an ironic form of poetic realism (finding meaning in the meaningless), vastly at odds with his neo-realist elements. His frame of reference recalls the blunt ironies of Jeff Koons's 'instant art' approach to the refuse of consumer culture (that is, that there is no refuse but rather an endless cycle of a consumption of the defecation). Indeed, Korine was first encountered in the Koons milieu, art and fashion magazines, rather than brought out as a precocious festival *cinéphile*.

Korine constantly hones in on the most superficial aspects of existence – a kind of anti-existentialism. He summons up the ambience of the American mid-west Heavy Metal life-styles in *Gummo*: the ridiculous posturing of the music overlapping the juvenile chants of the opening credits ('Peanut-butter-mother-fucker'), reflected in the style of the on-screen credits (1970s' album-cover Gothic). Korine bleeds the sense of authenticity from expressions of difference in these, his self-effacing début moments. His characters are defined by the commercial categories of difference that are on offer – they are products of the cultural assimilation of the supposed left-of-field. In this instance, the whole recalls the 'Judas Priest suicide' of the late 1980s – commodity-fetishised nihilism authenticated by an actual desire for annihilation:

> Sparks, Nevada – After James Vance demolished his face with a sawed-off shotgun at a church playground, he rode his bicycle around town shocking people with his grotesque disfigurement. Plastic surgeons had

been able to restore his ability to eat and breathe, but were not able to restore his smooth, youthful face. James' physical deformity stunned the town, but not as much as the message he later delivered: Heavy metal music drove him and his closest friend to strike a suicide pact, one that only James survived. "I believe that alcohol and heavy metal music, such as Judas Priest, led us or even 'mesmerized' us into believing that the answer to 'life was death,'" James wrote to his best friend's mother in 1986, quoting some of the album's lyrics. James, depressed and addicted to pain medications after the shooting, died last year in the psychiatric unit of the Washoe Medical Center from drugs and complications from his numerous surgeries. (Cooper 1989)

In the horizon of the inauthentic, actual difference is not so easily assimilated since its authenticity becomes all the more apparent.

Korine does not speak of the locale (the vantage point of the liberal agenda) but speaks the locale. He allows the nihilistic vision of the mid-west to mesmerise him – he 'opens himself up' to the influences, enters into the milieu, fashions an expression of it, not from it. He even engages in some grotesque disfigurement himself. In placing the film in a submissive position to the world around it, Korine finds a place in the freak-show parade of white trash. This cameo has neither the flourish of the Hitchcock 'signature' nor the effect of Welles's presence (which often reassembled the film around a sense of the *auteur* as present). Korine, as 'Boy on Couch', is utterly superfluous. He presents himself as a drooling, drunken supergeek, trying to seduce a streetwise gay Jewish African-American person of restricted growth, Midget. His voice is whispery and cracked, he slurs his way through stories of debasement, of being sexually abused as a child, and immerses himself in cheap beer. The sequence jump-cuts into, seemingly, alternative takes, creating the impression of an improvised scene with interchangeable anecdotes and voiding a suspension of disbelief. It is not as if Korine is presenting a fictional character that functions in any discernible way. It is not as if Korine is not himself noted in the process. (Indeed, critics of the film – such as David Prothero – tended to cast this scene as the 'final straw' in terms of evidence of exploitation.) Rather, the moment communicated a sense of Korine entering into the situation of the film, that his role is equally behind, and in front of, the camera (the final affirmation of the loss of the liberal vantage point). Both positions are engulfed by the world of the film and both are exercises in self-debasement. This is undoubtedly the lesson of Herzog. And, in the same exploratory manner, in interview, Korine noted the problems of such a methodology:

> As far as production design went, it was about taking things away to make it cleaner. At times the crew would refuse to film in those

conditions. We had to buy them those white suits like people wear in a nuclear fallout. I got angry with them because I thought they were pussies. I mean, all we're talking about is bugs and a disgusting rotty smell. I couldn't understand why they had no guts. I was like, "Think about what we have access to", but I guess most of them didn't really give a shit. But Jean Yves Escoffier, the cinematographer, was fearless. When the others were wearing their toxic outfits, he and I wore speedos and flip-flops just to piss them off. (Herzog 1997)

True or not, this represents the guiding notion of aspiring to a relatively unusual vantage point for the film – more that of reportage or documentary than underground. Yet even when such a notion is not directly verified by the aesthetic (a striking impressionistic equivalent of the milieu – anything other than objective framing), the aesthetic, in its difference, still speaks of the exploratory methodology.

The aesthetic stylisation cannot be read as a subjective construction. Rather, the stylisation seems, by default, to originate in the collective mind-state of the protagonists, themselves sometimes little more than colour in the wider milieu of the film. The diaegetic reason for the nature of the stylisation is unclear. It cannot be accounted for as point-of-view subjective stylisation (psychological realism) because the undigested mass of characters prevents the viewer from latching on to any one as the guide through the world of *Gummo*. Nor do schools of representation account for the approach, since Korine continually falls foul of the suggested neo-realist / ethnographic methodology with his aesthetic 'lapses' into bursts of impressionism. As with the continually differing textures of image, drawn from celluloid and video, the film has no constant. Rather, in entering into the milieu, the film seeks to reproduce such an experience in a mimetic fashion – modernism written over classicism.

In the first few moments of the film, Korine's technique is to de-establish information rather than to present the usual Establishing Shots. The implicit objectivity of the classical approach (which also allows the viewer to find a distance from the world by looking *on* it rather than having to look *with* it, from its own perspective) gives way to a classicism that is apparent at base but 'eroded' by elements associated with the world of the film. Here the film speaks *of* the mind-state more than a straightforward presentation of it. So Korine allows the characters to talk in voice-over, as if to guide the viewer through the world of the film (the camera as the 'psychic medium'). But the voice-overs then determine the course of the film – hijacking the narrative – and the film latches on to the minds rather than the characters in these voice-overs; we hear their ruminations rather than explanations, their fantasies rather than realities. There is plenty of evidence of addled mind-states throughout the film (from, for example, glue sniffing) but Eddie, when he talks of his 'attention disorder . . . [which] makes it hard to concentrate', seems to voice the central *raison d'être* of the flitting, *non-sequitur* structure of the film.

In the first instance, the film finds itself unable to 'concentrate' on any developing, linear narrative. Before Korine's appearance, the film's structure seems only to be concerned with clocking up sequences of ever greater degradation. It indicates an inability to focus on one line of narrative, or even to differentiate narratives as actual or imagined. Two skinhead brothers, body-building Jehovah's Witnesses, who playfully and brutally engage in bare-knuckle boxing in their kitchen, are present in the film only to illustrate a seemingly inconsequential voice-over anecdote. This thus tears the film away from a sense of the encountered reality, breaking a spatial and temporal unity or consistency to the narrative development. This boxing sequence is shot as fly-on-the-wall documentary; the brothers are defiantly real and present in terms of aesthetic presentation (albeit, disconcertingly, shot with a fish-eye lens). There is, therefore, a stylistic 'lie' in the way in which the film refuses to codify moments that seem not to exist other than in the imagination. Other moments lapse into the narrative codes or generic types of film-making: a coming-of-age narrative (signalled with voice-overs), Godard-like performing/ improvising for the camera; a neo-realist-like investigation of the world of the film; abstract video art; and even, at one point, a cable dating channel (an albino waitress talks about Patrick Swayze as the ideal man and dances around her car).

Such a narrative 'attention deficiency', combined with an aesthetic impressionism, make for the opening assault of the film: degraded video images, rhythmlessly cut together, detail 'the great tornado' hitting Xenia, Ohio. Over-exposed and differing speeds of film meld with the camcorder-like footage to render the whole stylistically timeless: neither 8 mm experimentation from the 1960s nor scratch video from the 1980s. This very precise event, the tornado, is decontextualised from any sense of a recent history. An unintelligible voice-over narrates a bizarre commentary, fading into a series of unreal, echoed aural digressions (a ditty with the refrain 'pussy'). The furious black mass of the tornado itself is briefly glimpsed with a shot of a tattooed crucifix, suggesting the event as a kind of biblical plague, an act of God. The tornado at the opening of the film recalls *The Wizard of Oz* (1939), another journey through an alien/familiar landscape. But such intertextual suggestions are themselves only momentarily thrown up in the miasma of the rapid bursts of montage, punctuated by glimpses of self-consciously outrageous imagery (a dog impaled on a TV aerial, for example). All this, and *Supergirl* (1984) too, is touched upon in the opening narration:

> Xenia, Ohio. A couple of years ago, a tornado hit this place. It killed the people left and right. Houses were split open, and you could see necklaces hanging from branches of trees. Dogs died. Cats died. I saw a girl fly through the sky . . . and I looked up her skirt.

The film, as it begins proper (in 35 mm definition), contrasts boldly with the frantic montage of the opening sequence; this is the calm after the storm (so calm that time seems to have stopped altogether). The pre-pubescent 'Bunny Boy' kicks his heels on a motorway flyover. Cars and lorries shoot by below, emphasising the nowhere-ness of the location. He is topless, his torso bruised and dirty, teeth cracked, fingers tattooed, shivering in the rain. He smokes like a pro and pisses and spits on the traffic below, all the time sporting a pair of filthy pink bunny ears. He kicks at the ripped bridge fencing (of the type installed to prevent would-be suicides). It is a full gamut of behavioural traits, as if from a Paul Morrissey film – and the sequence has all the grimy oppressiveness of *Flesh*, *Trash* and *Heat* (1968, 1970, 1972 respectively). But, whereas Morrissey's elegantly wasted low lifes seemed to follow a certain code of behaviour (as did the protagonists of the Korine-scripted *Kids*: updated Morrissey, a cut-price hedonistic odyssey of drugs and fucking, AIDs no objection), and hence their romanticism, *Gummo*'s occupants only drift. Not even a punk ethos (referenced via the iconic casting of Linda Manz, from Hopper's *Out of the Blue* [1980]) is apparent: the forty speaking parts in the film are united in a sump of complacency rather than rebellion – marginalisation rather than drop-out, glue rather than dope. The shammed Satanism of the snatches from Slayer videos adds another level of superficiality to the 'bad' behaviour – not even 'evil' is a constituency beyond commodification. No one does anything for any particular reason. And this crushing inertia pervades the calmness of the opening sequence.

Nor does the photographic imagery itself offer a sense of narrative (like Nan Goldin's or Larry Clark's photographs of comparable characters and situations) or suggest fragments ripped from a wider narrative (like, say, the Death Row photographs of Oliviero Toscani). Korine's moving images simply move the images away from narrative, leaving them stripped of any sense of a socio-historical resonance. And with that goes any sense of an imperative as to why Korine should show us such imagery. At times, heads are optically fogged (as if those filmed had not signed release forms), just as the eyes are scrubbed out from the Polaroids detailing sex parties. The whole is bathed in a urine yellow (achieved with banks of fluorescent Kino-Flos rather than standard lighting), broken by the fuzzy green globules that bubble to the surface of the distressed video images.

This approach manifests itself rapidly as the film 'moves on': cat drowning; teenage prostitution (interrupted by a lump found in her breast); cat hunting with pop guns – the protagonists on a couple of *ET* (1982) BMXs. Tummler is introduced with a montage of yellowed photos. He has the look of a potential mass murderer: gaunt, prematurely thinning hair, 'downright evil' as Solomon approvingly describes him. Tummler and Solomon spend the few dollars they make from selling dead cats (for human consumption) on strawberry milkshakes, glue, and sex with a Down's syndrome prostitute, pimped by her macho-sporty brother. Meanwhile, two platinum-blonde sisters use tape to expand their nipples and Bunny Boy re-enacts a Disney cartoon in a scrapyard: two small children in cowboy hats, smashing car windows, wielding toy guns, pretend to gun him down and scream 'fucking rabbit' as Bunny Boy, unmoved, lies on the filthy ground. It is a vision of rural squalor akin to Godard's *Le Weekend* (1967): a refuse-scape, the future as built from the junk of the past. Korine invites the viewer to read the idiosyncratic nuances as absurdist (the clown-like masks; the dialogue), situationist (the tornado as a perception-altering event) and, in a way, experiential in the manner of *Titanic*: both *Gummo* and *Titanic* are spectacles of destruction, served up by major studios.

Korine shoots in tableau (the two sisters, jumping up and down on an attic bed, for example) and in a frontal, 'naïve' way – often characters are introduced in such a fashion, approaching the camera. This composition recalls Pasolini's neo-realism in *Accattone* (1961), as does the ethnographic aesthetic component of the film, a constantly changing array of faces, predominantly drawn from non-actors. Llittle specific information can be read into the succession of faces, however; nor does the film document Xenia in much detail (it was, in fact, shot in Nashville). A collage approach alternates between image and sound: snatches of dialogue in voice-over – anecdotes, observations, incoherent drones that defy contextualisation in terms of a sense of an evolving narrative or even, sometimes, in terms of just who is speaking. It is a jigsaw: the viewer is invited to examine pieces at random so as to visualise the entire picture.

This technique is one long negation, an evolving denial of information for the viewer. The film is even named as such: Gummo was the Marx brother who 'didn't make it' and was forgotten, was negated. As the nature of Korine's own presence in the film suggests (and, in a more roundabout manner, the opening credits, or the Slayer footage) this negation is connected to the elimination of a vantage point that would allow a distance from the world of the film. In its place, a process of mimesis occurs. Korine 'writes' in a language that is not his own, one that is drawn from the space between classical reconstruction of the world of the film and a subjective-documentary approach to the world of the film. A kind of mimetic visual slang evolves. The vast lacunas of the film exist because of the fragmented nature of this language, the fragmenting attention-deficiency impressionism. It is an incomplete or broken vernacular system; a foreignness that cannot be reduced to a nuance or a quirk. Yet, in the absence of anything else, this mimetic visual slang constitutes the *mise-en-scène* in its entirety. In this way, it is ultimately the vernacular system that speaks of the place, a generic American mid-west. The mind-state is presented as evidence for the existence of the location rather than the location and milieu as reasons for the mind-state. Korine delivers a (literal) psycho-geographical portrait: a collective concentration that is continually disrupted by the inability to pull fragments and impressions together into a cohesive whole. This speaks of the lack of a non-befuddled perception, the lack of any ethical or, indeed, even motivational codes of behaviour. Korine's young protagonists may come across as latter-day equivalents of the child anti-hero of Rossellini's *Germania Anno Zero* (*Germany Year Zero*) (1947), wandering lost in a devastated landscape but, in reality, Korine's vision details the psychological or spiritual devastation of the characters rather than just showcasing a locale as defined by social problems and as defining those who dwell within it.

This is achieved via the structurelessness. Against this deadened and information-free approach, which works to eliminate a sense of depth to the world of the film, Korine fashions the material into moments – 'beats' – that break through the collaged, impressionistic aesthetic and stand out from the free-form structure. They glide in on the woozy, drugged-up ambience of the aesthetic: are they profound, or merely crass? These moments constitute the lasting impressions once the film has finished (or, rather, 'wound down'). They can be both cathartic or paralysed, both uppers (irrational, spontaneous acts of violence, seemingly engaged in only to verify the existence of those who commit them) and downers (nostalgic-sentimental; the suggestion of a meaning in imagery which does not actually manifest itself). Such moments include the two skinhead brothers fighting, the grandmother dying once Tummler has turned off her life-support machine, a group of bare-chested, beer-drinking men smashing a kitchen chair after a bout of arm-wrestling, a wired Tummler reproducing a humourless stand-up routine, a soapy Solomon eating spaghetti and chocolate in his murky bath. Such moments break through the collage, emerging from the aesthetic anarchy. The film eventually lapses into a run of these: the platinum sisters make out with Bunny Boy in an outdoor swimming pool, Solomon and Tummler repeatedly shoot a dead cat, Bunny Boy holds up a dead cat to the camera, an eyebrowless girl sings 'Yes, Jesus Loves Me' in bed. Most of these final scenes occur in the pouring rain and are accompanied by Roy Orbinson's song 'Crying'. Again this underscores the universality of the sentiment, the way in which Korine details non-specific perception. The repeated refrain – 'crying' – connects all images of water (the swimming pool, the pouring rain, the soaking dead cat). It is the whole milieu that is drenched in a 'crying', not the actions of the characters.

While *Titanic* detailed the destruction of the Titanic, *Gummo* details the destruction of *Gummo*. Via mimesis, the film articulates a perception that has itself been destroyed to contaminate all norms of film-making. Why is the impulse for this attempt at self-annihilation a necessity? All that is not contaminated is assimilated into the neo-underground. Korine negates his film before 'the bourgeois apparatus of production and publication' can, thus preserving, in the void, an innocence in the presentation of psychic devastation particular to such horrific socio-economic conditions. *Gummo* is a neo-realist nuance, as if set in amber, and so distorted to those who peer into it.

Note

The first version of this chapter, as 'What Is The Neo-Underground And What Isn't' (a paraphrasing of Pasolini), was published in late 2003 in *Underground USA* (ed. X. Mendik and S. J. Schneider). It had seemed to me that, by 2000, a shift in the terrain of the American 'indie' sector of film-making (here termed 'the underground' so as to find a critical context in the wider thesis proposed by Mendik and Schneider) was evident. Those films of Clinton-era America that, accepting the outward appearances of peace and prosperity as good coin and finding in this acquiescence the freedom to evolve expressions of hyper-individualism (where 'dropping out' was more to attain the post-'heroin chic' grungy ambience of the drop-out than any radical non-compliance with society), had finally broken into the mainstream with the critical and commercial success of *American Beauty*. Could it have been that in the so-called 'happy 90s' the traditional dynamic and concerns of indie / underground film-making (of the Cassavetes school) had withered and died? Was this success a final rearguard action against any residual legacy of the New Hollywood of the 1970s? For the conglomerates behind *American Beauty*, Sam Mendes had (unwittingly?) channelled various aspects of American indie film-making into the slightest of criticisms, into an expression of near inaction in the face of a very contemporary notion of alienation. Factoring out the virginal Mendes from this process, I was left with an impression of the things to come. I tentatively isolated this trend in late 2000 for the first, and somewhat convoluted, version of this chapter. When published in the midst of the capitulation of almost all areas of the American mass media, in the wake of 11 September 2001, to 'Axis of Evil'-era neo-colonialism, however, my contextual comments were merely a stating of the obvious. In 2000, the one bulwark seemed to be Korine. It seemed possible that, in his radical problematisation of form, he had fashioned a film, *Gummo*, which was intrinsically against this assimilating trend – that remained 'punk': the style of a radical will to dissent.

It is still too early to tell whether I was right on the first count. Certainly, there is a sense that American cinema cannot carry on in the current mode without failing to capitalise on its own distribution monopoly (so that, for one thing, the block-busters have been scaled back). This contradiction was apparent in the fumbling of distributors when confronted with Michael Moore's *Fahrenheit 9/11* (2004). And film-makers whose work speaks of the avoidance of a mature response to the crisis of the role of the American film-maker, such as Sofia Coppola, have come to the fore. But as to the second count . . . should American cinema be used as an instrument of peace and reconciliation after the George Bush era, I maintain that Korine will play no part in such anaesthetism.

13. REPO MAN: RECLAIMING THE SPIRIT OF PUNK WITH ALEX COX

Xavier Mendik

> [W]hile so many of his contemporaries have willingly exchanged their independent vision for major studio financing, Cox appears more than ever to embody the punk spirit which he first encountered while a film student in Los Angeles at the end of the Seventies. (Collins 2001: 35).

Alex Cox is very simply a punk-film phenomenon. He represents that rare breed of film-maker whose love of underground, off-centre and unseen cinema has resulted in him creating a series of defiantly independent works which continually fly in the face of the cinematic orthodoxy.

As a director, Cox first bedazzled and bemused mainstream Hollywood with his offbeat comedy/conspiracy-theory/road movie-inspired début *Repo Man*. The film featured an up-and-coming young Emilio Estevez as a disenfranchised punk rocker who is thrown into a number of surreal encounters after joining a vehicle-repossession agency hot on the trail of a nuclear-powered vehicle from outer space.

With its penchant for genre mixing, as well as its pounding Los Angeles underground music score, *Repo Man* was inextricably linked to the punk philosophy informing its creator. For cultural studies critics such as John Fiske, the subcultural activity of such marginal movements can be defined by the concept of '*bricolage*', whereby 'the subordinated make their own culture out of the resources of the "other"' (Fiske 1990: 150). As Fiske notes, this function was seen in the punk movement's unorthodox conflation of pre-existing styles and modes of performance which 'signifies their power to make their own style and to offend their "social betters" in the process' (ibid. p. 150). For such groups, *bricolage* is achieved by pro-active strategies including 'subcultural dress', where punks 'can combine workingmen's boots with bits of military uniform and mix Nazi and British insignia into a "new" style' (ibid. p. 150). It is a similar spirit which governs the 'cinematic mixing' of a movie such as *Repo Man*, which continually slides between differing genre film templates. For writers such as Fiske, the concept of bricolage indicates the essentially political nature of the punk movement. The activities of such groups offer a contested site of resistance to the mainstream, a factor which is confirmed by Clark Collins's definition of *Repo Man* as an 'hilarious genre-hopping indictment of consumerism in which, for example, all cans of drink in the supermarket are labelled simply "drink"' (Collins 2001: 36).

While *Repo Man* was dominated by a drive towards visual eclecticism, it was also noticeable for the ways in which it brought the motifs of underground musical *bricolage* to the fore. Cox's punk music credentials were further displayed in 1986 when he was at the helm of the infamous *Sid and Nancy*, a biopic on the rock's ultimate burn-out couple. The spirit of punk cinema was also later evident in his 1987 film *Straight to Hell*, a pastiche on the Italian western which brought together punk musicians, such as Joe Strummer with counter-cinema icons, such as Dennis Hopper.

Arguably, it was ultimately Cox's fiercely independent punk spirit (and political leanings) that lead him to be increasingly shunned by mainstream Hollywood (most famously in the case of his displacement from *Fear and Loathing in Las Vegas*). As Clark Collins has noted:

> . . . the concept of revolution, of kicking against the establishment, of never simply accepting the status quo, is one that is very close to Alex Cox's heart. Indeed, the merest glance at his filmography will confirm that the director's work has become not less but more independent minded. (Collins 2001: 35)

Order to retain this independent spirit, Cox has responded to a narrowing of mainstream studio tactics by increasingly embracing European film-making culture and funding as a way of making movies beyond the Hollywood machine. This has resulted in the proliferation of a diverse number of productions, including the Spanish-based *Highway Patrolman* (1992) and the more recent Dutch-funded *Three Businessmen* (1998).

While best known internationally for his off-beat and quirky productions, Alex Cox is also fondly remembered in Britain as the host of BBC televisions influential film show, *Moviedrome*. The series introduced eager audiences to American underground classics and European oddities, and effectively inspired a generation of would-be movie critics and fledgeling academics to endorse a love of trash and cult cinema.

In the following interview, Alex Cox discusses not only his films, but also the influence of the punk movement on his cinema and his politics. Cox's comments and his continued commitment to a socially aware system of cinema confirms Clark Collins's view of him as the 'last punk *auteur* in town', while also highlighting the strategies he employs as alternatives to the mainstream Hollywood machine. (Collins 2001: 37)

XAVIER MENDIK

Your film-training background came from the UCLA tradition of uniting film-production techniques with strong theoretical traditions. How useful did you find these approaches?

ALEX COX

I thought they worked really well actually. At that time, the way in which the entrance requirements worked meant that if you wanted to enter into the production department, you had to have made a film previously and be able to show it to the department. But if you wanted to enter into Critical Studies, you could use any kind of work at all as your introduction. So I actually entered into Critical Studies, which wasn't really what I wanted to do, but it was the easiest way to get into UCLA. So, until I was able to change over to production, I had to go to all these Critical Studies classes. However, this wasn't actually a bad thing, because the guy who ran the department was a great teacher. And so I found the whole interdisciplinary thing that was going on at UCLA a very interesting one. It's kind of genre breaking as well.

XM

In Britain we associate you with not only being a film-maker, but also hosting the ground-breaking film series *Moviedrome*, which strove to break down divisions between film production and critical interpretation/appreciation of trash and cult cinema.

AC

Yes, and I thought the series was good, precisely because it worked like a bit of a film-literacy class. Because the series was on late on Sunday nights nobody minded after a while what we did because by that time it had become this kind of institution. After a while, the BBC didn't even think about it, they just automatically reviewed the budget and kept on doing it. Even after I had decided I didn't want to do the show anymore because the direction had swung mainly in favour of American films, the budget remained after I left! One of the aspects of the series that I really liked was that we were able to screen some great movies that had rarely been seen before. For instance, we showed *Django* (1966), *Django Kill* (1967) and *The Big Silence* (1968). Nobody had ever shown *The Big Silence* in any English-speaking territory before. In fact, no one had ever seen *The Big Silence* anywhere outside of France, Italy, Spain or North Africa. So to be able to do that was a great opportunity.

XM

Watching *Moviedrome*, it is obvious that you have a great fondness for unusual, off-beat cult cinema. How much has this type of cinema affected your own productions, for example, *Repo Man*?

AC

Well, originally, *Repo Man* was supposed to be more of a road movie, going out of Los Angeles to New Mexico, but we lost the New Mexico part mainly for money reasons. However, half of the movie was on the road and so it was a road movie, like some of my favourites: *Easy Rider* and *Two-Lane Blacktop* (1971). These were the models we had in our minds when we made the film; we just wanted ours to include more jokes.

XM

Why did these two films make such an impact on you?

AC

They come out of that odd sort of cinema from the late 1960s and early 1970s, which was for me the great time of American cinema. I still believe that if you look back to the years between 1968 and 1973, they were just making these amazing films that were quite radical, surprising and unusual and they made me think 'Wow, I want to be in this business'. Whereas I don't think I would feel that now if I were going to the pictures a lot.

XM

Just to stick with *Repo Man* for a moment, why do you think the film became such a cult phenomenon?

AC

Well, I think it's really well photographed; the work of Robby Müller is really fluid. This impact of the film is also thanks to the work of Robert Richardson, who did fill in bits when Robbie had left, and these two cinematographers were superb. And I think the casting was very strong, as everybody just fitted straight into their roles. Also, the film's impact has a lot to do with the whole rockand-roll thing and the music of the period as *Repo Man* really manages to capture that feeling of Los Angeles during that time, so that today it still looks authentic.

XM

How would you compare *Repo Man* with the later punk biopic Sid and Nancy?

AC

Sid and Nancy had a fairly conservative narrative, with the flashback structure and everything. The only thing in it that is not that conventional is the weird stuff with their neighbour in the Chelsea Hotel, who is either a dwarf or a little boy, we are never sure who or what he is, and I like that aspect of it. But it is not the thing I feel the most proud of. It looks good and it's well acted but I don't feel any personal attachment to the film.

XM

It's interesting that both *Repo Man* and *Sid and Nancy* foreground the importance of punk music in your work. What do you feel was so significant about the punk movement?

AC

Well, this was a movement that encouraged the political. It encouraged anarchic tendencies because it had revolutionary expectations. Although punk's revolutionary tendencies may have been disappointed, its features fed through into a number of interesting films at the time. When we made *Repo Man*, Penelope Spheeris was making *Suburbia*, which is also quite an interesting film about the punk scene in a way. Punk was a dangerous thing outside of cinema as well. At the time that it was happening, there was still a thing called vinyl and people were making their own records and the record industry was being cut out of the distribution of music. So what did the record industry come up with, how did they regain control of the punk movement? By introducing two new bits of technology: the CD, which was well out of the recording ability of most punk bands, and the rock video. These two new media allowed them to take back control of the music business again. For instance, rock videos tended to be orientated towards groups that had a lot of money or bands that had pretty faces.

XM

I think you could extend this vinyl recuperation to a visual recuperation on the part of the major studios during the period. I am thinking here of Robin Woods's famous definition of Hollywood of the mid-1970s and early 1980s as 'Reaganite cinema', which attempted to seize power from the independents through big-budget block-busters which seemed to endorse the position of the *status quo*.

AC

Definitely. I think you can also see it in the career trajectory of an actor like John Wayne. As you may know, John Wayne began his career playing outlaws, he ended it playing reactionary cops. Equally, you can think of someone like Eastwood; he began his movie career in the 1960s, playing bounty hunters, in other words characters that are half way between an outlaw and a cop. So even in those days he was already being incorporated into the reactionary apparatus of the state, rather than being at odds with it. And he also ends his career playing reactionary cops. I heard a rumour that he is going to do another *Dirty Harry* movie, which would make his character the only eighty-year old policeman on the force in San Francisco. So as the 1970s wore on, it is interesting how the movie business switched from celebrating the rebel or the outlaw to celebrating the policeman. If you think of the remake of *Shaft* (2000), then those contradictions are there again. In the original film, Richard Roundtree is a private eye, while the new *Shaft* is a cop. Now, it's not that cops are bad necessarily, but the medium has increasingly come to celebrate the police state, where the police are the automatic hero of any activity that's going to be reported on film.

XM

You did go on to depict police figures in the movie *Highway Patrolman*, but they seem a world away from the reactionary Hollywood versions you describe.

AC

I had resisted doing a police film for a long time, precisely because I couldn't stand that kind of position. But then I became interested in such a story after talking to a guy who had been a policeman in Mexico. And I thought, 'This is a very interesting story.' He was like a rural highway patrolman. Most of this guy's story is about his domestic life and how he doesn't have enough money, so he has to do these little deals on the side to keep things going. And this is how he ends up running two families: the big house and the little house and shuttling between them. So this is a story about how the idealistic story of being a policeman gets beaten down.

XM
We have talked a lot about potential American influences, but both *Highway Patrolman* and *Straight to Hell* seem to be very influenced by European genre cinema.

AC
Well, *Straight to Hell* is supposed to be a Spaghetti Western and the reason for doing this was because apart from those American movies we discussed, the majority of films I was watching in the late 1960s and early 1970s were Spaghetti Westerns. I watched these movies endlessly. And it was through this interest that I saw other Italian films such as those by Francesco Rossi or the work of actors such as Gian Maria Volonté.

XM
These kinds of European genre films were also notable for their frequent fusion of art-house and experimental techniques. Your own works have also demonstrated an interest in this kind of European art/popular crossover. For instance, in 1996 you directed a film adaptation of Jorge Luis Borges's novel *Death and the Compass*.

AC
Yes, the Borges story that I really wanted to do was *The Aleph*, but I could not get the rights to do this at the time. So of Borges's stories available for option, I thought the easiest to do would be *Death and the Compass*, because it is a piece of classic detective fiction. This is a story that has been made into films or influenced films and other novels a lot. For instance, there was a murder novel called *Hawks Moor* that was written in England in the late 1970s or early 1980s, which was about a guy building the churches at the Tower of London, who also happens to be a serial killer and a Satanist. The novel ends up with a similar resolution as *Death and the Compass*, because the detective in the story gets sent a geographical map in the post and the fourth place on the map is where he will meet his apotheosis. So *Death and the Compass* is great to adapt because it is such a classic detective fiction piece as well as being an interesting parody and commentary on the genre.

XM
Sticking with the European angle for a moment, the other thing about European genre cinema is that it has never been afraid to incorporate

other media forms in quite startling ways. In particular, comic-strip art has been very influential on directors such as Jean Rollin and Mario Bava. I gather that you are also a director who has also dabbled in the idea of comic-strip adaptations.

AC

Yes, that's because I just love comic books. About six or seven times, people have come to me and said 'Don't you want to do *The Fabulous Furry Freak Brothers*', and my reply is always 'Yes, go and get the money and we can do it right away'. And that is the problem, who is going to pay to do *The Fabulous Furry Freak Brothers* as a film? Or rather, who would pay for such a movie without being judgemental about it? That is because in the story, these people are constantly on drugs all the time, and they don't get punished, and they are not only funny but they survive. You might not know that I also wrote a script with Stan Lee of all people called *Dr Strange*, based on the Marvel comic. But once again, it was impossible to fund this as a film, it was just a bit too weird for the studios. This is because the character was an odd creation for Marvel. He is not like *X-Men* or *The Fantastic Four* because *Dr Strange* is not part of any militaristic gang. He is just this kind of eccentric guy who lives in a weird house in New York with his houseboy. He would often sit there just meditating while a huge intercontinental battle between good and evil is going on all around, so I guess it is just a little too weird for a studio to take on.

XM

In the absence of studio support and funding, you are a director who has increasingly turned to new multimedia technology such as the Internet. What do you feel it offers you?

AC

It's a good sort of political tool because it is a way of providing a voice when one doesn't have one. It's a good activist medium for causes or sites that would not otherwise get a lot of attention. Yet, I don't necessarily think that it offers the way forward for young film-makers. There is this theory that all you need is a laptop and then everyone can be a film director. But that is not strictly true. You also need to engage with the collaborative effort that is film-making. You cannot make a film by yourself. So the idea that new media will help us tear down the studios actually misses the point. What it is more likely to do is to lead to a splintering of talent rather than bringing people together.

XM

Do you think your punk politics have affected recent projects like *Revengers Tragedy* or *Three Businessmen*?

AC

Well, I think we have been lucky really with *Revengers Tragedy* (2003). I don't really know why, but it has just kept afloat. It has gone through all these differing incarnations and has come back to pretty much what it was in the beginning, which is like a really weird low-budget British film featuring a clan war between Liverpool and London. However, if we had gone down the studio route, we would be still waiting to see if Anjelica Huston or Robert Downy Jr could be in it. And the problem with this is that our aspirations would then be to make *Richard III*, which is a decent film, but it does follow that Mid-Atlantic model: neither is it a big American film, nor is it a really ballsy, cutting-edge British film.

XM

It's interesting that you raise the British angle, as an English film-maker whose interests are much more international. Your films seem to contain too many fantastical and atypical elements to be considered as part of official 'British' film culture.

AC

Yes, but that's only because 'official' film culture has become so conservative. And that is largely a result of the American influence; we are so close by virtue of a shared language to the United States, that it is very hard for us to have our own independent culture and, when we do, it is very hard for us to maintain this. If you think about some of the really, really great British directors, like Nic Roeg or Ken Russell, they never had any problems incorporating elements of the fantastic into their work. I mean if you look at the films they made during the very early parts of their careers, these films were very unrestricted. Things were much more exciting then. Now, we are limited much more now into these traps, where you have to make much more conventional gangster films where everyone talks the same way and says things like [adopting exaggerated East End accent] 'sorted'! Or else you are forced to make these Merchant-Ivory-style productions with Tony Hopkins in a butler suit or one of those films from up North, where the factory has been closed and some dad says 'No lad of mine is going to a Ballet school!' And the problem with all of these scenarios is that we have seen them all before.

XM

Linked in with this fact is the fact that your films seem to emphasise the elements of fantasy over realism. How important are elements of the fantastical to your work.

AC

I think it's a really good hook to hang things on. It's a good excuse for why films are not normal. I think that films can be fairly restrictive in terms of people's genre expectations, and what they feel is appropriate to have in a film. What is good about that label is that it allows you to do things that you couldn't otherwise do. Otherwise we would be limited to making very conventional films, whether they were policeman movies or remakes of *My Dinner With Andre* (1981). Instead, the fantasy label allows the film-maker a little more fantasy freedom. In my opinion we need to free ourselves from realist restrictions and return to the fantastical and to our more surrealist roots.

XM

Which brings us back to European film influences and directors like Buñuel. Was he in any way an influence?

AC

Buñuel was the master, so you may as well imitate the best, you may as well steal from the best. The good thing about Buñuel was that he would not be categorised. No matter what film he was making, he would always put something into it that twisted it and surprised you. Things might lead from one thing to another and then another, but they would suddenly twist sideways and that, I think, is very exciting.

XM

How would you fit a movie like *Three Businessmen* into this?

AC

Three Businessmen could only have happened in Europe, because it's a kind of philosophical film where these characters talk all of the time, but never really communicate. I don't know anyone who would have produced that film except the Dutch.

XM

I cannot leave the interview without raising the issue of *Fear and Loathing in Las Vegas*. This is because independent directors such as yourself have been increasingly pushed out of the Hollywood system and I wondered if you had any closing thoughts on this?

AC

Well, it's kind of like a huge mill. The United States churns out something like 10,000 film directors a year from universities and film schools. So you have all of these people coming out of this system wanting to be directors, and that clearly makes it a buyer's market. And given that the Hollywood studios are still very similar to the top-down, heavy industry, war-machine-type mind-set they don't want to have old cynics like me working. I mean, I am forty-seven years old and you are not going to hire me when you can hire somebody who is twenty-two to do this film. Because at that age, people will do exactly what you ask them to without questioning it.[1]

Note

[1] I wish to offer my sincere thanks to Alex Cox for his time and enthusiasm during our interview. I also wish to express my gratitude to the staff of the Brussels International Festival of Fantastic Film for organising the above interview.

BIBLIOGRAPHY

Aarseth, E. (1997), *Cybertext: Perspectives on Ergodic Literature*. Baltimore: Johns Hopkins University Press.
'About *Mulholland Drive*' (2001), *Salon.com*, <dir.salon.com/ent/movies/feature/2001/10/23/mulholland_drive_analysis/index.html>, 23 October.
Adams, S. (2003), 'Screen Picks', *Philadelphia Citypaper.net*, <http://citypaper.net/articles/2003-09-18/screen.shtml>, 18–24 September.
'Ad Criteria' (2004), *MaximumRockNRoll*, 253, June.
Adorno, T. [1966] (2001), 'Transparencies on Film', in J. M. Bernstein (ed.), *The Culture Industry*, London: Routledge, 178–86.
The Andy Warhol Museum. Pittsburgh: The Andy Warhol Museum, 1994.
Anderson, P. T. (2000), *Magnolia: The Shooting Script*, New York: Newmarket Press.
Angell, C. (1994), 'Andy Warhol, Filmmaker', in *The Andy Warhol Museum*, Pittsburgh: The Andy Warhol Museum, 121–45.
Armes, R. (1971), *Patterns of Realism: A Study of Italian Neo-Realist Cinema*, New York: A. S. Barnes.
Balio, T. (1996), 'Adjusting to the new Global Economy: Hollywood in the 1990s', in A. Moran (ed.), *Film Policy: International, National and Regional Perspectives*, London: Routledge, 23–38.
Bangs, L. 'The White Noise Supremacists', in G. Marcus (ed.), *Psychotic Reactions and Carburetor Dung*, New York: Vintage, 1988, 272–82.
Barthes, R. (1977), 'Death of the Author', in S. Heath (ed. and trans.), *Image Music Text*, London: Fontana, 142–8.
Baudrillard, J. [1981] (1994), *Simulacra and Simulation,* trans. S. F. Glaser, Ann Arbor: University of Michigan Press.
Baudry, J. L. (1974-75), 'Ideological effects of the basic cinematic apparatus', *Film Quarterly* 28, 39–47.
Bazin, A. *What is Cinema?* (1967), H. Gray (trans.), Berkeley: University of California Press.

Benjamin, W. (1973), *Understanding Brecht*, A. Bostock (trans.), London: New Left Books.
Benjamin, W. (1978), 'The Author as Producer', in E. Jephcott, (trans.), *Reflections: Essays, Aphorisms, Autobiographical Writings*, New York: Schocken, 220–38.
Bennett, T. (1979), *Formalism and Marxism*, New York: Methuen.
Birch, I. (1977), 'Reading the Adverts', *Melody Maker*, 6 August 1977, <http://www.tvsmith.com/archives/press.php?prid=1&sort>.
Black, J. (2001), *The Reality Effect: Film Culture and the Graphic Imperative*, New York: Routledge.
'Blair Witch Project' (1999), *The Austin Chronicle*, <http://www.filmvault.com/filmvault/austin/b/blairwitchproject.1.html>.
Blank Generation (1976), dir. A. Poe, Poe Productions.
Blank Generation (1979), dir. U. Lommel, Anchor Bay Entertainment.
Bockris, V. (1998), *Beat Punks*, New York: Da Capo Press.
Bolter, J. D. and Grusin, R. (1999), *Remediation: Understanding New Media*, Cambridge, MA: MIT Press.
Bondanella, P. (1993), *The Films of Roberto Rossellini*, Cambridge: Cambridge University Press.
Bordwell, D. (1973), *La Passion de Jeanne d'Arc*, Bloomington: Indian University Press.
Bordwell, D. (1985), *Narration in the Fiction Film*, London: Methuen.
Bordwell, D. (1986), 'Classical Hollywood Cinema: Narrational Principles and Procedures', in P. Rosen (ed.), *Narrative, Apparatus, Ideology*, New York: Columbia University Press.
Bordwell, D. (2002), 'Film futures', *SubStance* 31:1, 88–104.
Borges, J. L. (1964), *Labyrinths: Selected Stories and Other Writings*, D. A. Yates and J. E. Irby (eds), New York: New Directions.
Bowen, M. J. (2002), 'Doris Wishman Meets the Avant-Garde', in X. Mendik and S. Schneider (eds), *Underground U.S.A.: Filmmaking Beyond the Hollywood Canon*, London: Wallflower Press, 109–22.
Boyle, D. 'A Brief History of American Documentary Video', in D. Hall and S. J. Fifer (eds), *Illuminating Video: An Essential Guide to Video Art*, San Francisco: Aperture, 1990, 51–69.
Brooks, X. (2000), Review of *Timecode*, *Sight and Sound* 10.9, September, 36–7.
Buñuel, L. (1983), *My Last Sigh*, New York: Knopf.
Carter, A. [1977] (1995), 'Ups and Downs for the Babes in Bondage', in H. Kureishi and J. Savage (eds), *The Faber Book of Pop*, London: Faber, 509–14.
Christensen, O. (2000), 'Authentic Illusions – The Aesthetics of Dogma 95', P.O.V. 10: 1–7, <http://imv.au.dk/publikationer/pov/Issue_10/section_4/artc2A.html>.
Clines, F. X. (1975), 'Beame Submits New Cuts', *New York Times*, 16 October: 1A.
Collins, C. (2001), 'Never Mind the Bollocks', *Uncut*, April 2001, 35–37.
Collins, J. (2002), 'Genericity in the Nineties: Eclectic Irony and the new sincerity', in G. Turner, (ed.), *The Film Cultures Reader*, New York: Routledge, 276–90.
Combs, R. and Durgnat, R. (2000), 'Rules of the Game', *Film Comment* 36.5: 28–32.
Cook, D. A. (1996), *A History of Narrative Film*, Third Edition, New York: W. W. Norton.
Coon, C. [1976] (1995), 'Rock Revolution', in H. Kureishi and J. Savage (eds), *The Faber Book of Pop*, London: Faber, 490–3.
Cooper, C. (1989), 'Subliminal messages, heavy metal music, and teenage suicide' *San Francisco Examiner*, <http://www.reversespeech.com/judas.shtml>.
Crass (1978), 'Do They Owe Us a Living?' *The Feeding of the Five Thousand*, Crass Records.

Curtis, J. (1987), *Rock Eras: Interpretations of Music and Society, 1954–1984*, Bowling Green: Bowling Green State University Popular Press.
'D-cinema: a timeline of experimental and mainstream uses of digital technology' (2004), *The Velvet Light Trap* 53, 55–8.
Demopoulos, M. (2000), 'Blink of an Eye: Filmmaking in the Age of Bullet Time', *Film Comment*, Fall 2000, 35–9.
Dienst, R. (2000), 'The Imaginary Element: Life + Cinema', in D. Wills (ed.), *Jean-Luc Godard's Pierrot Le Fou*, Cambridge: Cambridge University Press, 23–42.
Dixon, W. W. (2003), 'In Praise of Godard's *In Praise of Love*', *Film Criticism* 27: 3, 18–39, <http://app5.uwec.edu:2055/hww/results/results single.jhtml?nn11>.
'DIY Film Festival' (2004), <http://www.diyconvention.com>.
Eggers, D. [2000] (2001), *A Heartbreaking Work of Staggering Genius*, New York: Vintage.
Elsaesser, T. and Buckland, W. (2003), *Studying Contemporary American Film: A Guide to Movie Analysis*. London: Arnold.
Experience Music Project (2004), 'Riot Grrrl', 5 July, <http:www.emplive.com/explore/riotgrrrl/index.asp>.
Fight Club (1999), dir. D. Fincher, Fox 2000 Pictures.
Film Threat (2004), 'About *Film Threat*', <http://www.filmthreat.com/About.asp>.
Fiske, J. (1989), *Understanding Popular Culture*, London: Routledge.
'Flicktips / Intro. to Digital Flicks' (2004), <http://www.newvenue.com/flicktips/content/01intro-0000.html>.
Foreigner, The (1977), dir. A. Poe, Visions.
Frayling, C. (cited in) (2003), *Once Upon a Time in the West*, DVD Commentary, Paramount Home Video.
Friedberg, A. (1993), *Window Shopping: Cinema and the Postmodern*, Berkeley: University of California Press.
Frith, S. (1981), *Sound Effects: Youth, Leisure, and the Politics of Rock 'n' Roll*, New York: Pantheon.
Frith, S. [1986] (2004), 'Art vs Technology: The Strange Case of Popular Music', in S. Frith (ed.), *Popular Music: Critical Concepts in Media and Cultural Studies*, Vol. 2: *The Rock Era*. London: Routledge, 107–22.
Fugazi (1990), 'Merchandise', *Repeater + 3 Songs*, Dischord Records.
Gaggio, S. (1997), *From Text to Hypertext: Decentering the Subject in Fiction, Film, the Visual Arts, and Electronic Media*, Philadelphia: University of Pennsylvania Press.
Gaut, B. (2003), 'Naked film: Dogma and its limits', in M. Hjort and S. MacKenzie (eds), *Purity and Provocation: Dogma 95*, London: British Film Institute, 89–101.
Geffner, D. (2004), 'Write Now: Filling in the Gaps', in *RES Magazine*, vol. 7, no. 1, 44–6.
Geuens, J. P. (2001), 'Dogma 95: A Manifesto for Our Times', *Quarterly Review of Film & Video*, 18.2: 191–202.
Godard, J.-P. (2001), 'Michele Halberstadt Interview with Jean-Luc Godard', included in *In Praise of Love* press kit, 7 July 2004, <http://textz.gnutenberg.net/text.php?text=godard_jean-luc_eloge_de_l-amour&id=1034047963524>.
Grossberg, L. [1984] (2004), 'Another Boring Day in Paradise: Rock and Roll and the Empowerment of Everyday Life', in S. Frith (ed.), *Popular Music: Critical Concepts in Media and Cultural Studies*, Vol. 2: *The Rock Era*, London: Routledge, 311–42.
Gleick, J. (1987), *Chaos, Making a New Science*, New York: Viking Penguin.
Graham, R. (2000), 'Time Code', *Senses of Cinema* 9, <http://www.sensesofcinema.com/contents/00/9/time.html>.

Hack, J. (1999), 'Pure Vision: Interview with Harmony Korine', *Dazed and Confused Magazine*, May, <http://www.angelfire.com/ab/harmonykorine/dazed.html>.
Halligan, B. (2002), 'What is the Neo-Underground and What Isn't: A First Consideration of Harmony Korine', in X. Mendik and S. J. Schneider (eds), *Underground U.S.A.: Filmmaking Beyond the Hollywood Canon*, London: Wallflower Press, 150–60.
Harbord, J. (2002), *Film Cultures*, London: SAGE.
Harper, G. (2001), 'DVD: The Shift to Film's New Modernity', *Cineaction* 56, 20–5.
Hayles, N. K. (2004a), 'Living in Computational Spaces: Nature as Code, Code as Nature', keynote address, 32nd Annual 20th Century Literature Conference, University of Louisville, Louisville, Kentucky, 26–8 February.
Hayles, N. K. and Gessler, N. (2004b), 'The Slipstream of Mixed Reality: Unstable Ontologies and Semiotic Markers in *The Thirteenth Floor*, *Dark City*, and *Mulholland Drive*', *PMLA* 119, no. 3, 482–99.
Heath, S. (1978), 'Screen Images, Film Memory', *Edinburgh Magazine* 1, 33–42.
Heath, S. (1981), 'Film/Cinetext/Text', in *Screen Reader 2: Cinema and Semiotics*, London: SEFT, 99–124.
Hebdige, D. (1979), *Subculture: The Meaning of Style*, London: Methuen.
Hebdige, D. (1988), *Hiding in the Light*, London. Routledge.
Henry, T. (1989), *Break All Rules! Punk Rock and the Making of a Style*, Ann Arbor: UMI Research Press.
Hertzberg, L. (2001), *Jim Jarmusch: Interviews*, Jackson: University Press of Mississippi.
Herzog, W. (1997), 'Gummo's Whammo', *Interview Magazine*, <http://www.angelfire.com/ab/harmonykorine/interviewmag.html>.
Heylin, C. (1993), *From the Velvets to the Voidoids: A Pre-Punk History for a Post-Punk World*, New York: Penguin Books.
Hillier, J. (2001), 'Introduction', in J. Hillier (ed.), *American Independent Cinema: A Sight and Sound Reader*, London: British Film Institute, ix–xvii.
Hjort, M. and Bondebjerg, I. (2001), *The Danish Directors: Dialogues on a Contemporary National Cinema*, Bristol: Intellect Books.
Hjort, M. (2003a), 'Dogma 95: A Small Nation's Response to Globalisation', in M. Hjort and S. Mackenzie (eds), *Purity and Provocation: Dogma 95*, London: British Film Institute, 31–47.
Hjort, M. (2003b), 'The Globalisation of Dogma: The Dynamics of Metaculture and Counter-Publicity', in M. Hjort and S. Mackenzie (eds), *Purity and Provocation: Dogma 95*, London: British Film Institute, 133–57.
Hjorth, P. (2001), *Dancer in the Dark*, DVD commentary, New Line Home Entertainment.
Hoberman, J. and Rosenbaum, J. (1983), *Midnight Movies*, New York: Harper and Row.
Hoberman, J. (1985), 'Ten Years that Shook the World', *American Film* 10, June, 34–59.
Holland, J. H. (1998), *Emergence, From Chaos to Order*, Reading, MA: Addison-Wesley.
Horkheimer, M. and Adorno, T. [1944] (1993), *Dialectic of Enlightenment*, New York: Continuum.
Hurley, N. P. (1978), *The Reel Revolution: A Film Primer on Liberation*, Maryknoll, New York: Orbis.
Hutcheon, L. (1994), *Irony's Edge: The Theory and Politics of Irony*, London: Routledge.
In Praise of Love (*Éloge de l'Amour*) (2001), dir. J.-L. Godard, Avventura Films.
Jenkins, H. (1992), *Textual Poachers: Television Fans and Participatory Culture*, New York: Routledge.

Jeunet, J. (2001), 'An Intimate Chat with Jean-Pierre Jeanet', Supplemental material included with *Amélie* DVD, Mirimax Films/Mirimax Zoe.
Jones, K. (2004), 'Corridors of Powerlessness', *Film Comment*, vol. 39, no. 5, September/October.
Kaehler, S. D. (1998), 'Fuzzy Logic Tutorial', *Encoder: The Newsletter of the Seattle Robotics Society*, <http://www.seattlerobotics.org/encoder>.
Kael, P. (1994), *For Keeps*, New York: Penguin.
Kaufman, C. and Kaufman, D. (2002), *Adaptation: The Shooting Script*, New York: Newmarket Press.
Kelly, R. (2000a), *The Name of this Film is Dogma 95*, Channel 4, 12 August.
Kelly, R. (2000b), *The Name of this Book is Dogma 95*, London: Faber.
Kerekes, D. (1999), 'Tinseltown Rebellion: Punk, transgression, and a conversation with Richard Baylor', in R. Sabin (ed.), *Punk Rock, So What?* London: Routledge, 1999 68–80.
Kinder, M. (2003), 'Designing a database cinema', in J. Shaw and P. Weibel (eds), *Future Cinema: The Cinematic Imagery after Film*, Karlsruhe/Cambridge, MA: ZKM/MIT Press, 346–53.
Koc, A. (2004), '"*Vive le cinéma*": A Reading of *What Time is it There?*', *Cineaction*, Issue 62.
Koch, S. (1971), 'The Chelsea Girls', *Artforum* 10.1, September, 84–90.
Kundera, M. (1992), *Immortality*, New York: HarperCollins.
Landow, G. (1992). *Hypertext: The Convergence of Contemporary Theory and Technology*, Baltimore: Johns Hopkins University Press.
Leon, C. (2004), e-mail correspondence with N. Rombes, 27 May.
Lefebvre, M. and Furstenau, M. (2002), 'Digital editing and montage: the vanishing celluloid and beyond', *Cinémas* 13:1–2, 69–107.
Lumholdt, J. (ed.) (2003), *Lars von Trier: Interviews*. Jackson: University Press of Mississippi.
Lurie, P. (2003), 'Why the Web will Win the Culture Wars for the Left', *CTheory*, 14 April, <http://ctheory.net/text_file.asp?pick=380>.
McGrath, C. (2004), 'Not Funnies', *The New York Times Magazine*, 11 July: 24–56.
McKee, R. (2002), 'Critical Commentary' in *Adaptation: The Shooting Script* by C. Kaufman, New York: Newmarket Press, 131–5.
MacKenzie, S. (2003), 'Manifest Destinies: Dogma 95 and the Future of the Film Manifesto', in M. Hjort and S. MacKenzie (eds), *Purity and Provocation: Dogma 95*, London: British Film Institute: 48–57.
McLuhan, E. and Zingrone, F. (eds) (1995), *Essential McLuhan*, New York: Basic Books.
McLuhan, M. (1960), 'The Medium is the Message', in *Forum*, Summer, 19–24.
McNeil, L. and McCain, G. (1997), *Please Kill Me: The Uncensored Oral History of Punk*, New York: Penguin.
McSweeney's Quarterly, Number 11 (2003), D. Eggers (ed.), San Fransisco: McSweeney's.
Marcus, G. (1989), *Lipstick Traces: A Secret History of the Twentieth Century*, Cambridge, MA: Harvard University Press.
Mannes, B. (1999), 'Something Wicked', *Salon.com*, <http://www.salon.com/ent/movies/int/1999/07/13/witch_actor>.
Manovich, L. (1998), 'Towards an Archaeology of the Computer Screen', in T. Elsaesser. and K. Hoffmann (eds), *Cinema Futures: Cain, Abel or Cable? The Screen Arts in the Digital Age*. Amsterdam: Amsterdam University Press, 27–43.
Manovich, L. (2001), *The Language of New Media*, Cambridge, MA: MIT Press.

Manovich, L. (2002), 'Old media as new media: cinema', in D. Harries (ed.), *The New Media Book,* London, British Film Institute, 209–18.
Marie, M. [1997] (2003), *The French New Wave: An Artistic School,* R. Neupert (trans.), Oxford: Blackwell Publishers.
Martin, B. (2002), *Avant Rock: Experimental Music from the Beatles to Björk,* Chicago: Open Court.
Marx, K. [1867] (1990), *Capital,* vol. 1, trans. B. Fowkes, New York: Penguin.
Matthews, P. (2000), 'Dancer In the Dark', *Sight and Sound* 10.10, 41–2.
Metz, C. (1974), *Film Language: A Semiotics of the Cinema,* trans. M. Taylor, New York: Oxford University Press.
Minor Threat (1989), 'Minor Threat', *Minor Threat: Complete Discography,* Dischord Records.
Modleski, T. (1988), *The Women Who Knew Too Much,* London: Methuen.
Morowitz, H. J. (2002), *The Emergence of Everything, How the World Became Complex,* Oxford: Oxford University Press.
Moulthrop, S. (1991), *Victory Garden,* Cambridge, MA: Eastgate Systems, 1991.
Murray, J. (1997), *Hamlet on the Holodeck: The Future of Narrative in Cyberspace,* New York: The Free Press.
Murray, J. (2004), 'From Game-Story to Cyberdrama', in N. Wardrip-Fruin and P. Harrigan (eds), *First Person: New Media as Story, Performance, and Game,* Cambridge, MA: MIT Press, 2–11.
Murray, T. (1999), 'By way of introduction: digitality and the memory of cinema, or, bearing the losses of the digital code', *Wide Angle* 21:1, 3–27.
Myrick, D. (1999), '*The Blair Witch Project* Interview', *The Austin Chronicle,* 17 July, <http://www.filmvault/austin/b/blairwitchproject1.html>.
O'Pray, M. (1989), 'Warhol's Early Films: Realism and Psychoanalysis', in O'Pray (ed.), *Andy Warhol Film Factory,* London: British Film Institute, 170–7.
Orlean, S. (2002), 'Forward' to *Adaptation: The Shooting Script* by C. Kaufman, New York: Newmarket Press, vii–ix.
Oxholm, J. and Nielson, J. I. (2000), 'The Ultimate Dogma Film: An Interview with Jens Albinus and Louise Hassing on Dogma 2 – *The Idiots*', <http://imv.aau.dk/publikationer/pov/Issue_10/section_2/artc2A.html>.
Palahniuk, C. (1996), *Fight Club,* New York: W. W. Norton.
Paphides, P. (2000), 'It's Oh So Sad', *Time Out,* 16–23 August.
Peterson, J. 'Lens Crafter', *Filmmaker* 12, no. 13. spring 2004, 64–7.
Poe, A. (2001), 'Commentary Track', *The Foreigner* DVD, Oaks: Eclectic DVD Distribution.
Prigge, M. (2003), 'Blondie Ambition', *Philadelphia Weekly Online,* 32: 38, <http://www.philadelphiaweekly.com/archives/article.asp?ARTID=6174>.
Punking Out (1977), dir. F. Shore, M. Carson and J. Kossakowski.
Purdy, J. (1999), *For Common Things: Irony, Trust, and Commitment in America Today,* New York: Knopf.
'Ramones: Interview with John Holmstrom' (1976), in *Punk,* No. 3.
Ray, R. (1985), *A Certain Tendency of the Hollywood Cinema, 1930–1980,* Princeton, NJ: Princeton University Press.
Rechtshaffen, M. (2002), '*Ken Park*', *The Hollywood Reporter,* 27 September, <http://www.hollywoodreporter.com/thr/article_display.jsp?vnu_content_id=1723291>.
RES Magazine (2004), 'Handheld Cinema', vol. 7. nos 4, 9.
Robbe-Grillet, A. (1958), *The Voyeur,* trans. R. Howard, New York: Grove Press.
Roberts, M. (2003), 'De-coding *D-Day*: multi-channel television at the millennium', in M. Hjort and S. MacKenzie (eds), *Purity and Provocation: Dogma 95,* London: British Film Institute, 158–72.

Roddick, N. (1999), 'The Roddick Profile: Dan Myrick and Eduardo Sanchez', <http://www.filmfestivals.com/cannes99/html/interus12.htm>.
Rombes, N. [2002] (2004), 'Professor DVD', in A. Kroker and M. Kroker (eds), *Life in the Wires: The CTheory Reader*, Victoria, Canada: New World Perspective/CTheory Books, 343–47.
Rosen, P. (2001), *Change Mummified: Cinema, Historicity, Theory*, Minneapolis, MN: University of Minnesota Press.
Rosenbaum, J. (2000), 'State of the Art', <http://www.chireader.com/movies/archives/2000/>.
Sabin, R. (1999a), 'Introduction', in R. Sabin (ed.), *Punk Rock: So What?*, London: Routledge, 1–13.
Sabin, R. (1999b), ' "I won't let that dago by": Rethinking punk and racism', in R. Sabin (ed.), *Punk Rock: So What?*, London: Routledge, 199–218.
Sargeant, J. (1995), *Deathtripping: The Cinema of Transgression*, London: Creation Books.
Sargeant, J. (1999), *Cinema Contra Cinema*, Belgium: Fringecore.
Sato, K. (2001), 'Harmony Korine: The Anti-Dreamer', *Project A*, 15 January, <http://www.projecta.net/harmony.html>.
Savage, J. (1992), *England's Dreaming: Anarchy, Sex Pistols, Punk Rock, and Beyond*, New York: St Martin's Press.
Savage, J. (1998), liner notes, *Sid and Nancy*, dir. Alex Cox. Criterion DVD.
Schepelern, P. (2001), 'Film According to Dogma', <http://www.dogme95.dk/news/interview/schepelern.htm>.
Schepelern, P. (2003), ' "Kill Your Darlings": Lars von Trier and the Origin of Dogma 95', in M. Hjort and S. Mackenzie (eds), *Purity and Provocation: Dogma 95*, London: British Film Institute, 58–69.
Schrader, P. [1972] (1996), 'Notes on *Film Noir*', in A. Silver and J. Ursini (eds), *Film Noir Reader*, New York: Limelight, 53–63.
Scream (1996), dir. Wes Craven, Dimension Films.
Sex Pistols (1992), 'My Way', Kiss This, EMI/Virgin.
Shelley, M. [1818] (1980), *Frankenstein: or, The Modern Prometheus*, ed. J. Kinsley and M. K. Joseph, Oxford: Oxford University Press.
Siegel, F. (1997), *The Future Once Happened Here*, San Francisco: Encounter Books.
Silverman, K. and Farocki, H. (1998), *Speaking About Godard*, New York: New York University Press.
Simon, J. (1983), *Something to Declare*, New York: Clarkson N. Potter.
Sinker, M. (1999), 'The Trucam Show', *Sight and Sound* 9.7, July, 26–7.
Sleater-Kinney (2000), '#1 Must Have', All Hands on the Bad One, Kill Rock Stars.
Smith, E. (1999–2000), 'Thread Structure: Rewriting the Hollywood Formula', *Journal of Film and Video* 51, 3–4, fall-winter: 88–96.
Smith, M. (2003), 'Lars von Trier: Sentimental Surrealist', in M. Hjort and S. MacKenzie (eds), *Purity and Provocation: Dogma 95*, 111–21.
Sontag, S. (1966), 'Notes on Camp', in *From Against Interpretation and other Essays*, New York: The Noonday Press.
Sowell, T. (1997), *Fuzzy Logic for 'Just Plain Folks'*, <http://www.fuzzy-logic.com/Ch1.htm>.
Spencer, N. [1976] (1995), 'Don't Look Over Your Shoulder, but the Sex Pistols are Coming', in H. Kureishi and J. Savage (eds), *The Faber Book of Pop*, London: Faber, 489–90.
Stables, K. (2000), 'Scopophilia.com', *Sight and Sound* 10.2, February, 10.
Stam, R. (2000), *Film Theory: An Introduction*, Malden, MA: Blackwell Publishing.

Stark, J. (2000). 'It's a Punk Movie', *Salon.com*, 13 October, <http://www.salon.com/ent/movies/int/2000/10/13/aronofsky/>.
Stevenson, J. (2002), *Lars von Trier*, London: British Film Institute.
Sweet, M. (2004), 'The Cruel and Crazy World of Lars von Trier', *The Independent*, 5 May.
Taubin, A. (2004), 'Part of the Problem: Stepping into the Arena of High School. Gus Van Sant's *Elephant* Confronts the Specter of Columbine', *Film Comment*, vol. 39, no. 5, September/October.
Taylor, J. (2001), *DVD Demystified*, second ed., New York: McGraw Hill.
Thompson, S. (2001), 'Market Failure: Punk Economics, Early and Late', *College Literature*, 28: 2, 48–64.
Thompson, S. (2004a), 'Punk Cinema', *Cinema Journal* 43, no. 2: 47–66.
Thompson, S. (2004b), *Punk Productions: Unfinished Business*, Albany: State University of New York Press.
Thomsen, P. (1998), 'Rechristening The Kingdom', *American Cinematographer* 79.6: 24–8.
Thomsen, P. (2000), '*The Idiots* Plays By Von Trier's Rules', *American Cinematographer* 81.1: 19–26.
Time Code, Dir. Mike Figgis. DVD. Columbia/Tristar Studios, 2000.
'*Time Code*: Digital Storytelling in 4/4 Time', (2001), <http://www.apple.com/hotnews/articles/2000/04/timecode/>.
'*Time Code* Production Notes' (2000), <http://culture.com/article/item.phtml?ID=227>.
Trifonova, T. (2002), 'Time and Point of View in Contemporary Cinema', *CineAction* 58, 11–31.
Unmade Beds (1976), Dir. Amos Poe, Eclectic DVD Distribution.
Van Sant, G. (2003), interview with A. Kaufman, *RES.com*, <http://www.res.com/magazine/articles/>.
Villella, F. (2000), 'Circular Narratives', *Senses of Cinema*, Issue 3, February 2000 <http://www.sensesofcinema.com/contents/00/3/circular.html>.
Wallace, D. F. [1993] (1997), 'E Unibus Pluram: Television and U. S. Fiction', in *A Supposedly Fun Thing I'll Never Do Again*, New York: Little, Brown, 1997, 21–82.
Walsh, D. (1997a), 'Thoughts about the 1997 Toronto Film Festival: Film, Social Reality and Authenticity', *World Socialist Web Site*, <http://www.wsws.org/arts/1997/sep1997/tff-2.shtml>.
Walsh, D. (1997b), 'Thoughts about the 1997 Toronto Film Festival', *World Socialist Web Site*, <http://www.wsws.org/arts/1997/sep1997/tff-2.shtml>
Walters, T. (2004), 'Reconsidering *The Idiots*: Dogma 95, Lars von Trier, and the Cinema of Subversion?' *The Velvet Light Trap*, no. 53: 40–54.
Warhol, A. and Hackett, P. (1983), *Popism: The Warhol '60s*, New York: Harper and Row.
Waters, J. (1981), Shock Value, New York: Delta.
Welles, O. and Bogdanovich, P. [1992] (1998), *This is Orson Welles*, New York: De Capo Press.
'What is Microcinema?' (2004), <http://www.microcinemascene.com>.
Winston, B. (1998), *Media Technology and Society, A History: From the Telegraph to the Internet*, London: Routledge.
Wollen, P. [1972] (2002), 'Godard's Cinema and Counter Cinema: *Vent d'est* (1972)', in C. Fowler (ed.), *The European Cinema Reader*, New York: Routledge.
Wood, R. (1986), *Hollywood from Vietnam to Reagan*. New York: Columbia University Press.
Wyman, B., Garrone, M. and Klein, A. (2001), 'Everything You Were Afraid to Ask

About *Mulholland Drive*', *Salon.com*, October, <http://dir.salon.com/ent/movies/feature/2001/10/23mulholland_drive_analysis/index.html>.
Youngblood, G. [1989] (2003), 'Cinema and the code', in J. Shaw and P. Weibel (eds), *Future Cinema: The Cinematic Imagery after Film,* Karlsruhe/Cambridge, MA: ZKM/MIT Press, 156–61.
'X Offender' (1976), Blondie, private stock single #PS45 097, Chrysalis Records.

INDEX

Above the Below, 184
Accattone, 189
Adaptation, 76, 77–9, 136
Adorno, Theodor, 12, 85
The Adverts, 139–40
Amélie, 114, 118–25
American Beauty, 180, 181, 191
Anderson, Paul Thomas, 80
Anger, Kenneth, 172
Aronofsky, Darren, 3, 108
auteur theory
   The Blair Witch Project, 14–15
   Dogma 95, 104, 157, 158
   Fight Club, 134
   new punk cinema, 14, 128–31, 135, 137, 138, 195
   semi-underground 1990s cinema, 182–3

Bangs, Lester, 7
Barbaro, Umberto, 42
Bazin, André, 41, 105, 128, 170–1, 174
Baylor, Richard, 9
Being John Malkovich, 77, 130
Benjamin, Walter, 21, 24, 35, 180–1

Bergman, Ingmar, 157
Bertsch, Charles, 18
Beth B, 10, 39
The Biggest Heroes, 158
Black Flag, 32, 40
The Blair Witch Project, 2, 13,
   and irony, 64, 72
   and notion of *auteur*, 14–15
   similarity to Dogma 95, 14
Blank Generation, 11, 25
Bonnie and Clyde, 141
Bordwell, David, 126–7
The Boy Who Walked Backwards, 158
Brakhage, Stan, 172
Breaking the Waves, 64, 72, 162, 164, 165, 166
Breathless, 33, 57, 147
Browning, Tod, 44, 46
Buffalo 66, 168
Buñuel, Luis, 56, 202

CD-ROM format, 93–5, 97, 111
camp, 72, 81
Cassavetes, John, 30, 155
The Celebration, 2, 64, 153, 158–61

Index

DV cameras, 106, 155
magical psychological realism, 160–1
new punk cinema, 16, 154, 159
chaos theory, 116, 117
Chelsea Girls, 168, 169, 171–8
Cinema of Transgression, 9–10, 11
cinéma vérité, 39, 40, 47, 50, 107, 109, 175
Clark, Larry, 45, 47–51, 182
Clowes, Daniel, 73
Cox, Alex, 148, 149, 193–203
Cuarón, Alfonso, 65
Curtis, Jim, 6

D.O.A., 11
DV cameras
 Dogma 95, 12–13, 105–6, 159, 163
 new punk cinema, 12–13, 105–6
 realism, 107, 170, 175
 Time Code, 109–10
DVD format, 90, 93, 95–101
 and cinema of complexity, 96–100
 destabilises primary film text, 73, 97–8
 fosters cinematic deconstruction, 17, 74, 80–1, 92, 98–9
Dancer in the Dark, 2, 64, 161, 165
 challenges to *auteur* theory, 15–16
 DV cameras, 106, 163
 filmic self-awareness, 81
 irony, 84–5
David Boring, 73
Dead Boys, 74
Death and the Compass, 199
The Decline of Western Civilization, 11, 40
Demopoulos, Maria, 13
Dick, Vivienne, 10, 11
digital realism, 103–9, 169, 170–1, 175, 178
direct video, 175
Dod Mantle, Anthony, 160
Dogma 95, 103–7, 153–67
 challenges to *auteur* theory, 15, 104, 157
 DV cameras, 103, 105–7

do-it-yourself technology, 12–13, 156
and irony, 81–3, 143
masculinist bent, 158, 164
new punk cinema, 103, 154–6, 159, 167
realism, 105–7, 155
relationship to punk, 12, 143–4
response to globalisation, 154
war on spectacle, 104–5
Dogville, 163, 165, 166
Donnie Darko, 130, 131
Dreyer, Carl, 157, 165

Easy Rider, 141, 196
Eggers, Dave, 76–7, 81
The Element of Crime, 161, 164
Elephant, 51–5, 58, 145, 149
Epidemic, 161
Eraserhead, 10
Eternal Sunshine of the Spotless Mind, 14, 77, 136
Europa, 161
Even Dwarfs Started Small, 183
Every Man for Himself and God Against All, 183

Faces, 155
Female Trouble, 60
Figgis, Mike, 168–79
 and new punk cinema, 103, 156
Fight Club, 2, 83–4, 129, 130–1, 132–4, 136, 138
Filmmaker, 18
Film Threat, 17
Fincher, David, 129, 131, 132–4
Fitzcarraldo, 183
The Foreigner, 12, 26–31
 influence on Jim Jarmusch, 26
 lack of closure, 28–30
 punk technique, 30–1
Freaks, 44
French New Wave,
 influences on Dogma 95, 104, 155
 relationship to new punk cinema, 2, 57–8, 128–9, 137,
Friedberg, Anne, 73

214

Frith, Simon, 5, 12
Fugazi, 23

Germany Year Zero, 190
Geuens, Jean-Pierre, 74
Ghost World, 73
Glazer, Jonathan, 63
Godard, Jean-Luc, 67, 187
   and Dogma 95, 104
   and Harmony Korine, 189
   and punk sensibility, 31–7, 57, 128
The Great Rock 'n' Roll Swindle, 11
Grossberg, Lawrence, 16
Gummo, 2, 182–92
   formalism, 52
   New German Cinema, 183–4
   Pasolini, 189
   relationship to realism, 43–7
   Rossellini, 190
   voice-over, 186–7

Harper, Graeme, 73–4, 80
Hazan, Jack, 11, 25
A Heartbreaking Work of Staggering Genius, 76–7
Hebdige, Dick, 4, 8, 18, 59, 60, 75
Henry, Tricia, 3
Herzog, Werner, 44, 183–4, 185
Heylin, Clinton, 5
Highway Patrolman, 194, 198–9
Hill Street Blues, 175
Hoberman, J., 10
home computing, 89, 93–4
Homicide, 162
Hutcheon, Linda, 76
hypertext, 116, 123–4

The Idiots, 2, 154, 162, 166
   DV cameras, 106, 155
   mirrors Dogma 95, 81–4, 163
   punk aesthetics, 16
   sincerity and irony, 72
In Praise of Love, 31–7
In This World, 146
irony, 72–85, 137, 143
Italian for Beginners, 144, 154, 157
Italian neo-realism, 42–3, 170–1

and DV cinema, 107
and *Gummo*, 189
influence on *Ken Park*, 47
relationship to new punk cinema, 2, 43
and *Time Code*, 109

Jackie Brown, 62
Jarmusch, Jim, 26, 182
   on punk music and cinema, 3, 11
JenniCAM, 169, 176, 178
Jeunet, Jeanne-Pierre, 113
Jimmy Corrigan, 73
Le Joli Mai, 58
Jonze, Spike, 77–9
Jules and Jim, 68
julien donkey-boy, 2, 111, 154, 182, 184

Kael, Pauline, 141
Kaufman, Charlie, 77–9
Kempner, Scott, 6
Ken Park, 47–51, 52
Kern, Richard, 9–10, 39
Kids, 45, 48, 188
Kill Bill, 131, 137, 168
The Killing, 13, 62
The King is Alive, 154
The Kingdom, 161, 162, 165
Korine, Harmony, 111–12, 180–92
   and Jean-Luc Godard, 189
   and Lars Von Trier, 162
   and neo-realism, 43–7
   and new punk cinema, 40
Kowalski, Lech, 11
Kragh-Jacobsen, Søren, 153
Kubrick, Stanley, 13
Kundera, Milan, 104

Lachman, Edward, 47–51
Leon, Craig, 7
Letts, Don, 11
Levring, Kristian, 153–4
Lommel, Ulli, 25
Lost in Translation, 28–9
Lunch, Lydia, 9
Lurie, Peter, 79–80
Lynch, David, 10, 115, 181, 182

MTV, 13–14
McGain, Gillian, 5
McLuhan, Marshall, 73
McNeil, Legs, 5
McSweeney's, 81
Magnolia, 80, 130, 168, 169, 177, 178
Manovich, Lev, 107–8, 112, 168, 169–70, 176–7
Marcus, Greil, 4
El Mariachi, 61–2
Marker, Chris, 58
Martin, Bill
Marx, Karl, 23
Masculin/Féminin, 67
Maus, 73
Mean Streets, 142
Mekas, Jonas, 171
Memento, 14, 25, 147, 148
  as database narrative, 110
  narrative self-awareness, 80, 136
  noir tradition, 134–6
  spectator performance, 103, 110
microcinema, 17
Mifune, 154, 157
Mingay, David, 25
Minor Threat, 37
Mitchell, Eric, 10
Morrissey, Paul, 188
Moviedrome, 194, 195, 196
Mulholland Drive, 110, 115–16

Nares, James, 10
New German Cinema, 183
new punk cinema, 11–18, 107–12, 191
  alternatives to linear narrative, 14, 135
  challenges to director as *auteur*, 14–15, 128
  cinema of supplements, 97
  DV cameras, 13, 14, 105
  and Dogma 95, 81–5, 102, 105, 154–5, 167
  do-it-yourself sensibility, 12
  and film consumption practices, 92
  global character, 11–12
  influence of MTV on, 13–14
  irony, 13, 17, 130
  and microcinema, 17–18
  performance and technology, 107–8
  self-awareness, 16, 136–8
  self-imposed limitations, 15
Night and Fog, 58
Night Lunch, 11
nihilism, 131, 185
Nolan, Christopher, 134–6, 147

Open Hearts, 154
Ordet, 165
Orlean, Susan, 78
Out of the Blue, 45, 188

Pasolini, Pier Paolo, 189, 191
Pi, 2, 13, 108
Pink Flamingos, 59, 60
Poe, Amos, 11, 12, 26–31
The Police Tapes, 175
Polyester, 60
Pulp Fiction, 14, 63, 92, 110, 134–5
Punking Out, 74
punk cinema, 9–11, 24–31
  aesthetics of, 10, 11, 25
  and Alex Cox, 193–5
  and Cinema of Transgression, 9–10, 11
  early definitions of, 10
  economics of, 10
  and *The Foreigner*, 26–31
  resists commodification, 24
Punk Planet, 18
punk rock, 4–9, 58–60, 139–40
  and Alex Cox, 193
  and Dogma 95, 148, 156–61
  do-it-yourself ethic, 8, 74–5, 140, 156
  emergence during poor economy, 8–9, 22
  in *The Foreigner*, 27, 30
  minimalism, 6–7
  realism, 142
  resistance to corporatisation, 5, 23–4, 37, 197
Purdy, Jedediah, 76

Ramones, 4, 7, 8, 22, 59, 75, 103
Ray, Robert, 13, 73, 127
Repo Man, 148, 193–4, 196–7
Requiem for a Dream, 2, 3, 13, 65, 168
Reservoir Dogs, 62
Resnais, Alain, 58, 104
Revengers Tragedy, 201
Rock 'n' Roll High School, 10
Rodriguez, Richard, 61
Rome: Open City, 42, 44
Rossellini, Roberto, 40, 41, 190
Rude Boy, 11, 25
Run Lola Run
   and chaos theory, 116
   database narrative, 110
   experiments with classical narrative structure, 130, 147
   MTV editing style, 13–14
   new punk cinema, 2, 61, 103
   spectator performance, 103, 110
Russian Ark, 179

Sabin, Roger, 3, 7–8
Sargeant, Jack, 11
Savage, Jon, 5, 7, 8
Schalit, Joel, 18
Schrader, Paul, 3
Scorsese, Martin, 142
Scott B, 10
Scream, 17, 74
Sex Pistols, 4, 6, 7, 59, 72, 74, 93, 139, 148, 156
Shadows, 30
Short Cuts, 168, 177
Sid and Nancy, 145, 148, 194, 197
Sideburns, 21
Siegel, Fred, 9
Smith, Evan, 14
Smith, Jack, 171
Soderbergh, Steven, 63, 182
Sontag, Susan, 81
Spheeris, Penelope, 11, 25, 39–40, 197
Spiegelman, Art, 73
Stam, Robert, 41
Straight to Hell, 194, 199

Stroszek, 183
structural films, 131, 185
Suburbia, 25, 40, 197
Sweet Sweetback's Baad Asssss Song, 60

Tarantino, Quentin, 14, 62–3, 131–2
Temple, Julien, 11
Thompson, Stacy, 3, 5, 10–11
Three Businessmen, 194, 202
Time Code, 2, 136, 168–79
   DV cameras, 107, 109, 110
   digital neo-realism, 109, 170, 178
   multiple screens, 116–17, 169
   new punk cinema, 108–9, 156, 168–79
   performance and technology, 108–11
   real time, 176–7
   spectator performance, 103
Tristram Shandy, 74
24 Hour Party People, 146
28 Days Later, 13, 16
Twin Peaks, 162
Two-Lane Blacktop, 196
Tykwer, Tom, 61, 116, 147

Underground Film Bulletin, 11

Van Sant, Gus, 51–5, 58, 145, 149, 182
   on MTV, 13–14
   and new punk cinema, 40
Vertov, Dziga, 50
Vicious, Sid, 142, 148–9
videotape, 89–92, 96–7, 99, 170, 175, 186
Vinterberg, Thomas, 64, 104, 143–4, 153–67
   and DV cameras, 106
   and punk idiom, 159
Von Trier, Lars, 63–4, 153–8, 161–7
   challenges to *auteur* theory, 15, 104, 157
   emotional manipulation, 164–5
   irony, 77, 81–5
   and post-feminism, 166

INDEX

   and punk, 12, 143–4, 156, 161
   use of DV cameras, 106, 155, 163

Wallace, David Foster, 72, 74, 79
Ware, Chris, 73
Warhol, Andy, 1, 117, 168, 171–8
Waters, John, 11, 59, 60
Weekend, 189
Welles, Orson, 128–9, 170

Winick, Gary, 14
Winterbottom, Michael, 146
The Wizard of Oz, 187

Y Tu Mamá También, 65–71

Zavattini, Cesare, 41–3
Zedd, Nick, 9–10, 11, 39
Zentropa, 63